Strategic Relat
and Turkey, 19

Until ten years ago Turkey was seen as a close strategic ally of the US in the Middle East. However, since the beginning of the new century Washington has grown uncertain regarding the future course of the bilateral strategic co-operation.

Taking the period from the end of the 1970s to the end of the 1990s, this book critically examines the evolution of the strategic relationship between the US and Turkey with a particular focus on the Middle Eastern context.

Strategic Relations Between the US and Turkey employs interviews with US, Turkish and Israeli officials and archival research in order to offer an alternative reading of the realities that shaped bilateral co-operation. The unravelling of these realities enlightens the reader about the past course of events but also aids the understanding of the dynamics of the relationship today.

Essential reading for students and scholars of US and Turkish foreign policy, this study of co-operation between a superpower and a relatively weak state in the international system will also be of use to those interested in International Relations, Diplomatic History and World Politics more broadly.

Ekavi Athanassopoulou is Assistant Professor of International Relations at the University of Athens. She is the author of *Turkey: Anglo-American Security Interests, 1945–1952: The First Enlargement of NATO* (1999).

Routledge Studies in Middle Eastern Politics

1. **Algeria in Transition**
   Ahmed Aghrout with Redha M. Bougherira

2. **Palestinian Refugee Repatriation**
   Edited by Michael Dumper

3. **The International Politics of the Persian Gulf**
   Arshin Adib-Moghaddam

4. **Israeli Politics and the First Palestinian Intifada**
   Eitan Y. Alimi

5. **Democratization in Morocco**
   Lise Storm

6. **Secular and Islamic Politics in Turkey**
   Ümit Cizre

7. **The United States and Iran**
   Sasan Fayazmanesh

8. **Civil Society in Algeria**
   Andrea Liverani

9. **Jordanian-Israeli Relations**
   Mutayyam al O'ran

10. **Kemalism in Turkish Politics**
    Sinan Ciddi

11. **Islamism, Democracy and Liberalism in Turkey**
    William Hale and Ergun Özbudun

12. **Politics and Violence in Israel/Palestine**
    Lev Luis Grinberg

13. **Intra-Jewish Conflict in Israel**
    Sami Shalom Chetrit

14. **Holy Places in the Israeli-Palestinian Conflict**
    Edited by Marshall J. Breger, Yitzhak Reiter and Leonard Hammer

15. **Plurality and Citizenship in Israel**
    Edited by Dan Avnon and Yotam Benziman

16. **Ethnic Politics in Israel**
    As'ad Ghanem

17. **Islamists and Secularists in Egypt**
    Dina Shehata

18. **Political Succession in the Arab World**
    Anthony Billingsley

19. **Turkey's Entente with Israel and Azerbaijan**
    Alexander Murinson

20. **Europe and Tunisia**
    Brieg Powel and Larbi Sadiki

21. **Turkish Politics and the Rise of the AKP**
    Arda Can Kumbaracibasi

22. **Civil Society and Democratization in the Arab World**
Francesco Cavatorta and Vincent Durac

23. **Politics in Morocco**
Anouar Boukhars

24. **The Second Palestinian Intifada**
Julie M. Norman

25. **Democracy in Turkey**
Ali Resul Usul

26. **Nationalism and Politics in Turkey**
Edited by Marlies Casier and Joost Jongerden

27. **Democracy in the Arab World**
Edited by Samir Makdisi and Ibrahim Elbadawi

28. **Public Management in Israel**
Itzhak Galnoor

29. **Israeli Nationalism**
Uri Ram

30. **NATO and the Middle East**
Mohammed Moustafa Orfy

31. **The Kurds and US Foreign Policy**
Marianna Charountaki

32. **The Iran-Iraq War**
Jerome Donovan

33. **Surveillance and Control in Israel/Palestine**
Edited by Elia Zureik, David Lyon and Yasmeen Abu-Laban

34. **Conflict and Peacemaking in Israel-Palestine**
Sapir Handelman

35. **Arab Minority Nationalism in Israel**
Amal Jamal

36. **The Contradictions of Israeli Citizenship**
Edited by Guy Ben-Porat and Bryan S. Turner

37. **The Arab State and Women's Rights**
Elham Manea

38. **Saudi Maritime Policy**
Hatim Al-Bisher, Selina Stead and Tim Gray

39. **The Arab State**
Adham Saouli

40. **Regime Stability in Saudi Arabia**
Stig Stenslie

41. **Sacred Space in Israel and Palestine**
Edited by Marshall J. Breger, Yitzhak Reiter and Leonard Hammer

42. **The UN and the Arab-Israeli Conflict**
Danilo Di Mauro

43. **Sectarian Conflict in Egypt**
Elizabeth Iskander

44. **Contemporary Morocco**
Edited by Bruce Maddy-Weitzman and Daniel Zisenwine

45. **Political Regimes in the Arab World**
Edited by Ferran Brichs

46. **Arms Control and Iranian Foreign Policy**
Bobi Pirseyedi

47. **Everyday Arab Identity**
Christopher Phillips

48. **Human Rights in Libya**
Giacomina De Bona

Acknowledgements

There is a genuine pleasure in writing the acknowledgements page. This book is the fruit of many years of research and many people have offered valuable assistance along the way. I must begin with all those who granted me interviews. Each of the individuals I interviewed without exception showed a remarkable generosity of spirit and willingness to help me in this project. This study is of course my responsibility, but without their interest in my research, their candour and the information and thoughts they shared with me much of it could not have been written. I am indebted to them beyond words. Some of them asked that there should be no attribution to their name. Since I cannot thank everybody by name I have to restrain myself in offering only this collective note of gratitude. A few, however, must be mentioned individually.

I am particularly indebted to Mehmet Ali Birand, who recently left the concerns of this world. His guidance concerning my research and his insights into the relations between Turkey and the US were simply invaluable. Cengiz Çandar spared many long hours on different occasions to discuss aspects of Turkish foreign policy with me. Our discussions helped me reach a good understanding of a number of issues that troubled me in this project. I am immensely grateful to him for his intellectual aid and his indulgence. I also wish to express my deep gratitude to Alan Makovsky. He graciously shared his vast knowledge of the American-Turkish relationship and helped me put a lot of the jigsaw pieces into place whilst offering encouragement. I could not have asked for more solid support than that given by both Professor Henri Barkey and Dr. Ian O. Lesser. Not only did they provide me with precious insights into the dynamics of the bilateral relationship but also volunteered to help in my effort to build up the oral history material. I owe them a lot. Ambassador Morton Abramowitz gave me very generously the benefit of his knowledge of the US–Turkey relationship while demonstrating more than charming patience every time I returned to him with new questions. I am indebted to him. Ambassador Mark Grossman brought to life many of the issues that concerned the bilateral relationship during his tour of duty in Ankara and courteously helped me to better understand the realities concerning the formulation of US foreign policy towards Turkey. I wish to thank him profusely. As I was at the very final stage of completing this book

Thomas Dine agreed to see me on very short notice indeed. In an extremely stimulating marathon conversation he went over with me a number of details concerning the role of the pro-Israel lobby in Washington within the context of the US–Turkey relationship. His immense understanding of the political game in Washington and his sense of humour have been inspiring. I wish to express here a strong note of thanks to him.

Professor John Iatrides has over the years been an unfailing source of great moral and intellectual support. I cannot thank him enough for reading a draft of this study and for providing biting comments, constructive criticisms, questions and gently-put suggestions which helped me strengthen my arguments particularly in relation to the intricacies of US foreign policy making. I also wish to express my deep thanks to Professor Theodore Couloumbis, who never tired of discussing the issues that baffled me when working on this book. His hard questions and incisive comments on US foreign policy invariably helped me look at my material from different perspectives at critical points during the writing process. I should not have to add, of course, that all the shortcomings in this study are entirely my responsibility. I can only hope that the book does not fall too short of the expectations of both of them.

Naturally, studies are more widely read when they are published. I am grateful to Joe Whiting, Routledge's editor for Middle East Studies, for his confidence in this project and his soft touch during the publication process. Kathryn Rylance, editorial assistant at Routledge, has responded to my multiple questions and appeals for help with patience, kindness and utmost professionalism. I cannot thank her enough. Many thanks also go to Megan Hiatt for her outstanding copyediting of an often demanding text. Andrew Watts, production editorial manager at Routledge never failed to quickly and efficiently solve editing issues. I wish also to thank him. Finally, I reserve a special note of thanks for Andrew Humphrys, the editor of my very first book, who offered wonderful encouragement and invaluable advice while I was seeking to publish this study. I am most obliged to him.

Trying to establish the contents of archival material from afar is not always a straightforward process, as some of us know. The courtesy and professionalism of Eudes Nouvelot at the public disclosure unit of the NATO archives and the kind assistance of David Langbart at the US National Archives at College Park spared me expense, loss of precious time and multiple headaches. I thank them profusely.

I am also indebted to Duygu Öztürk in Ankara, who, while in the midst of her own doctoral research, with skill and courtesy helped me lay my hands on some of the secondary material I was looking for. Lia Deliyanni and Eleni Sarri in Athens – both extremely competent librarians – also came to my rescue when I had difficulties tracing secondary sources which could not be easily located. I note their support and kind interest gratefully.

My research in the US was partly funded by my home institution, the University of Athens. I am very appreciative of this financial help. As Greece has

Map 1 Major United States military installations in Turkey during the Cold War
Source: Congressional Research Service. Foreign Affairs and National Defense Division. *Turkey's problems and prospects: implications for U.S. interests*: report/ prepared for the Subcommittee on Europe and the Middle East of the Committee on Foreign Affairs, U.S. House of Representatives by the Foreign Affairs and National Defense Division Congressional Research Service, Library of Congress, Washington D.C.: U.S. Government Printing Office, 1980.

Map 2 Selected Major United States communication facilities in Turkey during the Cold War
Source: Congressional Research Service. Foreign Affairs and National Defense Division. *Turkey's problems and prospects: implications for U.S. interests*: report/ prepared for the Subcommittee on Europe and the Middle East of the Committee on Foreign Affairs, U.S. House of Representatives by the Foreign Affairs and National Defense Division Congressional Research Service, Library of Congress, Washington D.C.: U.S. Government Printing Office, 1980.

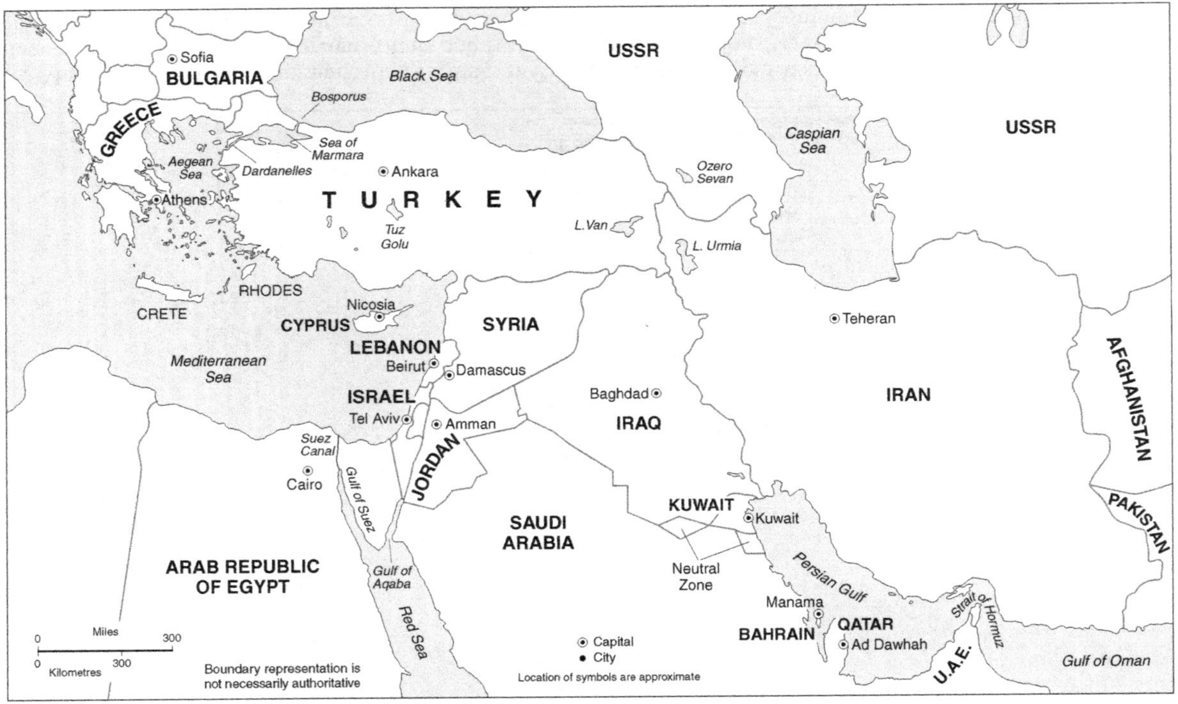

Map 3 Turkey and the Middle East during the Cold War Source: Congressional Research Service. Foreign Affairs and National Defense Division. *Turkey's problems and prospects: implications for U.S. interests*: report/ prepared for the Subcommittee on Europe and the Middle East of the Committee on Foreign Affairs, U.S. House of Representatives by the Foreign Affairs and National Defense Division Congressional Research Service, Library of Congress, Washington D.C.: U.S. Government Printing Office, 1980.

Ismet Inönü was asked about Turkey's relations with the US and he answered thus: 'To conduct politics with big states is like sharing the same bed with a tiger'.

HUNGARY
MOLDOVA
UKRAINE
KAZAKHSTAN
ROMANIA
RUSSIA
YUGOSLAVIA
BULGARIA
Black Sea
UZBEKISTAN
GREECE
GEORGIA
Caspian Sea
Ankara
ARMENIA
AZERBAIJAN
TURKEY
TURKMENISTAN
CYPRUS
SYRIA
Mediterranean Sea
LEBANON
IRAN
IRAQ
ISRAEL
JORDAN
LIBYA
EGYPT
SAUDI ARABIA
0 Miles 200
0 200 Kilometres

position at the crossroads of three areas of US strategic interest (the Caucasus, the Balkans, the Middle East) quickly resolved the issue of Turkey's loss of strategic value because of the end of the Cold War. Yet while geopolitics are undoubtedly important they cannot offer a fully satisfactory explanation for the new conceptualization of the US interest in Turkey without an account of the contribution of a number of domestic and non-domestic actors. Nor can they answer why US policy toward Turkey was formulated in the particular way it was. Therefore, this book seeks to illustrate that the renewal of US interest in Turkey in the second half of the 1990s was not an automatic response to new post–Cold War realities in the international environment. Rather, it was an interest that emerged more gradually from the beliefs and actions of US officials and also from the linkage between domestic and international politics that resulted from Turkey's decision to deepen its relationship with Israel.

For some of the literature Turkey's new strategic role in the post–Cold War era was highlighted early on when the Turks decided to support the military US-led allied effort against Saddam Hussein in 1991. The decision is attributed to Turkish President Turgut Özal, who, it is said, threw in Turkey's lot with the US against the opposition of the military leadership, the bureaucracy and the majority of political forces, who were all against Turkish involvement in the war; his main hope was allegedly to regenerate US interest in Turkey, whose strategic value was in decline after the end of the Cold War. In other words, according to the mainstream analysis, had it not been for Özal Turkey would not have agreed for its bases to be used for military operations against Iraq. This book, however, is meant to show that it was not one man, Turgut Özal, and his strategic calculations that determined Turkish participation in the war. Rather, Turkey's ambitious military-modernization plans, which were developed in the 1980s – with full US support and encouragement – could not be financed by Turkish resources alone, and this primarily decided the matter.

Over the course of some years I have studied the literature, worked in the archives and interviewed a good number of US, Turkish and Israeli officials as well as analysts of US–Turkey relations in order to form a picture of the bilateral relationship by employing an analysis at many different levels. My hope is that the reader will appreciate the existence of a great number of factors often interacting with each other, which account for the development of the strategic relationship between Washington and Ankara during the period under consideration. Also, I expect that those who read this book will keep in mind that its main purpose is to ask questions and generate discussion concerning only a number of these factors, those I feel are of particular importance but have not been given proper attention in the literature.

There is clearly much more that can be said about the issues that I address and about many others that I have not touched upon in this book. Hopefully in the years to come and as more archival material becomes available new research will correct omissions but also misapprehensions that occur in this study and offer a better understanding of the 'whys' and the 'hows' that help explain the course of the US–Turkey strategic relationship in the fascinating period between the late 1970s and late 1990s. What has become evident to me while working on this project is that a great deal more research is needed before we reach the stage of what we might call adequate scholarly understanding of the relationship between these two formal allies.

Most of the US and Turkish officials I interviewed (often more than once on account of the need for cross-referencing) had first-hand knowledge of the rationale behind decisions that shaped the interaction between US and Turkish officials. In fact, a number of them were directly involved in the decision-making process. For their part the American and Turkish analysts I spoke to were privy to much of Washington's and Ankara's inner thinking. And the Israeli officials I interviewed had an intimate knowledge of the dynamic between the US, Turkey and Israel which developed in the 1990s. Most of all, these officials were willing to share important pieces of information which are not to be found in the official accounts of the states concerned, enabling me to provide some important new pieces to the picture of the bilateral relationship. For example, this study is the first to show that the Clinton administration was instrumental in Ankara's decision to expand relations with Israel also into the security field. Furthermore, the book offers for the first time a comprehensive account of the role Mark Grossman, the US ambassador to Turkey, played in the renewal of the US interest in Turkey in the latter part of the 1990s.

In the course of the last decade US–Turkey strategic relations have reached a critical point. To the US officials' surprise and often frustration Turkish leaders – including members of the older guard – seek to re-shape the bilateral dialogue in a way that acknowledges Turkey's regional importance. A better understanding of the dynamics of the relationship seems more important today than perhaps ever before. This book suggests that the study of the realities which shaped relations in the 1980s and the 1990s can greatly help. In that sense hopefully the reader will find the history that is presented in the following pages more than a story of past events.

Part I

The 1980s

The rekindling of the relationship

1 A piece of real estate

Difficulties between allies

Since the proclamation of the Truman doctrine (1947) and throughout the Cold War the US interest in Turkey was shaped exclusively by strategic considerations. From Washington's point of view Turkey's strategic value was threefold.[1] For one, there was the large number of Turkish military forces which were available for NATO use since Turkey joined the North Atlantic Treaty in 1952. In addition, Turkey's location enabled its participation in three of the four major theatres of war in NATO's southern flank: the Mediterranean, eastern Turkey and eastern Thrace. Furthermore, Turkey could provide a host of bases and intelligence-gathering facilities in support of the interests of NATO but also of the US. Two of the biggest and most important of the Turkish intelligence facilities were located in Sinop on the Black Sea coast in north-central Turkey and in Pirinçlik near Diyarbakir in southeastern Turkey. Their importance lay in the collection of various data regarding Soviet military activities within the Soviet Union, the eastern Mediterranean and the Middle East. A smaller but equally important intelligence facility was Belbasi station, a US seismographic detection base near Ankara, which monitored Soviet nuclear tests. When it came to bases used by the US in support of NATO commitments the Incirlik air base in the southeastern part of Turkey was the biggest. A large number of US Department of Defense personnel worked and resided there (in the 1970s the number amounted to around 2,500 people).[2] It was a major tactical fighter base which served as a key deployment base for US Air Force Europe participating in NATO-related missions. Its significance was due to the fact that US fighters (capable of launching a conventional or a tactical nuclear strike) when located at Incirlik were the most forward deployed land-based aircraft in the eastern Mediterranean. In addition Turkey offered two important supply and storage centers for US military forces in the extreme eastern Mediterranean near the border with Syria. These were Iskenderun and Yumurtalik, close to Adana. During most of the Cold War almost 20 per cent of the Mediterranean-based fuel for the US Sixth Fleet was stored in Turkey.

It was because of the allure of these strategic assets that US officials considered a socially and politically stable, co-operative Turkey very important to their strategy of containing Soviet power. To protect the US strategic stake in Turkey the Americans developed a close dialogue not only with the Turkish governments but also with Turkey's military leadership. The running discussion over security issues between US military officers and their Turkish counterparts over time would gather a lot of momentum, partly due to regular contact through their participation in the various NATO bodies.

For most of the 1950s the Americans co-operated closely on security issues with the government of Adnan Menderes, not only with reference to the needs of the North Atlantic Treaty but also with regard to US strategic interests in the Middle East. Thus, Turkey played a leading role in the creation of the Baghdad Pact (1955), which was part of the US strategy of containing the Soviet Union along the Northern Tier.[3] At the time Ankara's wish to closely co-operate with Washington in the Middle East originated to a large extent in the belief of the Menderes' government that Turkey's security interests in the region were very close with those of the US.[4] The Turks' willingness to assist the Americans in their strategic plans for the Middle East was greatly facilitated by handsome amounts of US aid given to Turkey (although mainly for NATO-related purposes). The Americans saw that the Turks needed military assistance if they were to maintain and modernize their large army; also, they recognized that economic assistance was necessary to help Turkey maintain its stability. Between 1946 and 1961 Turkey received on average over 100 million dollars per year in military assistance and around 86 million dollars in economic assistance. Over the Menderes period alone (1950–60) US assistance had averaged a quarter of a billion dollars per year.[5]

Yet this state of affairs between the two allies did not last beyond the 1950s. By the end of the decade and mainly since the 1960s the bilateral relationship entered a new, less co-operative phase.[6] A number of interrelated factors accounted for this. Many analysts identify the differences of perspective between Ankara and Washington over Turkish policy regarding Cyprus as the main cause behind Turkey's new, less-engaged policy towards the US. According to this argument, because of these differences the Turks were deeply disappointed in their ally and their trust in the Americans was undermined.[7] However, a few scholars provide a more comprehensive explanation. They point out that while the Cyprus issue was undoubtedly a major contributing factor, the root causes of the distance that emerged between Ankara and Washington should rather be looked for in the easing of tension between the two superpowers.[8] In other words, under the influence of détente the US attitude towards Turkey changed both in qualitative and quantitative terms. It has been remarked that as the Cold War–tension between the US and the Soviet Union eased and the 'tight' bipolar system changed into a 'loose' one the bargaining position of many non-aligned weaker states was automatically undermined.[9] Turkey is a good example of how the same applied also to aligned weaker states. In the new international environment Washington no longer felt that its alliance with Turkey was serving pressing security needs as had been the case in the 1950s. Consequently, from the mid

1960s US aid to Turkey in the form of grants was drastically reduced. Turkey was now expected to assume most of the expenses necessary to support its defence budget (excluding expenses for the acquisition of supplies and equipment which incurred the use of foreign currency).[10] Moreover, Washington was contemplating ending all grant aid to Turkey from the 1972 fiscal year onwards (something that in the end did not happen).[11] In short, while successive American administrations continued to recognize Turkey's significance for US strategic interests they were less sensitive about upsetting the Turks.

The Turkish leadership regarded these developments as extremely adverse for both the country's economic development and its future military preparedness, for it was clear that they could not achieve their NATO-approved force goals without enough US assistance. Moreover, they firmly believed that Turkey could not take on the immense cost of supporting its military forces without seriously jeopardizing its economy.[12] Actually, as Walter Laqueur, the distinguished contemporary analyst of Middle Eastern affairs, observed at the time, 'to many Turks, the continuing economic and social backwardness of their country, in a world which is so much dependent on technology and productivity, was an even greater menace than the Soviet army or navy.'[13] Hence, it was not surprising that the Turks in their turn started re-examining their policy toward the US. Turkey's attitude was not solely a reaction to Washington's unwillingness to support Turkey financially (or politically regarding Cyprus) at least to the degree Ankara wished. It also reflected the easing of Turkish security concerns due to the reduction of the threat of a clash between the two superpowers and the improvement of Ankara's relations with Moscow.[14] Following Stalin's death (1953) the Soviets renounced their territorial claims against Turkey and towards the end of the decade bilateral relations began slowly to improve. As from 1963 trade relations between Turkey and the Soviet Union and a number of its East European satellites grew. Moscow was also offering economic help in the form of credits, which the Turkish governments were ready to accept, though the amount of help was not significant enough to replace the West as a source of credit for Turkey.[15] By 1968 the State Department was referring to the existence of a 'limited Soviet-Turkish détente'.[16] Naturally these developments allowed Ankara more room for maneuvering in their policy towards the US than in the tight bipolar environment at the height of the Cold War.

The change of political leadership in 1960 also contributed to the re-examination of Turkey's approach toward the US. After the 1960 military coup, which ousted Menderes's Democratic Party from power, and the 1961 general elections that followed, Ismet Inönü, the leader of the Republican People's Party became prime minister. Inönü, the older statesman who had steered Turkey through the extremely difficult course of neutrality during the Second World War, was against the 'Americanization' of Turkey's foreign policy. In the 1950s as head of the opposition he had repeatedly criticized Menderes for co-operating too closely with the Americans.[17] Inönü's perception was that Turkey's national interests did not fully coincide with those of the

US. On the contrary they demanded a more flexible Turkish policy towards the Third World, compared to the one dictated by America's hegemonic leadership. Inönü's approach resonated with a very large part of the Kemalist political and military elite,[18] who were the adherents to the republican strategic culture.[19] A central component of this culture was the avoidance of ties which undermined the independence of the country. Inönü's viewpoint was in fact vindicated by the Cuban Missile Crisis in 1962. When the US government decided to withdraw the Jupiter missiles from Turkey it was generally assumed in Ankara that this was part of a secret arrangement between the two superpowers,[20] in spite of the assurances of the US government that there had been no 'deal' with Moscow regarding the missiles.[21] Hence, Ankara began to think that in the midst of the new, more relaxed environment between the two superpowers Turkey ran the risk of becoming a pawn in the service of US interests and strategic calculations.[22] Many members of Inönü's government began to argue that if Washington put its own security above the interests of its allies, 'Turkey, too, should put its national interests first and regain some freedom of manoeuvre.'[23] These deliberations became more focused due to Washington's unwillingness to accommodate Turkish special interests in Cyprus, where a major crisis had began to unfold at exactly the time that Ankara was looking to regain some freedom of maneuver vis-à-vis the US. The US stance was epitomized in a blunt letter from President Lyndon Johnson to Prime Minister Inönü in 1964, which caused great indignation and provoked a strongly negative reaction against the US in Turkey. The letter stated that should the Soviet Union retaliate militarily against Turkey in the event of a Turkish invasion of Cyprus the US would not come to Turkey's assistance, despite NATO's commitments. Moreover, the attitudes of many cabinet members were affected by a wish to accommodate public opinion in Turkey, at least to some extent, where in the 1960s the call for independence from the US was heard loudly from left-wing intellectuals, many of whom were also ardent nationalists.[24]

This new phase in the bilateral relationship was only natural because 'no two states are alike and no two states can arrive at an identical appreciation of their national interest'.[25] In times of great international crisis the members of a coalition are willing to submerge their narrow national interests, but when the emergency passes and as the most likely leaders of the coalition seek to dominate, 'the willing sinking of interests is replaced by resentment and resistance',[26] as well as the pursuit of the national interest by the individual members. In the 1965 general election Inönü was defeated by Süleyman Demirel, the leader of the Justice Party, which to a large extent was the continuation of Menderes's Democratic Party. But Ankara's effort to reposition itself vis-à-vis the US continued under the successive governments of Demirel and Bülent Ecevit, the other major Turkish political leader of the 1960s and the 1970s, although Demirel was particularly careful not to cause any serious damage to the bilateral relationship. In practical terms this new attitude meant that while Ankara continued to fulfil Turkey's NATO obligations it was not willing, as had been the case during the Menderes period, to bind its foreign policy to that of the US and be a participant in American policy initiatives. On the contrary, Turkish governments made a conscious effort to disengage Turkey from any visible identification with US policy objectives in the Middle East.[27] Also, although the Turks were not seriously contemplating abandoning their basic security policy of alliance with the US and NATO, they pushed for a number of restrictions on the scope of their co-operation with the US. This effort was clearly reflected in the 1969 Defense Cooperation Agreement (DCA) – negotiated by the Demirel government – which restricted US privileges and freedom of action in all joint defense installations. In brief, during the 1960s it was not only Western Europe which gradually had become 'semi-Gaullist', to use Fritz Stern's expression,[28] but also Turkey, contributing thus to the 'neutralization of the Northern Tier', as Walter Laqueur pointedly observed.[29] Of course, the Americans, the US military in particular, did not welcome the new restrictions. Thus, the matter became an additional irritant for each of the two sides,[30] alongside other issues such as opium poppy cultivation in Turkey.[31] In the words of a State Department official and Turkey analyst: 'Only common lip service to the threat from the Soviet Union and the inertia of the military and economic aid systems concealed the gravity of the tensions from the leaders on both sides.'[32]

It was only to be expected that against this background the US Congress decision in February 1975 to impose a military embargo on Turkey (as punishment for the invasion of Cyprus)[33] would reinforce the Turks' distrust of the Americans and cause further damage to the bilateral relationship. Actually, this time the US action also led to a serious disruption of many aspects of the bilateral strategic co-operation: in reprisal the Demirel government unilaterally abrogated the 1969 DCA, which governed the operations at the Turkish facilities to which the US military had access. As a result the American use of four electronic intelligence-gathering facilities,[34] which were not directly related to NATO planning, was suspended. Moreover, the Turkish government announced that the Incirlik air base was to be utilized only for direct NATO purposes.[35]

Following these developments the US Pentagon took the view that due to the strategic value of these military facilities it was important that the bilateral relationship was restored to the status quo ante. Specifically, the US military used the four intelligence stations to monitor among other things the Soviet Union's air and naval activities in the Black Sea, Soviet missile-testing activities and other tests relevant to the Strategic Arms Limitation Talks (SALT).[36] So it was not surprising that the Gerald Ford administration pushed to lift the embargo and to conclude a new defence co-operation agreement with the Turks.[37] This effort led to the desired results at least at an initial phase. By September 1975 the administration succeeded in having the embargo partially lifted while it also negotiated and signed a new Defense Cooperation Agreement (DCA) with the Demirel government in March 1976. The 1976 DCA was similar to that of 1969, and following its conclusion the Ford administration expected that the US would be able to fully resume its activities in the Turkish military facilities.[38]

The key element behind the Turks' decision to sign the new agreement was one billion dollars in US military and economic assistance to Turkey over the four-year period that the agreement would be operative, in return for which the Americans would again be allowed access to all facilities. However, this was not meant to be. As Ellen Laipson succinctly put it, 'despite winning the partial lifting of the embargo, the Ford administration had not succeeded in removing the Cyprus issue from the attention of Congress.'[39] The agreement that both the US and the Turkish governments were so keen on was never ratified by Congress, which made it clear that Ankara had to make concessions over Cyprus *first*.[40]

As the Ford administration came to a close and Jimmy Carter took office full bilateral security cooperation was left in limbo because of Congress. The Carter administration also attached similar importance to the agreement, but being fully aware of the prevailing mood in the legislative body initially it did not attempt to exert pressure for its ratification.[41] So the suspension of American access to the facilities in Turkey continued. However, in 1978 the executive felt ready to battle in Congress over this issue.[42] In spring 1978 it made public its intention first to request from Congress the total lifting of the arms embargo without directly linking it to Turkey's stance regarding Cyprus and second to renegotiate with Ankara the 1976 DCA. The objective was to re-activate as soon as possible a satisfactory defence co-operation agreement with Turkey. The urgency was due to the fact that the intelligence data collected from the Turkish sites – which had become inaccessible to the US – was too important for in some instances it was unavailable from other sources. At least, that was what the US Department of Defense senior officials argued.[43]

On 26 September 1978, following a very well-organized by the executive campaign in Congress, the embargo was totally lifted. As a close observer of executive-congressional relations observed at the time: 'In recent memory only the Panama Canal treaties and the 1978 Middle East arms package rank as high' in terms of the efforts by the executive to achieve 'a contentious foreign policy objective in the Congress'.[44] In Ankara Bülent Ecevit's government was in power. Ecevit argued mostly at a rhetorical level for the reduction of Turkey's dependency on the US and the development of a new national security concept that implied a revision of Turkey's defense policy which was based on its NATO alliance.[45] As a matter of fact it was only in June that he stated during an official visit to Moscow that his government would limit Turkey's co-operation with the US and NATO because the Soviet Union was no longer a threat to Turkey's security.[46] But this was assuredly not the line he had held in Washington only at the end of May. At a meeting at the State Department while he pointed out that 'Turkey had a stake in détente and would like to enlarge it on a more sound basis' and also that it had been acting 'as a catalyst helping to bring about closer exchanges between East and West', 'without changing its own essence or basic posture', he stressed that 'Turkey's effectiveness in this respect could be seriously reduced if she could no longer act in a deterrent capacity and if NATO as a whole continued not to function in that region,[47] thus creating a dangerous and tempting vacuum.'[48] So, it was hardly surprising that Ecevit, putting rhetoric aside, allowed the US military to resume its activities in the four intelligence-gathering facilities for a year while the two countries negotiated a new defence co-operation agreement.[49]

'Turkey obviously occupies a key position within this Soviet strategic arc'[50]

During the latter part of Carter's term in office both Pentagon and State Department officials wished not only that relations with Turkey returned to the state of affairs existing before the embargo but also that they were further strengthened. The reason for this was that a tighter defense co-operation with the Turks was by now considered not simply desirable but imperative because of the activities of the Soviet Union in the broader area around the Persian Gulf. The Moscow-guided coup in Afghanistan (April 1978) expanded Soviet influence to a distance of only 560 kilometers (and less than an hour's flight from Afghan airbases) away from the Arab Sea. It is well known how those in the US who advocated the need to beef up defence viewed this coup as one end of a gigantic pincer which the Soviet Union was putting in place aiming at encircling the Gulf oil fields. At the other end of the pincer there was already the Soviet military presence in Ethiopia and in South Yemen; Moscow's pressure tactics on Pakistan (via the instigation of nationalist separatist movements); the increasing Soviet military presence in Syria, the influence of which was in turn growing in the Middle East.[51] In brief, as soon as the rivalry between the US and Moscow was renewed Turkey's strategic importance grew in Washington's eyes. The flight of the Shah in January 1979 and the rise to power of the Islamic government a few months later (1 April 1979) enhanced in Washington the sense of the development of a critical power vacuum in the 'Northern Tier' along which since the 1950s the US sought to contain the expansion of Moscow's influence in the Middle East. The Soviet invasion of Afghanistan in December 1979 gave a new urgency to the questions that were already exercising Washington regarding Moscow's designs for the Gulf region.

As one might expect, the answers to these pressing questions uncovered wide differences of perception among American strategic analysts. At the one end of the spectrum were those like Albert Wohlstetter who viewed developments in the periphery of the Persian Gulf as calculated Soviet moves, part of an expansionist design by Moscow. Others like Alvin Rubinstein saw the same developments as the result of changes within the states of the region.[52] Amidst these opposing views the Carter administration reached the conclusion that it did not matter whether the Afghanistan invasion was a pre-planned decision or the exploitation of an opportunity. The bottom line was, as the chairman of the NATO Military Command underlined in a message to all NATO's military commanders and chiefs of defence on 1 January 1980, that the invasion reflected the Soviets' 'calculation of Western and world reaction and perception of risk.'[53] And the prolonged instability in the periphery of the Persian Gulf offered the Soviet Union an excellent opportunity to penetrate the region. If this happened the energy interests of the West and by extension world stability would be endangered.[54]

As is well known, the invasion of Afghanistan delivered a fatal blow to the pursuit of Nixon's and Kissinger's realpolitik and the policy of détente. Its harsh critics, who all along had been advocating the containment of the Soviet Union, prevailed, détente collapsed and the policy of containment returned strong. On 23 January 1980, in his State of the Union Address, President Carter announced a new US policy that came to be called the Carter Doctrine. Referring to the invasion of Afghanistan, Carter warned that an attempt by an outside force to gain control of the Persian Gulf region would be regarded as an assault on the vital interests of the US and would be repelled by any necessary means, including the use of military force. The strong warning had been inserted in the speech upon the insistence of Zbigniew Brzezinski, Carter's national security adviser,[55] who believed that the Middle East constituted the third strategic zone of vital importance to the US next to Europe and the Far East.[56]

As these international developments were viewed in Washington as serious challenges to the security interests of the US they provided a strong argument in favour of re-focusing on security priorities in the Middle East. Within this context the Carter administration arrived at two main conclusions: first, US security policy in the vital Gulf region should take much more seriously into consideration the Soviet threat; second, the US should endeavour to strengthen the security of the Middle East. This was to be achieved by developing the military capabilities of friendly states in the region as well as the infrastructure to project at will American military power in the Persian Gulf. The latter point in practical terms meant that a concentrated effort had to be made to establish a Rapid Deployment Force (RDF), hence its establishment had to be given special attention by US strategic planners.

The Ronald Reagan administration – which magnified its global competition with Moscow – not only adopted these conclusions, the central proponent of which had been Brzezinski, but expanded and intensified the policy of its predecessor. Thus, after taking office it consistently emphasized the importance of improving the defenses of the Middle East vis-à-vis the threat of Soviet intimidation or aggression. In practice, this resulted in Washington's efforts to engage the strategic co-operation in the Middle East of its West European allies by trying to convince them (without much success in the end) that the mandate of the North Atlantic Treaty had to be expanded to also cover threats emerging in this area. But primarily the State Department and the Pentagon focused on how to develop the US military capability to repel a Soviet invasion of the Persian Gulf oil fields and on assisting the improvement of the self-defense capabilities of the US friendly Arab regimes and of Turkey. In parallel, US officials aimed at strengthening economic, financial and technological co-operation with these states.[57] These designs which were intended to enhance co-operation in every regard with Turkey and America's friends in the Middle East, were not a revival of the policy of regional alliances, one of the main feature of US national security policy during the 1950s at the height of the Cold War. Nor were they a return to Nixon's doctrine, which relied on proxy forces to act as the gendarmes of the US in the Persian Gulf. Since the end of the 1970s Washington was not looking for regional policemen and, in any event, there were no regimes in the Middle East keen on assuming such a role. The Americans were ready to police the area with their own military forces which, however, required that they were facilitated by local regimes. Specifically, the US needed to secure en route access to facilities, over-flight rights and bases for the deployment of US forces.[58] As a matter of fact it was widely presumed within the administration that a deployment of American forces in the Gulf would not be possible without the support of the friendly countries of the region.[59] So the strengthening of economic, military and technological ties with regional regimes aimed at solidifying Washington's influence, thus making it easier to build the material but also the psychological infrastructure for the planned Rapid Deployment Task Force. It was within this context that the belief that Turkey had a central role to play in the pursuit of American strategic interests in the Middle East was promoted and grew within the Pentagon and the State Department.[60]

Around 1980 Turkey's overall strategic value in the light of the new international security environment was epitomized by US officials as follows. First, its traditional strategic significance as a key element in the defence of NATO's southern flank as well as in the protection of the Western communication lines in the Eastern Mediterranean (mainly through Turkey's control of the Turkish Straits) was magnified. Second, the significance of Turkey's military installations and intelligence-collection bases gathering information on Soviet military activity had increased after the loss of similar facilities in Iran and was even bound to rise further due to expectations of instability in the Middle East and of increased Soviet activity in the area. Third, Turkey's potential role in the security of the Middle East in general and the Persian Gulf in particular was becoming increasingly relevant.[61] The Incirlik air base in southeastern Turkey was the most forward land base in the Eastern Mediterranean for the deployment of US fighters launching a conventional or tactical nuclear strike in the event of military operations in the Gulf. Also, the storage depots near the Syrian border were considered to be the most important supply and storage centers for US military forces in the extreme Eastern Mediterranean.[62]

Zbigniew Brzezinski and Paul Henze – a CIA official who had served in the US embassy in Turkey (1974–7) and became Brzezinski's deputy in the National Security Council (1977–80) specializing on Turkey, Greece and Cyprus – emerged as fervent advocates of Turkey's strategic significance for

US interests during this period.[63] Another prominent champion of Turkey was Albert Wohlstetter, the defense analyst who had noticeable influence on strategy-planning circles within the bureaucracy. Wohlstetter, a nuclear strategist, for decades at the RAND (the think tank of the US Air Force) held teaching positions at Berkeley and the University of Chicago. He had been a staunch opponent and critic of the policy of détente and was very active in making public interventions on issues of US security and foreign policy.[64] In 1965 and 1977 during the Johnson and Ford administrations respectively he was awarded the Department of Defense Medal for Exceptional Civilian Service, the highest honour paid to a civilian by the US Department of Defense. In 1985 President Reagan awarded him the Presidential Medal of Freedom, America's highest civilian award.

In the late 1970s Wohlstetter re-focused with intensity the strategic debate on Turkey and its potential role within the context of the new security challenges to US interests. Convinced of Moscow's expansionist designs in the Persian Gulf region he underlined Turkey's strategic value. He argued publicly in favour of lifting the embargo[65] in order to close the gap that, in his view, existed along the southern line of NATO defence. Actually he challenged NATO's defence planning which was based on the assumption that the major thrust of a Soviet attack would come through the centre of Europe. He argued, instead, that the allies were exposed in the south in Turkey (and in the north in Norway).[66] Wohlstetter not only confirmed Turkey's strategic importance within the context of the established strategic thinking, which held that its participation in the major theaters of war in NATO's southern region was vital to the success of the Western alliance, he also emphasized Turkey's potential contribution to the defence of the Persian Gulf. In hindsight we can say that his linking Turkey with Gulf security had a major impact on the US view of Turkey's strategic role and hence on the shaping of US policy toward Turkey in the following years.

Turkey, of course, had been an important and strong supporter of US strategic objectives in the Middle East back in the 1950s, as mentioned earlier. However, Turkey's role in this regard had been frozen in the eyes of US officials since the 1960s. This was mainly due to the more independent foreign policy that Turkish governments developed in the Middle East since the 1960s but also to the Shah's regime in Iran, which meanwhile had emerged as the chief policeman for US interests in the Gulf. But in the final days of the 1970s Wohlstetter, who believed that Turkey because of its location could play a crucial role in the protection of Persian Gulf oil fields, rekindled bureaucratic interest in Turkey. In his view Turkey's contribution to the successful defence of the area would be in the form of the following: first, fighters deployed from Turkish bases could interrupt the Soviet lines of communication in the event of Soviet aggression against the Gulf area via Iran. All the more remarkably, Wohlstetter thought that Turkey might provide the only bases in the area from which the origins of the Soviet attack could be attacked.[67] Second, he argued that operations in the Gulf area originating from Turkey would demonstrate allied involvement due to Turkey's NATO membership. Therefore, he thought it important that there should be joint defence preparations in Turkey's territory between other members of the alliance and Turkey against potential Soviet aggression in the Gulf to help deter any inclination by Moscow to move against this area.[68]

Wohlstetter's point of view regarding Turkey's role in the defence of the Gulf resounded particularly with Pentagon circles and found a welcoming ear within the Carter and even more so the Reagan administrations. As prominent American security analyst Lawrence Whetten characteristically observed in 1981 in *Strategic Review*,[69] the belief that NATO's southern flank constituted a second front as a result of the invasion of Afghanistan, and that Turkey after the loss of Iran was the only real barrier in the region against a Soviet military advance to the oil fields of the Persian Gulf, was held widely within the Pentagon.[70] Moreover, in the event of a Soviet incursion into Transcaucasia and Iran Washington expected that Turkey would be able to support Iranian resistance against the Soviets and thus add to the frustration of Moscow's ambitious plans.[71] In the early 1980s Wohlstetter emerged as one of the Pentagon's major sources of strategic analysis regarding the defence of the Gulf[72] and his views on Turkey were endorsed almost completely by the Reagan administration.[73] Certainly the appointment of Richard Perle to the position of assistant secretary of defense for international security policy (1981–87) greatly contributed to the dissemination of Wohlstetter's views inside the Pentagon. Perle had been Wohlstetter's student and was deeply inspired by him. As a young graduate he had also been exposed to and influenced by the foreign policy views of Dean Acheson – President Truman's secretary of state, who helped design the administration's policy at the beginning of the Cold War – and Paul Nitze – the chief architect of US policy towards the Soviet Union for most of the Cold War.[74] Perle had an engrossing interest in Turkey, due to Wohlstetter's strategic theory, which had shaped much of his own strategic perceptions.[75] And in the 1980s he would emerge as a staunch and successful advocate of Turkey's strategic role inside the bureaucratic apparatus.

Notes

1 The information that follows is based on: United States Congress, Senate Committee on Armed Services, *The Military Aspects of Banning Arms Aid to Turkey. Hearing before the Committee on Armed Services*, United States Senate, ninety-fifth Congress, second session, 28 June 1978, Washington DC: US Government Printing Office, 1978, passim; United States Congress, Senate Committee on Foreign Relations, *Fiscal Year 1980 International Security Assistance Authorization Hearings, February 28–April 30, 1979*, ninety-sixth Congress, first session on S. 584, To Amend the Foreign Assistance Act of 1961 and the Arms Export Control Act, and for Other Purposes, Washington DC: US Government Printing Office, 1979, pp. 480–82, 507.

2 J. W. Spain, *American Diplomacy in Turkey: Memoirs of an Ambassador Extraordinary and Plenipotentiary*, New York: Praeger Publishers, 1984, p. 35.

3 The other members of the pact were Iran, Iraq, Pakistan and the United Kingdom.

4 Department of State to the Embassy in Turkey, Washington, 28 May 1955, *Foreign Relations of the United States* [*FRUS*], *1955–1957, Near East Region; Iran; Turkey*, vol. XII, Washington DC: US Government Printing Office, 1991, pp. 59–60; National Intelligence Estimate, Washington DC, 21 June 1955, ibid., p. 83; notes prepared by the Secretary of State, Washington DC, 17 October 1955, ibid., p. 172; memorandum from the Assistant Secretary of State for Near Eastern, South Asian, and African Affairs (Rountree) to the Secretary of State, 4 April 1957, ibid., p. 487.

5 Memorandum of discussion at the 461st meeting of the National Security Council (NSC), Washington DC, 29 September 1960, *FRUS, 1958–1960, Eastern Europe; Finland; Greece; Turkey*, vol. X, part 2, Washington DC: US Government Printing Office, 1993, p. 886; Congressional Research Service, Foreign Affairs and National Defense Division, *Turkey's Problems and Prospects: Implications for U.S. Interests*, report prepared for the Subcommittee on Europe and the Middle East of the Committee on Foreign Affairs, US House of Representatives, Washington DC: US Government Printing Office, 1980, p. 38. It is difficult to calculate the exact amounts of overall assistance to Turkey during this period, because a lot of it fell under very many different types of assistance programmes which are not always accounted for in the relevant reports.

6 However, Turkey did not negate of any of its NATO commitments. G. S. Harris, *Troubled Alliance: Turkish-American Problems in Perspective, 1945–1971*, Washington DC: American Enterprise Institute for Public Policy Research, 1972, offers a first-rate account and analysis of the bilateral relationship and its problems during this period.

7 Among others, S. Taşhan, 'Turkey's Relations with the U.S.A. and Possible Future Developments', *Diş Politika* (Foreign Policy), vol. 8, 1979, p. 18; D. Bazoğlu Sezer, 'Turkey and the Western Alliance in the 1980s', in A. Eralp, M. Tünay, B. Yeşilada (eds) *The Political and Socioeconomic Transformation of Turkey*, Westport, CT: Praeger, 1993, p. 218 (on Sezer's views see also fn. 8 below); W. Hale, *Turkish Foreign Policy, 1774–2000*, London: Frank Cass, 2000, pp. 148–50; N. Uslu, *The Turkish-American Relationship between 1947 and 2003: The History of a Distinctive Alliance*, New York: Nova Science Publishers, Inc., 2003, pp. 184–6, 217.

8 This view (which the author shares) is offered by among others W. Laqueur, *The Struggle for the Middle East: The Soviet Union in the Mediterranean 1958–1968*, New York: Macmillan, 1969, pp. 26–7; comments by K. Karpat in 'Discussion on "Turkey between Alliance And Alienation"', *Dış Politika* (Foreign Policy), vol. 8, 1980, p. 132; M. L. Evriviades, 'Turkey's Role in United States Strategy during and after the Cold War', *Mediterranean Quarterly*, vol. 9, 1998, pp. 40–41. It should be mentioned that in the late 1970s D. Sezer (see fn. 7 above) also de-emphasized the importance of the Cyprus issue as the main factor shaping Ankara's stance towards the US: see comments by D. Sezer in 'Discussion on "Turkey between Alliance And Alienation"', p. 126.

9 M. Handel, *Weak States in the International System*, London: Frank Cass, 1990, pp. 192, 187–95.

10 Actually the US had been insisting since the end of the 1950s that Turkey should be using national resources to finance its defence budget instead of relying on US aid, National Security Council Report, NSC 6015/1, Statement of U.S. Policy toward Turkey, Washington DC, 5 October 1960, *FRUS, 1958–1960*, p. 894.

11 Congressional Research Service, *Turkey's Problems and Prospects*, pp. 37–38.

12 Telegram from the embassy in Turkey to the Department of State, Ankara, 13 July 1960, *FRUS, 1958–1960*, p. 856; Harris, *Troubled Alliance*, pp. 150–51. In response, the US encouraged the Turks to revise their force goals, taking into consideration Turkey's economic capacity as well as the amount of foreign

assistance, memorandum of discussion at the 461st meeting of the NSC, 29 September 1960, *FRUS, 1958–1960,* pp. 885–7; National Security Council Report, NSC 6015/1, 5 October 1960, ibid., p. 897.

13 Laqueur, *Struggle for the Middle East*, p. 25.

14 Laqueur, *Struggle for the Middle East*, pp. 26–7.

15 Laqueur, *Struggle for the Middle East*, p. 26; B. R. Kuniholm, 'Turkey and NATO: Past, Present, Future', *Orbis*, vol. 27, 1983, p. 427; Hale, *Turkish Foreign Policy*, p. 151.

16 Department of State research memorandum no. REU-35 to Secretary Rusk, 11 June 1968, *FRUS, 1964–1968, Western Europe Region*, vol.XIII, Washington DC: US Government Printing Office, 1995, p. 711.

17 Warren to Assistant Secretary of State for Near Eastern and South Asian Affairs (Jones), 11 August 1960, *FRUS, 1958–1960*, p. 873.

18 Warren to Assistant Secretary of State for Near Eastern and South Asian Affairs (Jones), 11 August 1960, *FRUS, 1958–1960*, p. 873.

19 M. Mufti, *Daring and Caution in Turkish Strategic Culture: Republic at Sea*, Houndmills, Basingstoke: Palgrave Macmillan, 2009, p. 41.

20 Laqueur, *Struggle for the Middle East*, p. 16. It was in 1968 following the publication of Robert Kennedy's account of the crisis that the Turks' suspicions were confirmed, Hale, *Turkish Foreign Policy*, p. 135.

21 Memorandum of conversation: subject, Turkish Missiles and the Cuban Crisis, 29 October 1962, *FRUS, 1961–1963, Eastern Europe; Cyprus; Greece; Turkey*, vol. XVI, Washington DC: US Government Printing Office, 1994, p. 733.

22 G. E. Gruen, 'Ambivalence in the Alliance: U.S. Interests in the Middle East and the Evolution of Turkish Foreign Policy', *Orbis*, vol. 24, 1980, p. 369.

23 Laqueur, *Struggle for the Middle East*, p. 16.

24 On the foreign policy approaches of the left in Turkey at the time, see Laqueur, *Struggle for the Middle East*, pp. 17, 19; Hale, *Turkish Foreign Policy*, p. 150. E. J. Zürcher, *Turkey: A Modern History*, London: I. B. Tauris, 1993, p. 289.

25 D. Vital, *The Inequality of States*, Oxford: Clarendon Press, 1967, p. 187.

26 Vital, *Inequality of States*, p. 187.

27 For a succinct account of how the Turkish leadership viewed relations with the US during this period and the adjustments in their policy toward the Middle East see Hale, *Turkish Foreign Policy*, pp. 150–54, 162, 170. See also K. H. Karpat, 'Turkish and Arab Israeli Relations', in K. H. Karpat *et al.*, *Turkey's Foreign Policy in Transition, 1950–1974*, Leiden: Brill, 1975, pp. 122–5; M. Hakan Yavuz, 'O Diismos stis Tourkoaravikes Sxesis ke to Palestiniako Zitima', in Faruk Sönmezoğlu (ed.), *Mythos ke Pragmatikotita: Analysi tis Tourkikis Exoterikis Politikis*, Athens: Infognomon, 2001, tomos B, pp. 187–8.

28 F. Stern, 'Germany in a Semi-Gaullist Europe', *Foreign Affairs*, vol. 58, 1980, p. 871.

29 Laqueur, *Struggle for the Middle East*, pp. 14–28.

30 Harris, *Troubled Alliance*, pp. 128–47, 160–69.

31 In the late 1960s and early 1970s, US administrations put a lot of pressure on Turkey to stop the opium-poppy cultivation, J. W. Spain, 'The United States, Turkey and the Poppy', *Middle East Journal*, 1975, vol. 29.

32 G. S. Harris, 'Turkish-American relations since the Truman Doctrine', in M. Aydin and Çağrı Erhan (eds), *Turkish American Relations: Past, Present and Future*, London: Routledge, 2004, p. 71.

33 During this period following the debacle in Vietnam and the Watergate scandal Congress sought to reassert its authority over the executive. Within this battle between the two institutions the Cyprus issue became partly a convenient stick to beat the executive with.

34 At Sinop, Pirinçlik, Belbasi, Karamursel.

35 *The Washington Post*, 26 July 1975. I use the British system when referring to dates of American publications and documents.
36 United States Congress, *Military Aspects of Banning Arms Aid to Turkey*, pp. 6, 8, 15, 17, 26, 50–51, 70–71, 75.
37 E. B. Laipson, *Congressional-Executive Relations and the Turkish Arms Embargo*, Congress and Foreign Policy Series, Washington, DC: US Government Printing Office, 1981, pp. 23–5.
38 United States Congress, Senate Committee on Foreign Relations, *United States-Turkish Defense Cooperation Agreement: Hearing before the Committee on Foreign Relations*, United States Senate, ninety-fourth Congress, second session, on S. J. Res. 204. 15 September 1976, Washington DC: US Government Printing Office, 1976, passim.
39 Laipson, *Congressional-Executive Relations*, p. 26.
40 Laipson, *Congressional-Executive Relations*, pp. 23–5.
41 Congressional Research Service, *Turkey's Problems and Prospects*, p. 26; Laipson, *Congressional-Executive Relations*, p. 26.
42 Laipson, *Congressional-Executive Relations*, pp. 26–7.
43 United States Congress, *Military Aspects of Banning Arms Aid to Turkey*, p. 8.
44 Laipson, *Congressional-Executive Relations*, p. 27.
45 Hale, *Turkish Foreign Policy*, p. 162.
46 Hale, *Turkish Foreign Policy*, p. 162. Ecevit was visiting Moscow in order to conclude a Political Document on the Principles of Good Neighbourly and Friendly Cooperation with the Soviet Union.
47 A reference to the reduced level of co-operation with the US in reaction to the embargo.
48 Summary record of a meeting with the participation of heads of states and government held in the State Department, Washington DC, on Tuesday, 30th May 1978, C-R (78) 22 part I, p. 21, NATO archives.
49 *The Washington Post*, 4 October 1978.
50 L. L. Whetten, 'Turkey and NATO's Second Front', *Strategic Review*, Summer 1981, p. 58.
51 *The New York Times*, 16 June 1978, p. 11; J. Phillips, *Afghanistan: The Soviet Quagmire*, Washington DC: The Heritage Foundation, Backgrounder 101, 25 October 1979, pp. 4–5, 7; J. E. Peterson, *Defending Arabia*, London: Croom Helm, 1986, p. 116.
52 For a brief but succinct presentation of this debate, see Peterson, *Defending Arabia*, pp. 97–9.
53 CHAMILCOM-1–80, 1 January 1980, pp. 1–2, NATO archives.
54 On US security concerns and defence strategy vis-à-vis the Soviet Union in relation to the Gulf region during the latter part of the Carter administration and in the early 1980s, see G. Sick, 'The Evolution of U.S. Strategy toward the Indian Ocean and Persian Gulf Regions', in A. Z. Rubinstein (ed.), *The Great Game: Rivalry in the Persian Gulf and South Asia*, New York: Praeger, 1983; G. Kemp, 'Strategic Problems in the Persian Gulf Region', in G. S. Wise and C. Issawi (eds), *Middle East Perspectives: The Next Twenty Years*, Princeton, NJ: Darwin Press, 1981; H. Brown, *U.S. Security Policy in Southwest Asia: A Case Study in Complexity*, Washington DC: Johns Hopkins University School of Advanced International Studies, Johns Hopkins Foreign Policy Institute, Occasional Paper, 1981 (Brown was Secretary of Defense under Carter); P. Jabber, 'U.S. Interests and Regional Security in the Middle East', *Daedalus*, vol. 109, 1980; also Peterson, *Defending Arabia*, pp. 87–142, 181–93.
55 Z. Brzezinski, *Power and Principle: Memoirs of the National Security Adviser, 1977–1981*, New York: Farrar, Strauss, Giroux, 1983, p. 444.
56 Sick, 'Evolution of U.S. Strategy', p. 74.

57 Congressional Research Service, *The Persian Gulf: Are We committed? At What Cost? A Dialogue with the Reagan Administration on U.S. Policy*, prepared for the use of the Joint Economic Committee, Congress of the United States with the assistance of the Congressional Research Service, Washington DC: US Government Printing Office, 1981, pp. 16–17 and passim; J. H. Sigler, 'Evaluating Reagan's Middle East Policy: A First Term Balance Sheet', in P. Marantz and B. S. Steinberg (eds), *Superpower Involvement in the Middle East: Dynamics of Foreign Policy*, Boulder, CO: Westview Press, 1985, pp. 250–51; Peterson, *Defending Arabia*, p. 99, 116–17.

58 Congressional Research Service, *Persian Gulf: Are We Committed?*, p. 34.

59 Peterson, *Defending Arabia*, p. 118.

60 For a good overview of the Pentagon and State Department views concerning Turkey's strategic significance at the end of the 1970s and during the first Reagan administration, see Congressional Research Service, *Turkey's Problems and prospects*, pp. 14–24, 48–9; G. S. Harris, 'Introduction', in G. S. Harris (ed.), *The Middle East in Turkish-American Relations*, Washington, DC: The Heritage Foundation, 1985; B. Kuniholm, 'Turkey in the World', in Harris (ed.), *The Middle East in Turkish-American Relations*; R. Burt, 'Turkey and the Reagan Administration', in Harris (ed.), *The Middle East in Turkish-American Relations*; R. Perle, 'Turkey and US Military Assistance', in Harris (ed.), *The Middle East in Turkish-American Relations*; United States Congress, House, Committee on Foreign Affairs, *United States-Turkey Defense and Economic Cooperation Agreement Hearing before the Subcommittee on Europe and the Middle East of the Committee on Foreign Affairs*, House of Representatives, Washington DC: US Government Printing Office, 1980, p. 5; S. Sayarı, 'Regional Security Issues and U.S.-Turkish Relations in the 1980s', paper presented at the conference on 'The History of American-Turkish Relations, 1833–1989', Boğaziçi University, Istanbul, 5–6 June 2006. I would like to thank Professor Sayarı for supplying me with a copy of his paper. Also, J. A. Philips, 'Turkey: An Increasingly Key Strategic Asset for the U.S.', Washington DC: The Heritage Foundation, Backgrounder 609, 1987.

61 Congressional Research Service, *Turkey's Problems and Prospects*, pp. 1–2, 4, 21–2; B. Kuniholm, 'East or West? The Geopolitics of Turkey and Its NATO Alliance', in A. L. Karaosmanoğlu, S. Taşhan (eds), *Middle East, Turkey and the Atlantic Alliance*, Ankara: Foreign Policy Institute, 1987, pp. 134, 140–45.

62 Congressional Research Service, *Turkey's Problems and Prospects*, pp. 19, 56.

63 M. L. Evriviades, *The U.S. and Cyprus: The Politics of Manipulation in the 1985 U.N. Cyprus High-Level Meeting*, Athens: Institute of International Relations, Occasional Research Paper no. 3, October 1992, p. 6. According to *The New York Times* Henze had served in Ankara as CIA station-chief, mentioned in Evriviades, *The U.S. and Cyprus*.

64 See the collection of his published (and unpublished) essays, R. Zarate, H. Sokolski (eds), *Nuclear Heuristics: Selected Writings of Albert and Roberta Wohlstetter*, Carlisle, PA: Strategic Studies Institute, 2009.

65 A. Wohlstetter, 'Lift the Turkish Embargo', *Wall Street Journal*, 14 June 1978.

66 A. Weisman, *Prince of Darkness: Richard Perle. The Kingdom, the Power and the End of Empire in America*, New York: Union Square Press, 2007, p. 116.

67 Mentioned in A. L. Karaosmanoğlu, 'Turkey's Security Policy in the Middle East', *Dış Politika* (Foreign Policy) vol. X, 1983, p. 10. (Karaosmanoğlu's article was also published but in somewhat more condensed form in *Foreign Affairs*: A. L. Karaosmanoğlu, 'Turkey's Security and the Middle East', *Foreign Affairs*, vol. 62, 1983).

68 Karaosmanoğlu, 'Turkey's Security Policy in the Middle East' p. 10; also Wohlstetter, 'Lift the Turkish Embargo'; *Discriminate Deterrence*, report of the Commission on Integrated Long-Term Strategy, Washington, DC: US Government Printing

Office, January 1988, p. 68. Wohlstetter was the principal author of the report. He and Fred C. Iklé, assistant secretary of defense for political affairs (1981–88) in the Reagan administration, were co-chairmen of the commission. Iklé was also a RAND strategist and had worked alongside Wohlstetter. The commission was created in the mid 1980s with the task of re-assessing US foreign policy.

69 The periodic publication of the United States Strategic Institute. The independent United States Strategic Institute expressed to a large extent the views of those among the US military leadership who gave special emphasis on the need to beef up US security.

70 Whetten, 'Turkey and NATO's Second Front', p. 57; US Congress, Senate Committee on Foreign Relations, *Fiscal Year 1980 International Security Assistance Authorization. Hearings, February 28 – April 30, 1979*, ninety-sixth Congress, first session on S. 584, To Amend the Foreign Assistance Act of 1961 and the Arms Export Control Act, and for Other Purposes, Washington DC: US Government Printing Office, 1979, pp. 480–82, 507; Congressional Research Service, *Turkey's Problems and Prospects*, p. 15.

71 Harris, 'Introduction', p. ix; Kuniholm, 'Turkey in the World', p. 14.

72 Zarate, Sokolski, *Nuclear Heuristics*, pp. 31, 47, 88, fn. 165; Evriviades, *U.S. and Cyprus*, p. 7.

73 Karaosmanoğlu, 'Turkey's Security Policy in the Middle East', p. 11; Evriviades, 'Turkey's Role in United States Strategy', p. 43.

74 In the summer of 1969 Perle as a graduate student worked in the Washington office of the Committee to Maintain a Prudent Defense Policy, which was created by Acheson and Nitze with the aim of lobbying Congress to continue support for antiballistic missile systems, James Mann, *Rise of the Vulcans: The History of Bush's War Cabinet*, New York: Viking, 2004, pp. 31–2.

75 J. Heilbrunn, *They Knew They Were Right: The Rise of the Neocons*, New York: Doubleday, 2008, pp. 98–9; Weisman, *Prince of Darkness*, p. 116.

2 When US interests and Turkish needs meet

Ankara's perception of threat ...

Most accounts of Turkey–US relations maintain that the significant political changes near Turkey's borders in 1979 gave rise to security concerns in Ankara which compelled Turkish leaders to close ranks again with their Western allies and to strengthen their defence co-operation and consultation with the US. The clearest sign of this change in Turkish policy, it is noted, was the signing of a new Defense and Economic Co-operation Agreement (DECA) (March 1980) after the quick settlement of very important controversies.[1] More specifically, it is argued that the abating of the Turks' suspicions and bitterness toward the US was mainly the result of the invasion of Afghanistan, which caused profound security concerns in Turkey as it was itself going through a period of instability and political violence: 'The Soviet Afghan policy was the single most important event for Turkey, possibly a watershed' because it aroused 'strong suspicions' in Ankara that 'its great northern neighbor returned to an interventionist and expansionist foreign policy.'[2] It invoked 'the specter of a similar move by the Soviet Union against its other neighbors, including Turkey.'[3] It caused fears in Ankara that 'may be only the first step in extending Soviet influence into the subcontinent, ... to gain control of all or part of Iran'.[4] A number of the same accounts also identify the Iranian Revolution and the establishment of a radical Islamist regime in Tehran as another cause of security concern for Ankara. The reason was that Turkish leaders regarded the political change in neighbouring Iran both as a source of regional instability and a threat to Turkey's internal order and security for it posed a significant challenge to the secular Kemalist ideology which legitimized the Turkish state. However, it is recognized that the influence of the Iranian Revolution on the Turks' decision to renew their defence ties with Washington was limited.[5] In short, mainstream accounts of the Turkey–US relationship concur with the view that in the beginning of the 1980s overall 'the graveness of the external environment in Southwestern Asia helped reconfirm for Turkish governments the continuing relevance of NATO, and in particular the special security relationship with the US'.[6] Change in Turkey's domestic politics, more specifically the

September 1980 military coup that brought the Turkish generals to power, has also been identified as an additional reason that was 'no less influential in the redirection of [Turkish] foreign policy' closer to the US[7] for a number of reasons. Thus, it has been argued that Turkey's new rulers 'were acutely conscious of the way their country's security had been affected by both internal and external developments … and desired to restore the old, stable Turkish–American relationship.'[8] Also, according to another argument, the conservative worldview of the Turkish military provided strong pro-American and pro-NATO policies.[9] Another explanation given is that because the military regime, which officially stayed in power from 1980–83, felt isolated in Europe, where it was heavily criticized by Turkey's European allies (but not by Washington), and it became dependent on the US for political backing internationally.[10] Furthermore, it is pointed out that the keen interest in greater co-operation with the Americans continued under the premiership of Turgut Özal (1983–89) due to the fact that he more than any other Turkish politician was much more favourably disposed towards the US and its regional and global policies.[11]

There is no doubt that the strengthening of Turkey's defence co-operation with Washington during the 1980s had a lot to do with the establishment of the military regime in Ankara, but *not only* for the reasons mentioned above, as we shall discuss later on. The smooth building of defence ties between Turkey and the US was also somewhat facilitated by Özal being in power. But the view that Ankara's re-engagement with the US at the down of the 1980s was mainly due to the Turks' perception of a renewed Soviet threat against the backdrop of instability in Turkey is not convincing. At first glance it seems self-evident to conclude this. However, it has to be said that in reality it is very difficult to establish with precision how the Turkish leadership considered developments in the periphery of their country. Even more importantly, it is hard to establish – solely on the basis of the available public statements of Turkish leaders and before the relevant archival documentation becomes accessible – how these considerations affected the Turks' perspectives concerning their policy toward the US.[12]

Actually what we do know suggests that the invasion of Afghanistan, however disturbing for Turkish leaders, did not have a catalytic effect on their minds concerning Turkey's security, which according to the established view triggered their decision to re-engage with the Americans. On 3 January, less than two weeks after the invasion, at the first 1980 meeting of the NATO Military Committee, Vice Admiral Sabahattin Ergin, the Turkish member of the committee, did not convey the message that his government or Turkish military authorities were particularly apprehensive about Turkish security. He rather made the blunt point that 'the dangers to Turkey and NATO were underscored by this latest Soviet move' in order to note that the alliance members had to 'ensure that this sensitive flank area received the economic and arms support it required to present a solid and credible deterrence',[13] which was actually Turkey's recurrent point – as far as its own needs were concerned – at NATO meetings. That the Turks were not disquieted so much as to overlook other considerations and support US military initiatives aimed at meeting the challenge of the Soviet threat in the area was illustrated at another meeting of the NATO Military Committee at the end of February. The meeting discussed a draft US paper on Afghanistan, which 'called for a capability to surge significant forces' into the Middle East, emphasizing that for this purpose 'extra resources were required' and suggesting that European allies could take additional measures 'such as increasing their reserve forces to strengthen Europe'.[14] This time Vice Admiral Ergin spoke at length in order to impress upon the Americans Turkey's different, calmer perspective. The Soviet invasion, he said,

> was a flagrant violation of International Law and a direct threat to peace. Moreover Soviet expansion into neighbouring countries would further aggravate this threat … . He emphasized, however, that in asking for contributions from NATO countries located close to the areas affected, the political situation, regional issues and long term national interests should be thoroughly evaluated. He stressed that it was not possible to maintain stability and security in the area by force alone … . With this in mind, he urged that national tendencies and the character of the legal [*sic*] Government in the area should be taken fully into account when determining deterrent measures, and particularly the military measures to be taken.[15]

Clearly if Soviet action in Afghanistan had helped remind the Turks of the value of the NATO alliance it did not cause them enough apprehension to make them close ranks with the US and accept the need to engage in strong military tactics with its ally. The memoirs of James Spain, the US ambassador to Ankara at the time (1980–81), fully confirm this. In fact, the US ambassador shows that the Turks' main preoccupation was not 'to provoke the Soviet Union'. In his own words 'condemning the Soviet action vigorously in words, the Turks were cautious in action.'[16] They insisted on keeping their ambassador in Kabul while other Western states were withdrawing their representations. They adopted an 'evasive' stance on the US request that Turkey join in a boycott of the summer Olympics in Moscow. In the end the Demirel government decided to join in the boycott, however only after considerable US diplomatic pressure including a letter to the Turkish prime minister from President Carter. But Demirel made clear to the Americans that the Turkish government wished to announce the decision first and in its own way.[17] The basic point that the Turks were not really uneasy concerning their own security following events in Afghanistan is also confirmed by another contemporary State Department official and Turkey analyst. The perceptive and well-informed director of analysis for the Near East and South Asia in the Bureau of Intelligence and Research at the State Department, writing not long after the invasion remarked that

> while Afghanistan raises for the present at least the Soviet threat factor, it does not alarm the Turks. They deplore the USSR's invasion and joined

> Islamic nations in demanding immediate Soviet withdrawal. Yet, the Turks do not fear invasion of their own country; the intense Cold War attitudes of the 1950s are still quite absent in Turkey.[18]

'Hence', concluded he insightfully, 'Ankara is unlikely to feel the need to subordinate other concerns in order to assure American support against the northern foe.'[19] Moreover, Turkish leaders had 'no appetite for heightened East-West tension, which could jeopardize Turkey's stable relations with the Soviet Union' as the US Senate delegation that visited Turkey a few months after the invasion stated in their report.[20]

Ali Karaosmanoğlu's very carefully crafted paper in *Foreign Affairs* (1983), which articulated Ankara's thinking, also helps illustrate the case in point. The distinguished Turkish security analyst on the one hand noted that the 'threat facing the southern flank of NATO in general and Turkey in particular had grown steadily in recent years' inducing Turkey to increase military co-operation with the US. But on the other he emphasized that Turkey had to act 'cautiously'. In other words, it had to be careful not to be 'provocative' to avoid being caught in a regional confrontation between the two superpowers.[21]

Such a cautious and cool-headed approach, which, by the way, was very similar to the one also taken by NATO's other European members, reflected an ambivalence that would have no place in an environment where the conviction of confrontation was prevailing. Had the Turks really been experiencing a deep-seated fear over Soviet intentions they would have been energized to take joint action with the US as had been the case in the 1950s. Instead they even concluded a trade pact with the Soviet Union in January 1982, exactly at the time when the Americans sought to convince their Western allies to cut down their economic dealings with Moscow because of the Polish crisis.[22]

The truth of the matter was that the Turks, like the European allies, did not want to give up the valuable fruits of détente because of the renewed tension between the two big powers. Ankara maintained a cautious but calm relationship with Moscow, in spite of difficulties and problems simmering under the surface, since the end of the 1960s.[23] The relationship had a significant economic side due to the Soviet aid to Turkey which had been increasing after 1974. In total from 1967 to 1979 Soviet aid to Turkey amounted to 650 million dollars, making Turkey the largest recipient of such aid outside the Soviet bloc.[24] Following the invasion of Afghanistan Ankara's interest in maintaining its correct relations with the Soviet Union remained strong and Moscow seemed to share the same objective.[25] In brief Afghanistan was not 'allowed to become a major problem in Turkish-Soviet relations.'[26]

It was not only that the Turks, in Bruce Kuniholm's words, 'were determined not to be intimidated by the threat of greatly increased Soviet capabilities in the region.'[27] The ongoing dialogue between the Turkish governments and the US executive during the embargo years clearly shows, as mentioned earlier, that since the mid 1970s – well before the Soviet moves in the periphery of the Gulf – Ankara wished to renew its strategic co-operation with the US at the desired level for both sides as long as the US Congress was willing to respond positively to Turkey's demands for military and economic assistance. This was the clear message that the Demirel coalition government sent to Washington soon after the implementation of the embargo.[28] Hence, in 1976 Demirel's government happily signed a new Defense Cooperation Agreement (DCA) with the Ford administration, which committed the US to multiyear security aid amounting to one billion dollars over the four-year life of the agreement, of which no less than 200 million would be in the form of grants.[29]

Clearly neither the Turkish ruling elites' indignation at its American ally nor accumulated bilateral tension had eroded the widely held view among Turkish leaders that the economic and political interests of their country demanded that Turkey remain in NATO and maintain its relationship with Washington.[30] Undoubtedly the fact that the Ford and later the Carter administrations sought to restore high levels of military assistance to Turkey in addition to the partial lifting of the embargo (Sept 1975) helped sustain this view.[31] Even more importantly, despite the adoption of a multi-dimensional foreign policy by the Turkish governments, the Turks' growing determination to keel aloof from US strategic initiatives and the lessening of American influence in Ankara since the 1960s, there had been no radical re-orientation of Turkey away from the West, the US or NATO. It is very telling that after the US Congress imposed a complete embargo on all arms deliveries Turkey did not withdraw in protest from NATO's military branch (as Greece did following Turkey's invasion of Cyprus in protest at the inaction of NATO and the US).

That in the end the 1976 Defense Cooperation Agreement was stillborn was not because of a negative backlash in Turkey but because Congress refused to ratify it when Ankara – which was negotiating very cautiously, as one might expect – declined to accept the condition that the Turks make concessions over Cyprus first. In other words while the Turkish governments showed a vivid interest in renewing security co-operation with the US the base that was necessary – from a Turkish perspective – to support such co-operation was not there: due to resistance in Congress the US was not prepared to give Turkey military and economic assistance but also indirect support for its Cyprus policy via the decoupling of military and economic aid from progress regarding Cyprus.[32] So, when in 1978 Congress decided to fully co-operate with the Carter administration by lifting the embargo and increasing the assistance to Turkey without linking, except in its rhetoric, assistance levels to Turkey with Turkish compromises over Cyprus[33] the path for re-building the defence co-operation opened up. In brief the Turkey–US security co-operation was renewed in the late 1970s and not earlier not because the Turks adjusted their policy due to increased security concerns but because the US did.

... and the more pressing economic reality

Receiving US 'stable' assistance was one of the main issues that preoccupied the Demirel government when negotiating the terms of re-newed defence co-operation with Washington since the mid 1970s.[34] US assistance was what determined, in the final analysis, the degree of the Turks' re-engagement with the Americans. This was hardly surprising as Turkey was experiencing an economic shock due to the 1973 oil crisis but also because of the multiple miscalculations and mistakes of the Turkish governments.[35] The economic crisis grew significantly worse after 1974. In the main it took the form of a balance of payments crisis, which resulted in a severe shortage of even basic commodities. In Ankara the urgency to secure external economic assistance alongside political support in order to restore Turkey's creditworthiness in the financial markets became more and more pressing after the mid 1970s. While in 1973 the country had a surplus of 484 million dollars, in 1977 it was faced with a deficit of more than 3.4 billion dollars. Turkey's ability to borrow in the international financial markets was dramatically reduced and the country was going to reach its nadir when it became obvious that in 1977 it would fail to make the payments on its huge external borrowings. By 1979 its foreign debt would reach almost 15 billion dollars. In the midst of this 'critical economic situation'[36] the main concern of the Turkish leadership, dwarfing any other consideration, could not but be how to get the country out of the crisis and help it stand back on its feet again.[37]

The economic crisis stung even more deeply because the country was simultaneously experiencing unprecedented political instability, which in its turn was made even more acute due to the dire economic conditions. Amidst political chaos Turkey was shaken by violent clashes between the extreme left and the extreme right (with the tolerance of the moderate right), clashes which reflected not only ideological but also social differences. 'Between 1975 and up to 1980 Turkey experienced a real descent into Hades.'[38] Under these circumstances the key motive driving Ankara's interest in re-newing its defence co-operation with the US should not be looked for in developments around Turkey's borders – which occurred at the end of the decade – but rather in its own domestic environment, punctuated by the utter and complete failure of the 40-year-old policy of economic statism.[39]

The Turks' unfailing insistence that substantial economic aid should be a major component of any new bilateral defence co-operation agreement[40] bore fruit in the end because of the renewed US–Soviet tension at the end of the 1970s. During the fiscal year 1978, and while the embargo was still in place, the total military and economic assistance to Turkey was 176.2 million dollars, of which economic assistance accounted only for 0.8 million. Following the lifting of the embargo Congress approved 225 million dollars assistance to Turkey for the fiscal year 1979. This time, economic assistance amounted to 50.3 million dollars, in other words about a fifth of the total sum. For the fiscal year 1980, and while the new defence agreement was under negotiation, the Carter administration succeeded in substantially raising the total amount of assistance to Turkey to around 402 million. Actually a bigger amount (452 million) would be authorized for the 1981 fiscal year. However, while military assistance increased only by 29 million and 76.7 million in FY 1980 and

FY1981 respectively – compared with that of fiscal year 1979 – economic assistance under the Economic Support Fund (ESF) programme[41] quadrupled, reaching over 203 million dollars in 1980 and 250 in 1981. In other words, it constituted more than 50 per cent of the total amount of US security assistance. Furthermore, in 1980 more than a third of total ESF funds, 75 out of the 203 million, were given to Turkey in the form of grants.[42]

At the end of the 1970s the principal argument the Carter administration employed in order to justify its request to Congress for increased economic assistance was that Turkey's future was of central importance for the protection of US strategic interests vis-à-vis the Soviet Union. Within this context it was stressed that Turkey's dramatic economic condition was undermining its role within NATO. The supporting argument that the dire economic situation was threatening the survival of the parliamentary form of government in the country was also made.[43] Of course, the underlying but clear message was that these amounts were absolutely necessary in order to secure the Turks' full co-operation in defence matters.

To sum up, developments in Afghanistan and in the broader Middle East had indeed a crucial role to play in the renewal of the strategic co-operation between Washington and Ankara and the abating of tension in the bilateral relationship. However, their importance lay more in that they made Congress bridge its differences with the US executive regarding the policy that Washington had to adopt towards Turkey, rather than in their effect on the minds of Turkish leaders.

The making of a strategic co-operation agreement

In the period following the lifting of the embargo (September 1978) and up to January 1980 Washington and Ankara completed much of the drafting of a new, five-year Defense *and* Economic Cooperation Agreement (DECA), which for the first time fully and formally recognized the interrelationship between a strong economy and a strong defence. On the Turkish part the handling of the negotiations with the US involved both Turkey's leading politicians, Süleyman Demirel and Bülent Ecevit, who represented Turkey's center right and social democratic political forces respectively. As the post-embargo negotiations for a new Defense and Economic Cooperation Agreement to upgrade and expand the 1976 DCA began, bilateral discussions were dealt first by the Ecevit coalition government (January 1978 – November 1979) and finally by the Demirel coalition government (November 1979 – September 1980).

According to American sources, negotiations were tough and a few particularly difficult issues remained on the table until the very end of the negotiations process. Principal among them was the question of the usage of the bases. The Turks, fearful that the US might use bases in Turkey for operations in the Middle East, insisted that the text of the agreement should incorporate a clear commitment on the part of the US to the effect that the bases would be used exclusively for NATO-related operations. The Americans on their part resisted such a definite restriction on operational use as Turkey figured in their strategic thinking in the event of a US contingency operation in the Gulf. Instead, they sought to obtain a phrasing that would be more flexible to interpretation. In other words, something that would read: the bases 'will be supporting the fulfilment of NATO commitments.'[44]

The economic dimension of the strategic co-operation was the other major thorny issue during negotiations. Significant disagreements between the two sides were produced by the levels of military as well as economic assistance that the Turks were requesting (between 2.5 and 3.6 billion dollars in the course of five years).[45]

In 1979 the Turkish economy had experienced almost a zero growth rate, inflation had reached above 70 per cent and the already high unemployment was further rising.[46] And although the Turkish government since the end of 1977 had taken measures to restore the country's external trade and payments positions these were going to take time before yielding the expected results, something that Turkey's allies also recognized.[47] There were estimations that the country would need external assistance amounting to at least 8 to 10 billion dollars for the next five years.[48] The amount the Turks asked for during the DECA negotiations far exceeded the amount of one billion dollars they had settled for in the 1976 DCA. Turkish leaders sought to exploit to their maximum advantage the strong bargaining position Turkey found itself in due to the renewal of tension between the two superpowers. In his memoirs, Ambassador Spain gives a taste of the difficulties that arose concerning the issue of US assistance up to the very last minute.[49] The Turks also insisted on a specific financial commitment of US assistance covering several years. This was difficult to achieve. Nevertheless, the American executive was not unsympathetic to Turkish demands because of their own assessment of Turkey's huge military needs, which were seen as being interrelated with its domestic economic problems. Since 1978 the US and the other NATO members repeatedly recognized that the modernization and maintenance of the Turkish armed forces was imperative (something that the Turkish leaders persistently focused on during their talks with the Americans).[50] US officials estimated that almost 50 per cent of Turkey's military equipment badly needed repair and realistically it would be difficult to operate. Actually their conclusion was that the Turkish armed forces had been weakened to the point that they would find it difficult to fulfil their NATO obligations.[51]

The Turks blamed the state of their military preparedness on the embargo to justify their requests for large amounts of US assistance. But the Pentagon and the State Department were not convinced that the embargo, which was limited[52] both in its scope and duration, had been the major reason accounting for the weakness of Turkey's military forces which, they reasoned, had always been 'significantly' lagging behind those of the other NATO allies, despite the large amounts of military assistance provided to the country since it joined the North Atlantic Treaty in 1952.[53] For US officials there were many other causes with far greater impact which accounted for Turkey's 'inadequate and outdated military equipment'.[54] The list was rather long and reminiscent of the problems identified by US officials dealing with Turkey in the late 1950s and the early 1960s: already obsolete equipment, inflation in weapons costs, the lack of usable US excess defence articles, poor Turkish logistics planning for many years, a weak economy which resulted from accumulated mistakes in economic planning, the persistent trend of inward-looking economic development that the Turkish leadership was so attached to and Turkey's 80 per cent dependence on foreign oil. The worldwide US shift from military assistance in loans rather than grants was also thought to have had extremely serious effects because it required repayment of high-interest loans when Turkey was experiencing a shortage of foreign currency in the 1970s. On top of all this, US officials pointed out, there was the burden on Turkey's economy of its 566,000 men in the armed forces, the largest standing army in NATO after that of the US.[55] Their viewpoint was that this force produced 'an inherently inefficient military structure' which in turn demanded 'an irrational allocation of scarce resources'.[56] So there was a large gap between Turkey's military needs and available funds although Turkey was spending over 5 per cent of its gross national product, the third highest in NATO, on military expenditures.[57]

In the wake of the post-embargo period the Pentagon reached two main conclusions regarding assistance to Turkey. The first one was that the US would have to provide Turkey with significant amounts of military assistance over a good length of time in order to upgrade its military forces, although the details of how much and for how long were not yet determined. At the US Senate Foreign Relations Committee hearing on international security assistance authorization for the fiscal year 1980 the chairman of the joint chiefs of staff, General David Jones, stated that the Pentagon had discussed an amount of 4.5 billion dollars over a five-year period as a possibility. Still, according to the US military officials this staggering amount would hardly constitute a proper remedy for Turkey's military problems. As a matter of fact it was not expected that such an amount would provide Turkey with large amounts of new, current-generation equipment. Rather, it would mainly improve Turkey's existing equipment. So although the US general could not tell what specific requests might be made for Turkey by the Pentagon in future years it was 'obvious' to his department that Turkey was going 'to require some continuing assistance'.[58] The second conclusion reached was that besides military assistance the US would also have to support Turkey with substantial economic assistance, not only because its economic growth and its military preparedness were obviously linked but also in order to secure Turkey's co-operation. As an insightful and well-researched report produced by the Foreign Affairs and National Defense Division of the Congressional Research Service in 1980 put it succinctly,

> in view of the significant problems facing Turkey, it seems clear that, for the foreseeable future, Congress will be asked to appropriate substantial

> economic and military assistance to help restore Turkey's military preparedness and economic viability. The position that Congress takes on aid requests is likely to have a profound effect on future United States-Turkish relations and US interests in the eastern Mediterranean.[59]

Besides asking for military and economic aid Ankara placed also on the negotiating table requests for co-production of defence hardware. These related to seven industrial defence projects that aimed to develop Turkey's defence industry and produce locally American defence items.[60] The development of an indigenous defence industry was an ardent desire of Turkish military and political leaders. This keen interest was mainly borne of the shock they experienced when the embargo restricted Turkish access to US weapons. The long-term primary goal was to limit dependency for the modernization of Turkey's armed forces and consequently enhance Turkish security as well as achieve greater freedom of manoeuvre in the pursuit of national interests.[61] But apparently there was more to it. Determination to lessen the country's dependency on foreign weaponry dovetailed nicely with ambitions for Turkey to enter the international arms market as an exporter.[62]

The new agreement

On 29 March 1980 the new Defense and Economic Cooperation Agreement was finally signed and this time Congress ratified it. Six months later there was a military coup in Turkey which brought to its end the Demirel government and the military to power. This development did not affect the implementation of the agreement either by Ankara or by Washington in the least. This was hardly surprising as far as the Turks were concerned. The leader of the coup, General Kenan Evren, was the Turkish general chief of staff (1978–83) whose office had been the military interlocutor during the DECA negotiations. The US administration for its part felt a sense of relief when the coup took place for it promised stability following a long period of political turbulence and street violence in the country.[63] Washington, in stark contrast with most West European capitals, showed a sympathetic understanding of the reasons that had led to the coup. Therefore, the Carter administration adopted a low-key reaction to Turkey's domestic political developments. Furthermore, in its first official post-coup statement the US administration although it emphasized the importance of a speedy return to democracy did not turn this development into a condition for the provision of US assistance.[64] During the following months Washington also offered diplomatic support to the military regime in Europe, where US senior officials lobbied to prevent Turkey's expulsion from the Council of Europe.[65]

According to the well-informed Turkish journalist and political commentator Mehmet Ali Birand, the US intelligence services were responsible for the coup.[66] While this allegation still remains to be proved undoubtedly the Americans did not lack motive. As a matter of fact, before the coup Turkey's political and economic problems were identified in American foreign policy-making circles as the most immediate threat to US interests in the eastern Mediterranean.[67]

The 1980 Defense and Economic Cooperation Agreement provided the new legal and institutional supporting framework for renewed security cooperation between the two countries. For both sides it was the happy end of a long, almost five-year, on-and-off negotiating process (since 1975) which had involved two US administrations that had to negotiate not only with Ankara but also with Congress.

The new agreement repeated the provision in the 1976 DCA[68] which stated that 'the extent of the defence co-operation envisaged … shall be limited to obligations arising out of the North Atlantic Treaty.'[69] The phrasing was more open to interpretation than the provision in the 1969 DCA, which noted that mutual defence cooperation 'will never exceed the limits of NATO commitments',[70] but still specific Turkish approval was required for non-NATO uses of facilities in Turkey. Although it was not what the US was exactly aiming for, it was again a compromise between the clear restrictions the Turks wished for and the Pentagon's desire to get 'the broader possible flexibility' on usage and access to the Turkish facilities.[71] For Ambassador Spain 'the resolution of these contradictory needs was one of the greater achievements of the U.S.-Turkish negotiating teams.'[72]

On the equally thorny issue of US assistance the Carter administration in the end did not commit the US to multi-year aid programmes – something that the 1976 agreement provided for – because, as was pointed out to the Turks, Congress would be unlikely to authorize such a long-term commitment.[73] As the Turks were very unhappy with this a mutually acceptable formula was finally found: the US government agreed to insert more than once in the text of the agreement the pledge that it would 'exert its best efforts to provide mutually agreed financial and technical assistance' to Turkey.[74] Such was the importance Ankara attached to this commitment that the Turks insisted upon receiving also a letter reaffirming the 'best effort' pledge by President Carter to Prime Minister Demirel.[75]

The US commitment to provide technical assistance meant US–Turkey co-operation in the field of research, development and production in order to help Turkey advance its industrial and technological defence capabilities. At the Turks' request the DECA committed US support for seven industrial defence projects.[76] These specifically aimed at the improvement of Turkey's capability in re-building aircraft, in constructing modern warships, in upgrading tanks and producing anti-armour ammunition, fuses and rockets. The overall objective was to assist the Turks in accelerating the development of their defence industry infrastructure through the provision of American technical data packages as well as the leasing of industrial equipment.[77]

The 'best effort' pledge of the American government was the cornerstone upon which the DECA stood. Yet against Ankara's wishes, but in keeping with the desires of Congress, no minimum amounts were identified. In reality it would not always be easy for the US executive to keep this pledge as Congress would have to approve every amount negotiated between the Turks and US officials and requested by future administrations. But at the time the 'impetus' to satisfy Ankara's wishes 'was strong' within the Carter administration,[78] so it was willing to mobilize in order to convince Congress.[79] In any event in 1980 the prospects for substantial levels of future assistance to Turkey looked good. The Americans were prepared to pay handsomely for a number of reasons. First, they wished to satisfy their security objectives as envisaged by the DECA without any further delay. In other words, they wanted to revitalize their ties with the Turks and advance a strong security relationship with them. Even more importantly, they were extremely keen to regain full access to all intelligence and communication installations and secure an increased US military presence.[80] As a matter of fact, according to the new DECA the number of US aircraft allowed to station in Incirlik Air Base doubled (from 18 to 36, a number matching the support capacity of the base). Also, these could be from more than one unit stationed in Europe, while prior to the new agreement only aircraft from one unit in Europe at a time were allowed. For the Americans one of the major reasons for assigning units to Incirlik was to use the Konya range for weapons training. The Konya range was one of the three primary ranges available to US Air Force units stationed in Europe, and its use was considered very important if weapons training requirements were to be met.[81] The other reason that urged Washington to provide Turkey with large sums of assistance on a continuing basis was the Pentagon officials' conclusion that its ability to meet its NATO responsibilities was directly linked with its economic viability and development.[82] In short the US was prepared to give large military and economic aid in return for Turkey's co-operation and in order to secure stability. But also there was a wish to send a message of strength and resolve to the entire region. As the Chairman of NATO's military committee stressed in his message to the allies a week after the invasion of Afghanistan, 'military aid to Turkey could have a most helpful effect, both in a real sense and as a matter of perception, throughout the region.'[83]

To be sure, at the end of the 1970s and in the early 1980s the US supported Ankara financially both directly and in other less direct ways. The Americans backed Turkey at the International Monetary Fund and the World Bank. They also exercised continuous pressure on their wealthier allies to provide Turkey with funds (grants and loans at low interest rates).[84] This pressure was effective. Consequently, many European allies, as well as Japan, were prepared to provide Turkey with substantial funds in order to assist it to get over its 'critical economic problems', due to its strategic importance.[85] For the years 1979 and 1980 they gave Turkey around 1.7 billion dollars in economic assistance; the US and West Germany contributed about 50 per cent of the total amount.[86] This assistance was primarily in support of an economic stabilization and modernization plan in accordance with the 1979 IMF-Turkey stand-by agreement, which mainly required major currency devaluation and the reduction of the state budget deficit. In short the allies' economic assistance was essentially pegged on Turkey's opening up its economy to market forces.[87] The economic stabilization and modernization plan was first announced by the Demirel government in January 1980 and was fully implemented by the military regime that assumed power in September. Following the announcement of the plan the World Bank authorized a loan of 200 million to Turkey, while in June 1980 the IMF pledged economic assistance of about 1.6 billion dollars.[88] In short, in the years 1979–80 Western assistance programmes and pledged funds amounted to a total of 4 billion dollars. Of equal importance was the US role in helping Turkey reschedule its debts, which by 1979 were close to 15 million dollars – servicing them ran close to half of the country's total export earnings. As the existing repayment schedule clearly was leading the country to bankruptcy Washington responded to the Turks' pressure and 'broke traditional rules' by agreeing to reschedule debts that had already been rescheduled once, setting an example which other state and private creditors followed, lowering thus the debt-service burden to manageable levels.[89]

Washington's persistent effort to galvanize Western collective assistance to Turkey with grants and loans at interest rates lower than the market levels continued up until 1983. By then Turkey's creditworthiness in the international financial markets had been restored and Turkey could borrow abroad at current market rates. In short, Turkey managed to get out of its dire economic crisis mainly thanks to Western economic support orchestrated to a very large extent by the Americans.[90] It has been observed that increased tension between the bigger powers works very often in favour of the weak states.[91] Undoubtedly at the end of the 1970s Ankara was able to reap substantial benefits because of the renewed rivalry between the two superpowers.[92]

The dizzying heights of assistance

The Reagan administration proved even more eager to fulfil the Carter administration's commitment to making the 'best effort'. From the moment the new administration came to power and against the backdrop of the vast rise in its defence spending it made a persistent and consistent effort to obtain from Congress authorization for ever increasing assistance to Turkey. For fiscal year 1982 the Reagan administration requested 815 million dollars assistance for Turkey (465 million was military aid and 350 million in ESF funds). Congress approved most of it, only cutting military aid down to 400 million.[93] It was a massive increase when compared to the total security assistance of 402 and 452 million dollars allocated to Turkey in fiscal years 1980 and 1981 respectively.[94]

The US executive justified this vast rise on the basis of the argument that the assistance Turkey received was not adequate to meet its great military needs as registered and assessed by Pentagon and State Department officials.[95] However, an increase in the assistance levels to Turkey raised serious question marks when examined from the perspective of the strategic objectives that Washington sought to satisfy under the 1980 DECA.

The comptroller general observed in his 1982 report to Congress – a review of the DECA – that both Pentagon and State Department officials were 'generally satisfied' with the implementation of the agreement. Although it limited 'US activities to NATO-related areas, unless approved by the Government of Turkey' and despite some differences in the interpretation of the language of the agreement[96] the Americans had regained access to military facilities as well as to intelligence and communication installations, they maintained a military presence and the US–Turkey relationship had been revitalized. The report essentially noted that even though Turkey's needs were considerable and exceeded US security assistance programmes the country was already 'receiving substantial assistance for US rights under the DECA'.[97] The report recognized that 'there were no easy solutions to Turkey's problems' and that the country would require significant amounts of assistance for many years to come, but it remarked that in the final analysis 'how much, on what terms and who would provide the assistance' should be a matter of consideration. In this context it was noted that the US had borne most of the cost of the assistance to Turkey with relatively small amounts being provided by other NATO members, although this assistance had been 'justified primarily on the basis of Turkey's commitment and importance to NATO.'[98] In short, the report argued that Turkey was a 'NATO problem' although it accepted that the US might have to increase its security assistance programme if Turkey was considered vital to US interests, unless the other members of the alliance were willing to increase their contributions. Moreover, it pointed out that the United States must consider the impact of increased assistance to Turkey on the balance of power in the Aegean and US interests in the Middle East.[99]

The Pentagon and the State Department adopted a different perspective. They placed more emphasis on the need to solve Turkey's military and economic problems and they focused on the fact that the DECA currently applied only to NATO-related activities. Actually, a number of US officials who regarded Turkey as important for staging US military operations in the Gulf wanted to supply the Turks with extensive military aid in return for a clearer commitment that the bases in eastern Turkey could be used in non-NATO contingencies in the Middle East.[100] Hence, Pentagon officials in particular adopted the position that increased aid to Turkey should not be an 'either/or' depending on the response of the NATO allies, but that the US administration should increase pressure on NATO allies to contribute more to Turkey *as well as* do more for Turkey.[101]

In short the US executive had come to the conclusion that the current 'best effort' under the DECA could not satisfy Turkey's projected needs or apparently US defence requirements in the Gulf and so the future levels of security assistance would have to rise.[102] Taking this conclusion into consideration the report pointed out that Congress might be expected to be asked by the administration to either approve increased security assistance to Turkey or to approve other 'alternatives', including 'debt forgiveness/and or concessionary terms as a further extension of U.S. "best efforts", or security assistance on a grant basis which would increase U.S. control on how funds are spent.' Any such action, the report suggested, might well be provided, but under the condition that Turkey grant additional concessions to the US.[103]

To be sure the Reagan administration requested much higher levels of assistance to Turkey in the following years. These levels reached a dizzying height in the beginning of 1983 when Congress was asked to authorize almost a billion dollars (930 million) for fiscal year 1984, of which 755 million constituted military assistance. A comparable request was put forward for the following fiscal year as well as for fiscal year 1986.[104]

Thus, in just a few years following the lifting of the embargo the total amount of US assistance steadily increased. Between the years 1982 and 1985 the increase was staggering when compared to the 293 million per year that Turkey received on average during the years 1950 to 1974 (during the embargo period it was reduced to 132.5 million).[105] Even though after 1985 assistance fell from the high peak it had reached Turkey was still receiving half a million dollars per year.[106] All this was new. Turkey had become after Israel and Egypt the biggest recipient of US assistance in the world. Put simply, as Turkey was regarded as 'an extremely valuable ally'[107] Congress internalized the message underlined by the executive that the position it took on aid requests was 'likely to have a profound effect on further United States–Turkish relations and U.S. interests in the eastern Mediterranean.'[108]

Huge amounts of assistance were not the only new element in the bilateral relationship. Also co-operation in the defence industry was significantly upgraded when in late 1983 Washington authorized the sale to Turkey of 160 F-16 aircraft following a strong recommendation by the Pentagon. These new generation multi-role combat aircraft were initially earmarked for sale to the Shah while Turkey was to be sold the oldest F-4, which was designed as an interceptor for defence, even though it had been used as the principal US fighter towards the end of the Vietnam War.[109] Co-operation in this field reached its pinnacle in 1984 following a decision between General Dynamics and the Turkish Aircraft Industries for joint production of the F-16,[110] a significant achievement within the broader context of Turkish ambitions to build its own defence industry. Washington's decision to upgrade its co-operation with the Turks in this field dovetailed with Albert Wohlstetter's belief that the strengthening of Turkey's defence capabilities and particularly of its air force would inhibit possible Soviet plans for operations in the Gulf area.[111]

Were these new elements in the relationship related to greater flexibility by the Turks concerning the use of their facilities by the US for the defence of the Gulf? The straight answer is that we do not know for sure on the basis of the material that has been made available so far. However, it is reasonable to assume that there was at least an implicit linkage between the two. If this were not the case, how could the administration justify its request for a dramatic rise in assistance while the amounts that were already provided secured US objectives under the DECA? Both the Carter and Reagan administrations believed that Turkey had a central role to play in the defence of the Gulf.

From early on the Reagan administration consistently emphasized the vital importance of the Middle East and underlined that the administration's 'overarching aim' was to build regional security mainly by improving US military capabilities in the region as well as by assisting friendly states to improve their own defensive capabilities.[112] Furthermore, it is clear that Pentagon and State Department officials were not happy with the fact that the DECA limited US–Turkey security co-operation to only NATO-related activities. For sure, already, the Carter and Reagan administrations employed an implicit, rather than an explicit, linkage between US military credits/financial assistance and access to military facilities with the approval of the host country, when it came to US military agreements with a number of states like Oman, Somalia, Kenya and Egypt.[113] But this is not all. Actually the staggering levels of US assistance to Turkey and Washington's decision to sell F-16 aircraft to Turkey coincided with the successful negotiations and signing of a US–Turkey collocated operating base (COB) agreement (November 1982) – much desired by the Americans – which marked Turkey's willingness for the first time to make military preparations for contingencies in the Gulf. Negotiations between the civilian and military authorities of the two countries had been languishing for years until the Pentagon took them over from the State Department after Reagan assumed office.[114] The Pentagon's chief negotiator was Assistant Secretary of Defense Richard Perle. As Perle notes, 'it was vital' for Washington to move forward on this agreement, which would allow the US 'the use of certain key air bases' in the event of a conflict with the Soviet Union.[115] In his words the establishment of a high-level US–Turkish consultative group, which he proposed, co-chaired by the Pentagon and the Turkish general staff, was 'an unprecedented encroachment on the State Department's monopoly control of state-to-state relations.' According to Perle the American ambassador in Ankara, Robert Strausz-Hupé, proposed that Perle took over the negotiations because he 'understood the importance that [the] Turks attached to the security relationship with the U.S. and Turkey's need for assistance from the U.S. to modernize its military forces.' Also Strausz-Hupé, notes Perle, 'knew that the Department of Defense was far better positioned to gain the confidence of the Turkish government', or, rather more accurately, of the Turkish military who were in power, 'than was his own department.'[116]

Hardly anything is known about the negotiations which produced the COB agreement, whose exact provisions are still unknown. But we have enough information to know that it provided for the modernization of ten Turkish airbases, including the ones in eastern Turkey at Erzerum and Batman, as well as the construction of a new one at Muş (also in eastern Turkey), and for the joint use of some of them (including ones located in eastern Turkey) with the objective of accommodating long-range bombers and cargo planes.[117] As Kuniholm remarked, these air fields would put 'fighter bombers within striking distance of the Transcaucasus, and the Rapid Deployment Force (RDF) within 700 miles of Abadan: much closer to the head of the Persian Gulf than any of the facilities to which the U.S. Central Command (CENTCOM) now has access.'[118] Both Ankara and Washington publicly maintained that the bases would be used for NATO purposes. But actually many contemporary observers underlined that this infrastructure was built in order to allow the rapid deployment of US forces in concert with *or without* its NATO allies, with an eye also to Soviet action in the Persian Gulf.[119]

Undoubtedly through the COB agreement the Americans managed to secure a bit more of what they wanted out of the relationship with the Turks. Also almost certainly the agreement gave the US executive valuable bargaining power in negotiating with Congress for new levels of assistance. It is doubtful, however, that the Turks committed themselves to allowing US usage of the bases for non-NATO operations in the Middle East without prior Turkish approval. Such a commitment would be tantamount to giving up the greatest point of leverage Turkey had over the US. From a Turkish point of view the whole issue of the use of the bases was not only a matter of foreign policy independence, it also represented a powerful bargaining card the Turks had in their constant negotiations with the US. Therefore, it could only yield maximum advantage when it was not entirely given up.

A new momentum in the bilateral relationship

The tension and bitterness caused by the embargo seemed to have been dissipated already during the first Reagan administration. Both sides were essentially satisfied with their co-operation. The Americans had secured their military objectives, if not fully certainly to a very large extent. The Turks for their part were receiving increasing assistance and technological know-how in the field of military industry. Furthermore, the Reagan adminisration like its predecessor avoided harassing the Turkish military – who remained in power until the end of 1983 – for a speedy return to democracy, in contrast to most European allies who heavily criticized the Turkish regime of fear and repression.[120] Actually General Kenan Evren, the leader of the military coup who assumed the powers of head of state, in his memoirs mentions that in 1982 he expressed to the US secretary of state his gratitude for the consistent understanding and support shown by the Reagan administration.[121] The regime's appreciation for the US approach was also clearly stated publicly when the foreign minister, Ilter Türkmen, declared in October 1982 that the bilateral relationship had never been better.[122]

Turkey's relative isolation in Europe, which contributed to Ankara's moving even closer to Washington, continued following the election of the centre-right Motherland Party of Turgut Özal after the military stepped down from power in 1983 (but only once they had made sure that their supervising role over political authority was institutionalized). Özal – who was not the generals' political choice – basically governed according to the rules designed by the military. He was in discreet co-operation with them until he was elected president of the republic in 1989. Özal was permitted a largely free hand in running the economy but the military continued to have the 'decisive role' in the formulation of security policy.[123] Repeated violations of human rights by the Turkish state and new adverse developments regarding the Cyprus issue accounted for the continuous rift between Ankara and many European capitals. On 15 November 1983, just before the generals handed power to Özal (and a day after President Reagan had signed a bill authorizing US assistance to Turkey for the 1984 fiscal year),[124] Turkish Cypriots in northern Cyprus, which was occupied by Turkish armed forces, declared their independence. The new state was immediately recognized by the Turkish military regime (but by no other government in the world). Özal's government did not repudiate the Turkish Cypriots declaration. Therefore his government was held responsible in many European capitals for the refusal of the Turkish Cypriots to nullify their decision, which was generally regarded as undermining efforts to find a mutually acceptable solution to the Cyprus issue. To be sure the Turkish government was similarly held responsible by a substantial part of Congress, but in the end, largely thanks to the Reagan administration's intensive lobbying, Turkey's critics failed to prevail.[125] As a matter of fact the Reagan administration did call for the reversal of the declaration of Turkish Cypriot independence, yet it showed no intention of changing its policy towards Ankara. Moreover, it strongly argued in favour of separating diplomacy over Cyprus from US assistance to Turkey.[126]

In 1985 Turgut Özal, who was keen to maintain the new tempo in the bilateral relationship, paid an official visit to Washington. It was the first visit by a Turkish prime minister in fourteen years. Already by then it was evident that there was a growing momentum in the bilateral relationship, which engendered hope among Turkey's supporters in Washington that it could lead to a deeper, stronger strategic relationship.[127]

What was creating this momentum? Undoubtedly there was a constellation of interrelated contributing factors. In Ankara, ties with the US occupied again a central place in Turkish foreign policy, for the reasons discussed earlier. In Washington, the conviction of the renewal of the Soviet threat created the right environment for a substantial increase in defence spending, the hallmark of the Reagan administrations. Under these circumstances the administrations' requests of assistance for Turkey had a favourable reception in Congress. The new co-operation between the legislative and the executive branches had a major positive impact on bilateral relations. There was also a noticeable change within the administration. For sure the interest of the executive in strengthening relations with Turkey had remained consistent throughout the difficult decade of the 1970s, feeding into the conviction of Turkey's strategic importance. President Gerald Ford, for instance, wrote in his memoirs that he considered Congress's decision to impose an arms embargo on Turkey 'the single most irresponsible, shortsighted foreign policy decision Congress had made in all the years'[128] he had been in Washington.[129] Among the first initiatives of President Carter and his secretary of state, Cyrus Vance, was a request to Congress for assistance to Turkey to be increased.[130] However, political decisions and the way they are implemented are not one and the same thing. In brief, while there was no really dramatic change in the executive's interest in Turkey the enthusiasm and intensity of the effort to generate further co-operation with Ankara were unprecedented. Another big change was the remarkable strengthening of military-to-military ties, something that would significantly determine the pace and nature of the bilateral relationship for much of the 1980s.

Both this newly found enthusiasm and the deepening of military-to-military relations were undoubtedly the result of the actions and initiatives of Richard Perle, the dynamic assistant secretary of defense for international political security (1981–87), who emerged as an important player within the bureaucracy concerning US–Turkey defence co-operation.

Neoconservative Perle made his name in Washington in the 1970s as a strategic analyst. From his position as an assistant secretary of defence, a position that he chose himself,[131] he sought to apply to policy the ideas of his mentor Wohlstetter regarding Turkey.[132] Being a middle-ranking officer in the foreign policy bureaucracy he was well positioned in this respect. As Henry Kissinger points out, 'if one wishes to influence American foreign policy, the time to do so is in the formative period, and the level is the middle level of the bureaucracy – that of the assistant secretary and his immediate advisers.'[133] Moreover, Perle's Office of International Security Policy (ISP) was a mid-level office of the Office of the Secretary of Defense, which was an important source of influence on foreign policy formulation. In the 1980s the ISP even gained in prominence because it assumed a more extended role within the Pentagon as a source of policy analysis and guidance for the Office of the Secretary of Defense, Caspar Weinberger (1981–87), who due to his ties with President Reagan had a major involvement in foreign policy formulation.[134]

The prominent status of the ISP within the foreign policy bureaucracy gave Perle a platform from which he could lead the effort to multiply US assistance to Turkey, a controversial matter in Congress, in order to turn Turkey into a major US ally. But as analysts of bureaucratic politics know the effectiveness of a player does not solely depend on one's position within the apparatus.[135] As a matter of fact Perle combined most of the attributes that define an effective player. He had expertise (as a strategic analyst) coupled with strong interest and an excellent knowledge of the action channels within the bureaucracy and Congress; he was a master of building coalitions; he knew how to work on connections; and he was aggressive.[136] On top of all this he had the ear of the secretary of defense. According to Dov Zakheim, who worked for Perle at the time, he was probably one of the most powerful assistant secretaries in history because Weinberger was comfortable with him, so he had 'tremendous clout.'[137] There was another factor of almost equal importance. Many of Perle's co-believers and friends staffed Reagan's government. This helps explain the well-orchestrated and unprecedented lobbying of Congress by the White House, the Pentagon and the State Department in 1983 over the authorization of almost one billion dollars assistance to Turkey for the 1984 fiscal year, in spite of the adverse developments over the Cyprus issue. Apparently many of Perle's friends were given jobs in the government to a large extent as a result of his persistent efforts. Alan Weissman notes that Perle was effective in placing 'those who shared his views in positions that matter' because he sat in three Reagan transition teams – State, Defence and Export-Import Bank – which helped with recruitment for the administration.[138] Paul Wolfowitz and Elliot Abrams are two characteristic examples of Perle's co-believers and friends who found themselves in major jobs in the State Department. Wolfowitz, also one of Wohlstetter's students and follower of his ideas, had worked as an aide alongside Perle in the office of Democratic Senator Henry Jackson. Abrams for his part had been Jackson's special counsel. Wolfowitz was appointed director of policy planning at the State Department (1980–82)[139] and Abrams, assistant secretary of state for human rights and humanitarian affairs (1981–85). During his tenure in this position Abrams was accused of covering up serious violations of human rights by countries friendly to the US regimes. One of them was Turkey, whose human rights abuse was well documented by human rights groups in Europe. Yet Abrams publicly defended the Turkish state in 1984 in the American press and in a speech while he was on a visit to Ankara by seeking to discredit the 'ill-informed and self-righteous' human rights community.[140]

Of course what determined Perle's success, perhaps more than anything else, was that the policy he was advocating toward Turkey did not really represent change. Rather, it was the natural outcome of the belief in Turkey's strategic importance that many US officials and strategic analysts within and without the bureaucracy shared for years. Furthermore, the re-surfacing of Cold War attitudes created a fertile ground for Perle's initiatives.

US officials and observers with good knowledge of US–Turkey relations in the 1980s underscore Perle's central role in the creation of the momentum that carried relations between the two countries particularly during the first half of the 1980s. The strengthening of bilateral defence co-operation both at a policy formulation and at an implementation level is regarded as his handiwork. He is considered the key player behind the dramatic increase in US security assistance to Turkey, for which he worked hard.[141]

Perle was responsible for enhancing the Pentagon's already strong interest in Turkey. But more importantly he was instrumental in building fresh ties between the Turkish military and the US Department of Defense.[142] In Perle's words, the high-level consultative group co-chaired by the Pentagon and the Turkish general staff, which was formed at Perle's suggestion during the COB agreement negotiations,

> quickly became the central venue for the conduct of U.S.-Turkish relations and the mutual confidence between the United States and Turkey that grew out of its deliberations played a vital role in the conclusion first of the base agreement and then the Defense and Economic Cooperation Agreement.[143]

Thus, essentially, the management and further development of defence co-operation between the two countries passed into the hands of the defence establishments on each side, a development which would have a long-term influence on the course of the bilateral relationship.

Notes

1 J. C. Campbell, 'The Superpowers and Turkey: An American View', in A. L. Karaosmanoğlu and S. Taşhan (eds), *Middle East, Turkey and the Atlantic Alliance*, Ankara: Foreign Policy Institute, 1987, pp. 60–62; D. Bazoğlu Sezer, 'Turkey and the Western Alliance in the 1980s', in A. Eralp, M. Tünay and B. Yeşilada (eds), *The Political and Socioeconomic Transformation of Turkey*, Westport, CT: Praeger, 1993, p. 220; Y. Çelik, *Contemporary Turkish Foreign Policy*, Westport, CT: Preager, 1999, p. 61; W. Hale, *Turkish Foreign Policy, 1774–2000*, London: Frank Cass, 2000, p. 165.

2 Sezer, 'Turkey and the Western Alliance', pp. 218–19.

3 S. Sayarı, 'Regional Security Issues and U.S.-Turkish Relations in the 1980s', unpublished paper presented at a conference on 'The History of American-Turkish Relations, 1833–1989', Boğaziçi University, Istanbul, 5–6 June 2006, pp. 1, 6.

4 I. Barutçuoğu, 'Evolution of Turkey's Security Role in the Middle East', in G. S. Harris (ed.), *The Middle East in Turkish-American Relations*, Washington, DC: The Heritage Foundation, 1985, pp. 65–6. Çelik, *Turkish Foreign Policy*, p. 61, attributes the re-alignment of Ankara's foreign policy with US interests to 'a deteriorating sense of security in Turkey' combined 'with growing support for increased military spending in the United States'. Hale, *Turkish Foreign Policy*, p. 163 also attributes Ankara's 're-engagement in the Western alliance' to the Turks' renewed sense that the Soviet Union constituted a threat. Although he comments that it was improbable that the Turkish leaders thought the Soviets were on the point of invading Turkey, he points out that the invasion weakened the case of those who argued for detachment from the Western alliance 'by demonstrating to the Turks what could happen to a relatively weak nation on the borders of the Soviet Union that opted for neutrality.'

5 Sezer, 'Turkey and the Western Alliance', p. 220; Sayarı, 'U.S.-Turkish Relations in the 1980s', p. 7.

6 Sezer, 'Turkey and the Western Alliance', p. 220.

7 Hale, *Turkish Foreign Policy*, p. 163.

8 Campbell, 'The Superpowers and Turkey', p. 61.

9 Sezer, 'Turkey and the Western Alliance', p. 220; Çelik, *Contemporary Turkish Foreign Policy*, p. 62. Hale, *Turkish Foreign Policy*, pp. 163–64 makes the same point but in a less clear way.

10 George S. Harris, *Turkey: Coping with Crisis*, Boulder, CO: Westview Press, 1985, p. 198; Sayarı, 'U.S.-Turkish Relations in the 1980s', pp. 7–8.

11 Sayarı, 'U.S.-Turkish Relations in the 1980s', p. 8.

12 In Turkey a 30-year rule applies before official documents are opened to the public. However, upon the completion of this book the classification of the documents for the period 1976–81 at the Turkish State Archives was still taking place and there was no access to the full collection or to individual documents. The archives officials could not provide an approximate date by which the classification process would be over.

13 Summary record, MC-CBX-1-80, 4 January 1980, 1st meeting of the Military Committee in 1980, held on 3 January 1980, p. 3, North Atlantic Military Committee (MC), MC records, NATO Archives.

14 Summary record, MC-CBX-10-80, 5 March 1980, 10th meeting of the Military Committee in 1980, held on 28 February 1980, pp.4–5, North Atlantic Military Committee (MC), MC records, NATO Archives.

15 Ibid, p. 3.

16 J. W. Spain, *American Diplomacy in Turkey: Memoirs of an Ambassador Extraordinary and Plenipotentiary*, New York: Praeger Publishers, 1984, p. 62.

17 Spain, *American Diplomacy in Turkey*, p. 63.

18 G. S. Harris, 'Turkey between Alliance and Alienation', *Diş Politika* (Foreign Policy), vol. 8, 1980, p. 123. It is worth mentioning that Turkey had been living with the fear of Soviet indirect invasion for at least a decade. In the late 1960s the fear of a Soviet-inspired coup was very much present in the minds of Turkish leaders as the country was in the midst of right- and left-wing extremists' shooting matches in the streets and the university campuses: M. Kaylan, *The Kemalists: Islamic Revival and the Fate of Secular Turkey*, New York: Prometheus Books, 2005, p. 264.

19 Harris, 'Turkey between Alliance and Alienation', p. 123. Professor Ali Karaosmanoğlu made the same point in his conversation with the author. For the dates and places of the author's interviews/conversations, see the bibliography section in this book.

20 United States Senate, *Perspectives on NATO's Southern Flank: Senate Delegation Report, April 3–13, 1980*, a report to the Committee on Foreign Relations, United States Senate, Washington DC: US Government Printing Office, 1980, p. 11.

21 A. L. Karaosmanoğlu, 'Turkey's Security and the Middle East', *Foreign Affairs*, vol. 62, 1983, pp. 158–9.

22 G. F. Treverton, 'Managing Alliance Politics', in Karaosmanoğlu and Taşhan (eds), *Middle East, Turkey and the Atlantic Alliance*, Ankara: Foreign Policy Institute, 1987, p. 177.

23 W. Laqueur, *The Struggle for the Middle East: The Soviet Union in the Mediterranean 1958–1968*, New York: The Macmillan Company, 1969, pp. 21–8; G. S. Harris, 'The Russian Federation and Turkey', in A. Z. Rubinstein and O. M. Smolansky (eds.), *Regional Power Rivalries in the New Eurasia: Russia, Turkey, and Iran*, Armonk, NY: M.E. Sharpe, 1995, pp. 7–10.

24 Congressional Research Service, Foreign Affairs and National Defense Division, *Turkey's Problems and Prospects: Implications for U.S. Interests*, report prepared for the Subcommittee on Europe and the Middle East of the Committee on Foreign Affairs, US House of Representatives, by the Foreign Affairs and National Defense Division, Congressional Research Service, Library of Congress, Washington DC: US Government Printing Office, 1980, p. 45; W. Weiker, *The Modernization of Turkey. From Ataturk to the Present Day*, New York: Holmes & Meier Publishers, 1981, p. 213.

25 G. E. Gruen, 'Turkey between the Middle East and the West', in R. O. Freedman (ed.), *The Middle East from the Iran-Contra Affair to the Intifada*, Syracuse, NY: Syracuse University Press, 1999, pp. 402–3. Harris, *Coping with Crisis,* pp. 198, 201–2; Harris, 'Russian Federation and Turkey', pp. 10–12.

26 A. L. Karaosmanoğlu, 'Turkey's Discreet Foreign Policy between Western Europe and the Middle East', in A. L. Karaosmanoğlu and S. Taşhan (eds), *Middle East, Turkey and the Atlantic Alliance*, Ankara: Foreign Policy Institute, 1987, p. 117. It is worth noticing here that soon after Mikhail Gorbachev's rise to power in 1985 and as tension between the US and the Soviet Union began gradually to subside an effort by both the Turkish and Soviet leadership to further improve bilateral relations became noticeable, Harris, 'Russian Federation and Turkey', in Rubinstein and Smolansky (eds.), *Regional Power Rivalries*, pp. 12–15. Nonetheless, the Turks' demands for high levels of US assistance continued.

27 B. Kuniholm, 'Turkey in the World' in G. S. Harris (ed.), *The Middle East in Turkish-American Relations*, Washington, DC: The Heritage Foundation, 1985,

p. 15. Professor Bruce Kuniholm was another well-informed American expert on Turkey and former official in the State Department Bureau of Intelligence and Research. He made his remark at a high-profile Heritage Foundation Conference on Turkey-US relations (1984).

28 The American Embassy in Ankara to the Secretary of State, Washington DC, Telegram 2755, 7 April 1975, Electronic Telegrams 1/1/1975–12/31/1975, no. 21, USA National Archives, online public access, available online at http://aad.archives.gov/aad/createpdf?dt=2476&rid=70336&dl=1345 (accessed 12 September 2007); The American Embassy in Ankara to the Secretary of State, Washington DC, Telegram 6209, 11 August 1975, Electronic Telegrams 1/1/1975–12/31/1975, no. 43, USA National Archives, online public access, available online at http://aad.archives.gov/aad/createpdf?dt=2476&rid=133390&dl=1345 (accessed 12 September 2007).

29 Congressional Research Service, *Turkey's Problems and Prospects*, p. 26.

30 American Embassy, Ankara to Secretary of State, Washington, Telegram 2584, 1 April 1975, 'Demirel Government's Coalition Protocol: Foreign Policy and National Security Section: Implications for USG-GOT Security Relationship', Electronic Telegrams 1/1/1975–12/31/1975, no. 14, USA National Archives, online public access, available online at http://aad.archives.gov/aad/createpdf?dt=2476&rid=70336&dl=1345 (accessed 12 September 2007); American Embassy in Ankara to the Secretary of State, 2 March 1975, Telegram 2621, Electronic Telegrams 1/1/1975–12/31/1975, no. 18, USA National Archives, online public access, available online at http://aad.archives.gov/aad/createpdf?dt=2476&rid=46974&dl=1345 (accessed 12 September 2007). For a good concise account of the views of the Turkish leadership on this issue, see Hale, *Turkish Foreign Policy*, pp. 148–62.

31 American Embassy, Telegram 2584, 1 April 1975, 'Demirel Government's Coalition Protocol'.

32 Author's interview with Peter Marudas, chief of staff, office of Senator Paul S. Sarbenes. Also author's interview with Michael Ledeen, expert on US foreign policy, consultant to the National Security Council during the Reagan administration.

33 E. B. Laipson, *Congressional-Executive Relations and the Turkish Arms Embargo*, Congress and Foreign Policy Series, Washington, DC: US Government Printing Office, 1981, p. 27.

34 The American Embassy in Ankara to the Secretary of State, Washington, Telegram 6209, 11 August 1975, USA National Archives, online public access, available online at http://aad.archives.gov/aad/createpdf?dt=2476&rid=133390&dl=1345 (accessed 12 September 2007).

35 On the development of the economic crisis in Turkey in the 1970s and for relevant economic data, see Z. H. Hershlag, *The Contemporary Turkish Economy*, London: Routledge, 1988, pp. 22–3, 38–40, 79–80; Z. Önis and S. Özmucur, *Capital Flows and the External Financing of Turkey's Imports*, OECD Development Centre, working paper no. 36, July 1991, pp. 17–18; W. Hale, *Turkish Politics and the Military*, London: Routledge, 1994, p. 223. For a less detailed overview, see E. J. Zürcher, *Turkey: A Modern History*, London: I. B. Tauris, 1993, pp. 280–82.

36 From Secretary General to Permanent Representatives (Council), 'Economic Co-operation and Assistance within the Alliance: Report on the Present Situation', 30 November 1979, p. 2, PO/79/127, NATO archives.

37 Comments by Ilter Turan, on the panel, 'Turkey, after Iran and Camp David', *Diş Politika* (Foreign Policy), vol. VIII, 1980, p. 130.

38 H. Bozarslan, *Istoria tis Sihronis Tourkias: Apo tin Epanastasi ton Neotourkon Mehri Simera*, Athens: Savalas, 2008, p. 85, see also pp. 81–94 for an overview of domestic political developments in the second half of the 1970s and during the 1980s; Zürcher, *Turkey*, pp. 275–330; Hale, *Turkish Politics and the Military*, pp. 231–300.

39 One cannot help but wonder what would have happened had the US Congress continued to insist in the late 1970s that aid to Turkey should be conditional on Turkey making concessions over Cyprus first.

40 Harris, *Coping with Crisis*, p. 196.

41 ESF programme funds were a strong indirect subsidy, structured to achieve US political objectives by enhancing political stability in countries of strategic importance through alleviating the burden of the cost of the purchase of US weapons.

42 For the relevant economic data, see Congressional Research Service, *Turkey's Problems and Prospects*, p. 38; United States General Accounting Office, *The Defense and Economic Cooperation Agreement – U.S. Interests and Turkish Needs,* report by the comptroller general of the United States, Washington DC, Gaithersburg, MD: US General Accounting Office, 1982, pp. i, 2; United States Congress, House Committee on Foreign Affairs, *United States Political-Military Relations with Allies in Southern Europe: Report of a Staff Study Mission to Portugal, Spain, Greece and Turkey, October 15–30, 1986, to the Committee on Foreign Affairs, U.S. House of Representatives*, Washington DC: US Government Printing Office, 1987, p. 33.

43 Congressional Research Service, *Turkey's Problems and Prospects*, pp. 4–5, 56; United States General Accounting Office, *U.S. Interests and Turkish Needs,* p. 43.

44 Congressional Research Service, *Turkey's Problems and Prospects*, p. 28; Spain, *American Diplomacy in Turkey*, p. 44; S. Taşhan, 'Turkey's Relations with the U.S.A. and Possible Future Developments', *Diş Politika* (Foreign Policy) vol. 8, 1979, pp. 26–7; United States Congress, Senate Committee on Foreign Relations, *Perspectives on NATO's Southern Flank, Senate Delegation Report, April 3–13, 1980: A Report to the Committee on Foreign Relations,* Washington DC: US Government Printing Office, 1980, p. 11.

45 *The Washington Post*, 27 December 1979.

46 'Economic Co-operation and Assistance within the Alliance: Report on the Present Situation', 30 November 1979, p. 2, PO/79/127, NATO archives; Weiker, *The Modernization of Turkey*, p.181.

47 'Economic Co-operation and Assistance within the Alliance: Report on the Present Situation', 30 November 1979, p. 2, PO/79/127, NATO archives.

48 According to the Turkish tycoon Vehmi Koç, whose comments were invited by *The New York Times*, 31 May 1979.

49 Spain, *American Diplomacy in Turkey*, pp. 31–2.

50 NATO, *Final Communiqué*, 05 December 1978–06 December 1978, 15 May 1979–16 May 1979, 11 December 1979–12 December 1979, available online at http://www.nato.int/cps/en/natolive/officialtexts.htm.U.S (accessed 15 January 2010); United States Congress, Senate Committee on Armed Services, *The Military Aspects of Banning Arms Aid to Turkey. Hearing before the Committee on Armed Services,* United States Senate, ninety-fifth Congress, second session, 28 June 1978, Washington DC: US Government Printing Office, 1978, pp. 7, 9, 12, 23–4, 45–6, 48; United States Congress, House Committee on Foreign Affairs, Subcommittee on Europe and the Middle East, *Suplemental Aid Requests for Fiscal Years 1979 and 1980 for Turkey and Oman. Hearings, May 15 and 31, 1979*, ninety-sixth Congress, first session, Washington DC, Washington Government Printing Office, 1979, p. 72.

51 Senate Committee on Armed Services, *Banning Arms Aid to Turkey*, p. 50.

52 Reminder: the total arms embargo that was imposed in February 1975 was partly lifted in September of the same year.

53 According to the 1982 report of the United States General Accounting Office, *U.S. Interests and Turkish Needs*, pp. 15–16. This report was reviewed by the Pentagon and the State Department before being submitted to the Subcommittee on Europe and the Middle East of the House Foreign Affairs Committee.

54 United States General Accounting Office, *U.S. Interests and Turkish Needs*, p. 15.
55 Senate Committee on Armed Services, *Banning Arms Aid to Turkey*, pp. 7, 9, 12, 23, 24; Congressional Research Service, *Turkey's Problems and Prospects*, pp. 20, 29–31, 39; United States General Accounting Office, *U.S. Interests and Turkish Needs*, pp. ii–iii, 15–16.
56 United States General Accounting Office, *U.S. Interests and Turkish Needs*, p. 16.
57 United States General Accounting Office, *U.S. Interests and Turkish Needs*, pp. 16, 24.
58 United States Congress, Senate Committee on Foreign Relations, *Fiscal Year 1980 International Security Assistance Authorization: Hearings, February 28–April 30, 1979*, ninety-sixth Congress, first session on S. 584, To Amend the Foreign Assistance Act of 1961 and the Arms Export Control Act, and for Other Purposes, Washington DC: US Government Printing Office, 1979, pp. 501–2.
59 Congressional Research Service, *Turkey's Problems and Prospects*, pp. 3–4.
60 *The Washington Post*, 22 January, 9 May, 7 September 1979, 9 January 1980; *The New York Times*, 19 March, 10 June, 6 September 1979.
61 V. Erdem, 'Turkish Defense Industries and DIDA', *Diş Politika* (Foreign Policy), vol. XIV, 1988, p. 113. Vahit Erdem was first undersecretary of Undersecretariat for Defense Industries, from 1986 to 1993. See also M. Şimşek, 'Defense Industry in Turkey', *Diş Politika* (Foreign Policy), vol. XV, 1989, pp. 36–7.
62 On this particular point, see United States General Accounting Office, *U.S. Interests and Turkish Needs*, p. 26.
63 J. M. Goshko, 'From the Allies: Patience', *The Washington Post,* 13 September 1980.
64 Spain, *American Diplomacy in Turkey*, pp. 23–4.
65 Spain, *American Diplomacy in Turkey*, p. 217.
66 M. A. Birand, *12 Eylül, Saat: 04.00*, İstanbul: Karacan Yayınları, 1984, p. 104.
67 Congressional Research Service, *Turkey's Problems and Prospects,* p. 5.
68 The relevant provision of the 1976 agreement is quoted in Congressional Research Service, *Turkey's Problems and Prospects*, p. 26.
69 U.S.-Turkey Defense and Economic Cooperation Agreement, March 29, 1980, article V.4. Available online at http://photos.state.gov/libraries/turkey/461177/pdf/32t3323.pdf, (accessed 15 January 2010).
70 G. S. Harris, *Troubled Alliance: Turkish-American Problems In Historical Perspective 1945–1971*, Washington, DC: American Enterprise Institute for Public Policy Research, 1972, p. 229.
71 Spain, *American Diplomacy in Turkey*, p. 32.
72 Spain, *American Diplomacy in Turkey*, p. 32
73 Spain, *American Diplomacy in Turkey*, p. 31; Congressional Research Service, *Turkey's Problems and Prospects,* pp. 26, 28.
74 U.S.-Turkey Defence and Economic Cooperation Agreement, Art. II and *passim.*
75 Spain, *American Diplomacy in Turkey*, p. 32.
76 U.S.-Turkey Defence and Economic Cooperation Agreement, Supplementary Agreement Number 2 between the Governments of the United States of America and of the Republic of Turkey on Defense Industrial Cooperation. Actually two of these projects dated from the pre-embargo period, while three others were initiated in 1979 before the signing of the 1980 DECA: United States General Accounting Office, *U.S. Interests and Turkish Needs*, pp. 25–6.
77 United States General Accounting Office, *U.S. Interests and Turkish Needs*, pp. 25–6, 30; R. N. Perle and M. J. McNamara, 'The U.S. Security Assistance for Turkey and the Challenge of Aid for the Southern Flank', *NATO's Sixteen Nations,* vol. 32, 1987, pp. 95–6.
78 Harris, *Coping with Crisis*, p. 196.
79 Author's interview with Peter Marudas.
80 United States General Accounting Office, *U.S. Interests and Turkish Needs*, p. 5.

81 United States General Accounting Office, *U.S. Interests and Turkish Needs*, p. 6.
82 Congressional Research Service, *Turkey's Problems and Prospects*, pp. 38, 56; United States General Accounting Office, *U.S. Interests and Turkish Needs*, pp.ii–iii and passim.
83 CHAMILCOM-1–80, 1 January 1980, p. 2, NATO archives.
84 Congressional Research Service, *Turkey's Problems and Prospects,* pp. 34–5, 38; Harris, *Coping with Crisis*, p. 198; Spain, *American Diplomacy in Turkey*, pp. 73–4.
85 From Secretary General to Permanent Representatives (Council), 'Study on Economic Co-operation and Assistance within the Alliance', 8 November 1978, pp. 5–6, PO/78/116, NATO archives; 'Economic Co-operation and Assistance within the Alliance: Report on the Present Situation', 30 November 1979, p. 2, PO/79/127, NATO archives.
86 These sums were of a mixed nature: they consisted of grants, loans and credits. 'Study on Economic Co-operation and Assistance within the Alliance', 8 November 1978, pp. 9–11, PO/78/116, NATO archives; 'Industrial Allies Offer Turkey $1.45 Billion', *The New York Times*, 31 May 1979; Congressional Research Service, *Turkey's Problems and Prospects*, pp. 34–8; United States General Accounting Office, *U.S. Interests and Turkish Needs*, pp. 32–6; Önis and Özmucur, *Capital Flows*, pp. 13, 35–36.
87 'Study on Economic Co-operation and Assistance within the Alliance', 8 November 1978, pp. 6–7, PO/78/116, NATO archive.
88 J. Roy, 'The Turkish Economy: Assessment of a Recovery under a Structural Adjustment Program', EDI Working Papers, Washington, DC: The Economic Development Institute of the World Bank, 1989, pp. 13–14, pp. 47–8. Between 1977 and 1979 the efforts of the Turkish governments to implement the economic programmes agreed with the IMF failed. As a result, the Ankara/IMF negotiations collapsed. At the time the countries that were prepared to extend financial assistance to Turkey were not willing to pledge long-term assistance because they were not convinced that the Turkish government was able or willing to undertake the necessary economic reforms. The military coup ensured the political stability which was a prerequisite for the implementation of the reform programme declared by the Demirel government. The reform programme put an end to the prevailing étatist economic model: Önis and Özmucur, *Capital Flows*, p. 18.
89 Spain, *American Diplomacy in Turkey*, pp. 73–5.
90 Önis and Özmucur, *Capital Flows*, p. 84.
91 M. I. Handel, *Weak States in the International System*, London: Frank Cass, 1981, p. 181.
92 These benefits were not free of cost (political but also economic) to Turkey in the longer run. Did Turkey on balance do well? The answer to this question is beyond the scope of this book. However, it is a question that needs to be properly discussed.
93 B. Kuniholm, 'East or West? The Geopolitics of Turkey and Its NATO Alliance', in Karaosmanoğlu and Taşhan (eds), *Middle East, Turkey and the Atlantic Alliance*, Ankara: Foreign Policy Institute, 1987, p. 152, n. 19. Congress cut the military aid request in order to maintain the 7 to 10 ratio concerning military aid to Greece and Turkey (on this ratio, see Chapter 3 in this book). The $400 million of military aid consisted of Foreign Military Sales credits. The $350 million of the ESF funds were a mixture of loans and mostly grants. The remaining $3.5 million were earmarked for military education and the training of Turkish military officers: United States General Accounting Office, *U.S. Interests and Turkish Needs*, p. 3.
94 Congressional Research Service, *Turkey's Problems and Prospects*, p. 38; United States General Accounting Office, *U.S. Interests and Turkish Needs*, pp. 2–3.
95 United States General Accounting Office, *U.S. Interests and Turkish Needs*, pp. 15–24, 45.

96 United States General Accounting Office, *U.S. Interests and Turkish Needs*, p.ii and passim.
97 United States General Accounting Office, *U.S. Interests and Turkish Needs*, pp. ii, 40, 48 and passim.
98 United States General Accounting Office, *U.S. Interests and Turkish Needs*, p. 43.
99 United States General Accounting Office, *U.S. Interests and Turkish Needs*, p. ii, 40.
100 B. Kuniholm, 'Turkey in the World', p. 15; Campbell, 'Superpowers and Turkey', pp. 62–3.
101 United States General Accounting Office, *U.S. Interests and Turkish Needs*, pp. 46–7 and passim. The comments and objections that the Pentagon and the State Department raised after having reviewed a draft of the report, as well as the the General Accounting Office's responses, are included in the report. Even though parts were sanitized before its public release at least certain aspects of their views emerge clearly.
102 United States General Accounting Office, *U.S. Interests and Turkish Needs*, pp. 46, 48.
103 United States General Accounting Office, *U.S. Interests and Turkish Needs*, pp. 42–3.
104 Congress in the end approved a total of $853 million and $875 million for the fiscal years 1984 and 1985 respectively. These amounts did not include the Military Education and Training Program assistance that Turkey received, which added about another three million $ each year: Kuniholm, 'East or West?', p. 139; T. Gabelnick, W. D. Hartung, and J. Washburn, with research assistance by M. Ciarrocca, *Arming Repression: U.S. Arms Sales to Turkey during the Clinton Administration*, a joint report of the World Policy Institute and the Federation of American Scientists, October 1999, available online at http://www.fas.org/asmp/library/reports/turkeyrep.htm (accessed 4 March 2000).
105 H. Binnendijk and A. Friendly, Jr., *Turkey, Greece,and NATO: The Strained Alliance,* staff report to the United States Senate Committee on Foreign Relations, Washington DC: US Government Printing Office, March 1980, p. 17; Congressional Research Service, *Turkey's Problems and Prospects*, p. 38. Besides the well-established annual US security assistance amounts there were also other significant sources of US aid to Turkey, including US Navy ships transfers and military construction funds.
106 For the levels of assistance in the second half of the Reagan administration, see Chapter 3.
107 G. S. Harris, 'Introduction', in G. S. Harris (ed.), *The Middle East in Turkish-American Relations*, Washington, DC: The Heritage Foundation, 1985, p. x.
108 Congressional Research Service, *Turkey's Prospects and Problems*, p. 56; Spain, *American Diplomacy in Turkey*, p. 44.
109 Dissatisfaction with the performance of the F-4 in Vietnam as a fighter aircraft eventually led to the development of the F-16, which became operational in 1979 and was purchased by the US Air Force as a multi-role aircraft.
110 General Dynamics was succeeded as a manufacturer of the F-16 by Lockheed Martin in the 1990s. The first jointly built American-Turkish F-16 made its first official flight in the autumn of 1987. For an interesting account of the story of this joint production, see M. R. Hickok, 'Peace Onyx: A Story of Turkish F-16 Co-Production', in P. C. Wood and D. S. Sorenson (eds), *International Military Aerospace Collaboration*, Aldershot: Ashgate Press, 1999, pp. 153–81.
111 Commission on Integrated Long-Term Strategy (US), *Discriminate Deterrence: Report of the Commission on Integrated Long-Term Strategy*, Washington, DC: US Government Printing Office, January 1988, p. 26.

112 Congressional Research Service, *The Persian Gulf: Are We Committed? At What Cost?: A Dialogue with the Reagan Administration on U.S. Policy*, prepared for the use of the Joint Economic Committee, Congress of the United States, with the assistance of the Congressional Research Service, Library of Congress, Washington DC: US Government Printing Office, 1981, p. 17.
113 Congressional Research Service, *The Persian Gulf: Are We committed?* pp. 18–19. Such an approach made it easier to co-operate with local regimes that were weary of explicit co-operation with the U.S. due to internal political and security problems of their own.
114 R. Perle, 'A Turkish Story', the first annual Robert Strausz-Hupé lecture, Foreign Policy Research Institute, FPRI Wire, Sept 1999, vol. 7, available online at http://fpri.org/fpriwire/0711.19909.perle.turkishstory.html (accessed 20 June 2010).
115 Perle, 'A Turkish Story'.
116 Perle, 'A Turkish Story'.
117 Kuniholm, 'Turkey in the World', p. 14; R. Perle, 'Turkey and US Military Assistance', in G. S. Harris (ed.), *The Middle East in Turkish-American Relations*, Washington, DC: The Heritage Foundation, 1985, p. 26; Campbell, 'Superpowers and Turkey', p. 63; E. L. Evriviades, *US–Turkey Contingency Planning and Soviet Reaction 1978–1983*, Athens: Defense Analyses Institute, 2001, p. 42. I wish to thank Euripedes Evriviades for providing me with a copy of his occasional paper; United States Congress, House Committee on Armed Services, Subcommittee on Military Installations and Facilities, *Hearings, on H.R. 1816 (H.R. 2972) To Authorize Certain Construction at Military Installations for Fiscal Year 1984, and for Other Purposes*, ninety-eighth Congress, first session, 1983, Washington, DC: US Government Printing Office, 1983, pp. 452–3, 467–79.
118 Kuniholm,'East or West?', p. 144.
119 G. Wislon, 'US – Turkey Sets Air Forces Nearer USSR', *The Washington Post*, 7 November 1982; M. Demirsar, 'U.S. Upgrades Military Links to Turkey with Eye to Soviet Union and Mideast', *The Wall Street Journal*, 12 January 1983; Evriviades, *US–Turkey Contingency Planning*, pp. 31, 40–41.
120 For a good account of how the Europeans viewed the Turkish military regime and of the counter-reaction of the Turkish military, see I. D. Dagi, 'Democratic Transition in Turkey, 1980–83: The Impact of European Diplomacy', in S. Kedourie (ed.), *Turkey: Identity, Democracy and Politics*, London: Frank Cass, 1996, pp. 124–41.
121 K. Evren, *Kenan Evren'in Hatıraları*, vol. 3, İstanbul: Milliyet Yayınları, 1991, p. 168.
122 N. S. Ludington and J. W. Spain, 'Dateline Turkey: The Case for Patience', *Foreign Policy*, no. 50, 1983, p. 163.
123 'The Turkish Economy under Ozal', 29 March 1985, Central Intelligence Agency, European and Soviet Affairs Directorate, series II, NSC Records, File Folder: Ozal Visit – April 2, 1985 (2) RAC Box 15, pp. 1, 6, Ronald Reagan Presidential Library.
124 M. L. Evriviades, 'The U.S. and Cyprus: The Politics of Manipulation in the 1985 U.N. Cyprus High Level Meeting', occasional research paper no. 3, Athens: Institute of International Relations, 1992, p. 7.
125 A fascinating account of this struggle by the administration with Perle as its main protagonist can be found in Evriviades, 'The U.S. and Cyprus', pp. 7–8. Also author's interview with Andrew Manatos, president, Manatos and Manatos Lobbying Firm.
126 Harris, *Coping with Crisis*, p. 199; Evriviades, 'The U.S. and Cyprus', p. 8 and passim.
127 Author's interviews with Michael Ledeen and Andrew Manatos.
128 G. R. Ford, *A Time to Heal*, New York: Harper and Row, 1979, p. 302
129 Ford, *A Time to Heal*, p.302

130 L. Stern, *The Wrong Horse: The Politics of Intervention and the Failure of the American Diplomacy*, New York: Times Books, 1977, p. 157.
131 A. Weisman, *Prince of Darkness: Richard Perle. The Kingdom, the Power and the End of Empire in America*, New York: Union Square Press, 2007, p. 69.
132 M. L. Evriviades, 'Turkey's Role in United States Strategy during and after the Cold War', *Mediterranean Quarterly*, vol. 9, 1998, p. 40.
133 H. A. Kissinger, 'Bureaucracy and Policymaking: The Effects of Insiders and Outsiders on the Policy Process', in H. A. Kissinger and Bernard Brodie, *Bureaucracy, Politics, and Strategy*, Los Angeles: University of California, Security Studies Project, Security Studies Paper no. 17, 1968, p. 1.
134 T. H. White, 'Weinberger on the Ramparts', *New York Times Magazine*, 6 February 1983, p. 18; J. M. McCormick, *American Foreign Policy and Process*, Boston: Wadsworth, 2005, p. 415.
135 A classic analysis of bureaucratic politics is still by G. T. Allison and P. Zelikow, *Essence of Decision: Explaining the Cuban Missile Crisis*, New York: Longman, 1999; also M. Halperin and P. A. Clapp, with A. Kanter, *Bureaucratic Politics and Foreign Policy*, Washington DC: Brookings Institution Press, 2006.
136 Weisman, *Prince of Darkness*, passim; J. R. Wedel, *Shadow Elite: How the World's New Power Brokers Undermine Democracy, Government, and the Free Market*, New York: Basic Books, 2009, pp. 147–64. Also, author's interview with Andrew Manatos. Perle also played a prominent role in the negotiations and policy formulation on arms control. On this see S. Talbot, *Deadly Gambits: The Reagan Administration and the Stalemate in Nuclear Arms Control*, New York: Vintage Books, 1985, passim; and Weisman, *Prince of Darkness*, pp. 87–110.
137 Quoted in J. Mann, *Rise of the Vulcans: The History of Bush's War Cabinet*, New York: Viking, 2004, p. 120.
138 Weisman, *Prince of Darkness*, p. 66.
139 In 1982 Wolfowitz was promoted to the position of assistant secretary of state for East Asian and Pacific affairs.
140 T. Jacoby, 'The Reagan Turnaround on Human Rights', *Foreign Affairs*, vol. 64, 1986, pp. 1081–2.
141 Author's interviews with Peter Marudas, Michael Ledeen, Andrew Manatos and Ian Lesser, strategic analyst and expert on Turkey; Weisman, *Prince of Darkness*, p. 116.
142 Author's interviews with Andrew Manatos and Mehmet Ali Birand, journalist and political commentator.
143 Perle, 'A Turkish Story'. Perle refers to the renegotiation of the 1980 DECA that was to expire in 1985.

3 Co-operation and discord

The renewal of bilateral security ties could not conceal the fact that it would be hard to maintain the smooth co-operation that the Americans desired. For this to happen it was necessary to meet the Turks' high expectations concerning security assistance.[1] But Congress was not prepared to assume a major commitment to Turkey on a long-term basis as in the 1950s. There was another more serious reason that threatened the agreement reached between the US administrations and Ankara guaranteeing a balance of interests between the US and Turkey. Congress did not share the executive's view of the terms under which assistance should be given to Turkey. In sum, in the post-embargo period the legislative branch resisted the executive's pressure to approve a substantial part of military aid to Turkey in the form of grants. Instead, Congress tended to authorize a major part of the military assistance requests in the form of loans, though usually at lower than market rates, but permitted some of the economic aid to be a grant.[2] The financial strain on the US did not allow for the level of military and economic assistance requested by Ankara and supported by the US military mission in Turkey. The latter estimated that an annual sum of around $1.5 billion was needed for Turkey to fully meet its NATO obligations. This was a point repeatedly stressed by those in Washington who advocated in favour of US largesse toward Turkey.[3]

Nonetheless, the significance of these issues would only be seriously felt in the latter part of the 1980s. Until the middle of the decade military and economic assistance levels to Turkey remained high, despite the 1980 military coup, the military's political tutelage and gross violations of human rights. The main reason was that the administrations' argument that Turkey possessed strategic importance in the renewed power contest with the Soviet Union appealed to a significant number of congressmen.[4] This is not to say that Congress paid no attention to the slow process of democratization in Turkey and violations of human rights. Indeed it would have been difficult not to. The European Community was growing increasingly critical of the harsh policies of the Turkish military and slowed down aid to Turkey. Amnesty International and Helsinki Watch were producing a stream of reports concerning the use of extended torture by the Turkish police[5] and the violation of a large number of civil rights by the new 1982 constitution,[6] the handiwork of the Turkish military regime. In early 1984 four political prisoners died in Turkey, following two and a half months of hunger strike in protest against torture in prisons. The Turkish military after the coup had promised the return of the country to parliamentary democracy once law and order had been restored and a new constitution had been enacted. They kept their promise, but only partly. The military members of the National Security Council, which was formed following the coup, exercised legislative and executive power for around three years. General Kenan Evren, the leader of the coup, assumed in 1982 the office of the president of the Turkish Republic for seven years; only three parties that were chosen by the military were allowed to contest the parliamentary elections, which finally were allowed to take place in November 1983. For those watching developments in Turkey, what seemed to be of even greater concern was that the military institutionalized its supervisionary role over political life through the new constitution.[7] Human and civil rights abuses, the slow return to representative democracy and the limits imposed on its institutions[8] attracted the interest of those members of Congress who had an interest in Turkey[9] either as its critics or indeed as its supporters. Thus, in Congress an environment of resistance was being cultivated, in contrast to the unreserved embrace of Ankara that the Reagan administration was promoting.[10] Nonethelesss, in the early 1980s no noteworthy attempt was made by any group in Congress to make assistance to Turkey contingent upon the quick pace of full return to parliamentary democracy. Washington needed Turkey to perform its role in international politics as a US military ally, and Congress like the White House was accustomed to this kind of compromise.

It was developments over Cyprus that led to an effort by Congress to use military and economic assistance as a means to put pressure on Turkey's leaders. The declaration of independence by the Turkish Cypriots (15 November 1983) in the occupied northern part of Cyprus mobilized American representatives and senators who were interested in the balance of power between Greece and Turkey as well as in the Cyprus issue. What followed was a quick reaction both in the House and the Senate as the declaration of independence was widely perceived as further aggravating the already tense situation between Turkey and Greece over Cyprus and therefore posing a threat to future stability in the area. Thus, both chambers condemned the Turkish Cypriots' declaration of independence, and during their deliberations in 1984 they proposed cuts in assistance to Turkey for the 1985 fiscal year. This attempt reflected two major strands of thought within Congress.[11] The first one was that the levels of assistance to Turkey that the administration requested ($934 million)[12] should maintain the seven to ten proportional allocation of military aid between Greece and Turkey. After 1978 Congress linked military aid to Greece to aid to Turkey in order to achieve a 'balance of military strength between the two'.[13] Since 1980 this linkage had taken the form of a seven to ten ratio, and Congress supported it even though the Reagan administration like the Carter administration before strongly opposed it, on the basis of the argument that Turkey did not pose a military threat to

Greece. As a result, the ratio, which partly resonated with the wider contest of wills between the two branches of the US government, had already shaped the Congress's position in relation to the levels of assistance to Turkey the Reagan administration had asked for in the previous fiscal year. But many members of Congress also wished to cut aid to Turkey further in order to send the Turks a message that the Reagan administration seemed only too reluctant to convey. The message was that the US Congress considered Ankara's policies at least partly responsible for the deterioration of the Cyprus issue as a result of the declaration of independence of the «Turkish Republic of Northern Cyprus» and its recognition by Ankara. In the end differences between the administration and Congress were squared off. The seven to ten ratio was maintained without any drastic cuts in aid to Turkey but through the increase of aid to Greece. Moreover, to the great relief of the Turks only $15 million, a small part of the military aid that the administration had asked for, was cut, once the seven to ten ratio had been applied, as a reminder to Ankara of its co-responsibility for the Cyprus issue taking another turn to the worse.[14]

The Reagan administration's efforts to ensure that the high levels of military assistance and economic aid to Turkey continued for the 1985 fiscal year were successful. Total assistance for that year would reach again almost $1 billion ($878,000,000). This was lower than the administration's requested amount of $934 million, but as a matter of fact $22 million more that the $856.3 million of total authorized assistance for the previous fiscal year.[15] Yet this success could not conceal that there was a reaction in Congress against the very high levels of assistance to Turkey, which the administration overcame only after a lot of intense and persistent effort. For Ankara and Turkey's supporters in Washington, 1984 was a year of great suspense.[16] It was also to be proved prophetic. The cornerstone of the renewed US–Turkey strategic co-operation was the willingness of the US government to provide Turkey with military and economic aid on a grand scale. What had become obvious was that the ability of the US government to secure the amounts Ankara was pressing for was not guaranteed. Thus, Ankara grew more and more concerned about the inability of the Reagan administration to fend off domestic obstacles in order to obtain authorization for expanded military and economic aid programmes.[17] For its part, the US administration sought to ease this concern. In early April 1985, while Turgut Özal, the Turkish prime minister, was on his official visit to Washington, President Reagan promised that his administration would request that year a 'record' level of assistance on better terms and would oppose the seven to ten ratio and the linkage to Cyprus.[18] The pledge that his administration would continue to seek high levels of assistance was also made publicly. In the press conference immediately following his meeting with Özal Reagan stated: 'Let me also assure you that the United States remains committed to high levels of security assistance for Turkey to speed the modernization of your armed forces and to support your economic reform program. And, of course, this assistance serves the interests of both our countries.'[19] Then Reagan added that he had reiterated to the Turkish premier that he would 'continue to urge the Congress to fund my full security assistance request for Turkey in fiscal year 1986'.[20] The US government kept its promise. It asked for authorization of a total record amount of $939 million, which was even $5 million over the request for the 1985 fiscal year. Military assistance accounted for the lion's share, $789 million, of which 73 per cent was in either grant form or on concessional terms, while the remaining $145 million was requested in the form of economic aid. Actually, the economic aid request was reduced by $25 million from the fiscal year 1985, and although it was mostly in the form of a grant[21] it amounted to only 50 per cent of the economic aid Turkey actually received in the fiscal years 1983 and 1984 ($300 and $285 million respectively). But this was a reflection of the changed economic reality in Turkey. According to the State Department, although the Turkish economy was still faced with very serious problems, the extreme conditions that prevailed in Turkey in the early 1980s due to the crisis of the late 1970s were eased as growth and Turkey's international creditworthiness had been restored.[22] The Reagan government proved as good as its word, but naturally whether it could actually deliver on it was a different matter. This time it failed to build within Congress the consensus it needed. When the legislative branch eventually decided on the amount of assistance for Turkey, it authorized $735, in other words $140 million less than the amount authorized in the previous fiscal year.[23]

Insistence by Congress that the seven to ten ratio should be maintained when it came to the authorization of assistance for Turkey and occasional criticisms by some of its members of Turkey's violations of human rights were by no means the only issues that vexed Ankara. Perhaps nothing infuriated and embittered the Turks more in 1984 than what they saw as an increasing congressional willingness to satisfy Armenian-Americans (another force critical of Turkey alongside the Greek-Americans and the Cypriot-Americans), who pressured to have the Armenian genocide, a taboo subject for the Turkish state,[24] commemorated and taken into consideration when formulating US policy.[25] In that year Congress deliberated over two resolutions on the Armenian issue and the adoption by the House of one of them it was seen by the Turks as '"a mini Johnson Letter"'[26] that 'created a universal public outcry in Turkey against the US'.[27] In the view of many members of Congress the importance of the resolutions was minimal because they were not a major part of legislation. They were rather 'symbolic, rhetorical gestures to special groups', 'not binding on day-to-day policy makers.'[28] Therefore, according to the wider congressional view, Ankara had no reason to concern itself. This was even more true because the importance of the bilateral relationship was reflected in the much more substantial foreign aid legislation. But none of these arguments eased negative Turkish perceptions of these congressional actions, which sometimes 'had almost a hysterical treatment.'[29] Ankara expected (and in a sense demanded) its strategic ally to show much more understanding when it came to an issue of such great sensitivity to the Turkish state.[30] So it was left to the Reagan administration to do its utmost to prevent passage of these resolutions out of fear that they would harm relations with Ankara.[31]

'Either there will be adequate security assistance to Turkey or … '[32]

Turkish officials and the Turkish media loudly expressed Ankara's intense indignation at congressional interference with Turkey's interests, the product of 'alien influences',[33] as Ankara liked to think of the Greek-American and Armenian-American lobbies. This discontent initially undermined the tone but not the substance of the bilateral relationship.[34] However, this began to change in the second half of the 1980s as Ankara grew more and more frustrated because the levels of US security assistance did not meet Turkish demands.[35] When the US authorized $615 million in military assistance for the fiscal year 1986 ($735 million security assistance in total) the Turks became highly critical of the US for not living up to the 'best efforts' commitment it undertook in the 1980 DECA concerning military financing. So, in September 1985, just prior to the expiration of the DECA, the Turkish government asked the US for a review of the agreement. Their basic goal was to find ways to improve the agreement by receiving more specific commitments concerning future levels of US aid. Once again the process of laborious negotiations began. It was going to last for 14 months. In the meantime, as Congress authorized $490 million in military assistance to Turkey for the fiscal year 1987[36] (about $100 million less than in the previous year) Ankara sharply reacted to the reduction. Turkish military officials argued that the military assistance appropriations for fiscal year 1987 fell significantly below the low projection of US assistance that was contained in their five-year military modernization plan and which was prepared in consultation with US officials.[37] The Turks' main rationale for their position was built on statements and documents prepared by the US Pentagon and reiterated by General Bernard Rogers, NATO's supreme allied commander, Europe – and former US chief of staff (1973–9) – according to which $1.2 billion in annual assistance was necessary for a thorough, effective modernization of Turkish armed forces in order for Turkey to fulfil its NATO mission.[38] At the same time, all this was accompanied by heavy criticism of congressional action to cut administration requests and to maintain a seven to ten ratio on certain categories of US assistance to Greece and Turkey. For the Turks, this attitude of Congress was 'illogical' and even 'anti-Turkish'.[39] There was another aspect to the whole issue, however, that excruciated the Turks. It was the simple fact that Turkey's debt burden as a recipient of Foreign Military Sales assistance was growing while US security assistance was declining. As Turkish officials noted in 1987 they would be paying the US a total of $421 million in military debt while Turkey would be receiving only $490 million in fresh military aid the same year. Therefore, the Turks refused to renew the Defence and Economic Cooperation Agreement unless they received stronger guarantees on aid levels and other forms of assistance that would help Turkey with its military modernization.[40] The Americans sought to deal with the Turks' grievances by pointing out that while levels of assistance were under extreme budgetary pressures the military assistance provided was on increasingly favourable terms. Turkey was the largest recipient of grants under the Military Assistance Program. In fact, since 1980, almost half of the total military assistance Turkey had received was in the form of grants.[41] US officials also based their logic on another important consideration. The US 'best efforts' concerning the provision of US military assistance to Turkey should not only be measured, they argued, on the basis of just the level of funds authorized and appropriated. The US strengthened Turkey's military through a variety of other forms of assistance, including leases, waivers of non-recurring costs, excess equipment, military industrial co-operation, pre-payment of NATO infrastructure funds and co-production agreements. According to US officials' estimations, these forms of assistance provided Turkey with over $1 billion over and above appropriated security assistance funds during the first five-year life of the 1980 DECA. To those US officials who dealt with Turkey it was clear that the executive exercised 'broad authorities available to the Department of Defense to help Turkey in ways that it does not for other NATO countries in southern Europe.'[42] In addition to all this, the Americans were ready to discuss Turkey's options under a military debt restructuring proposal developed by the US.[43] Eventually the hard bargaining came to an end and the renewal of the DECA was initialled in December 1986. The authorization under the 1986 Defense Authorization Act for the transfer to southern-flank NATO countries (Turkey, Portugal, Greece) of equipment in the US inventory certified by the US president to be in excess of US needs for the next two fiscal years apparently significantly contributed to the Turks' decision to renew the agreement.[44] Through an exchange of letters on 16 March 1987 the Özal government accepted a five-year extension of the agreement until the end of December 1990 (the agreement was backdated to the 1985 expiration of the 1980 DECA). This was accepted only after the Turkish government had first secured in writing by Secretary of State George Shultz the unusual pledge that the Reagan administration would lobby Congress with 'vigor and determination' to help Turkey meet its NATO obligations.[45] It was a battle that both the US executive and the Turks were going to lose.

In April 1987 Congress further reduced assistance to Turkey to the total amount of $522 million for the 1988 fiscal year.[46] This was still a significant amount, but it represented a major cut to the administration's aid request of $913 million.[47] A few weeks later Richard Perle resigned from the administration. Everybody in Washington agreed that Turkey lost one of its crucial allies within the administration at a critical period.[48] (Actually, Perle would continue to work in favour of Turkish interests through different channels of influence.[49]) But had he remained in government it would not have made much difference as far as congressional cuts were concerned. These reductions reflected primarily the staggering rise of the US public debt (around $250 billion on average per year during the Reagan presidency[50]), which set serious limits to the amounts of foreign aid that Congress was predisposed to authorize. Hence, between the years 1987 and 1990 security assistance to Turkey was reduced to an average of $550 million per year. However, a higher percentage of it was in terms of outright grants.[51] So, assistance for Turkey returned to the levels of the Carter presidency in the post-embargo period. These were still pretty high, but far lower than what the Turks bargained for and certainly had been accustomed to expect in the previous years of the Reagan presidency.

The Turks' reaction to the congressional decision to reduce by almost 36 per cent the administration's assistance request for the 1988 fiscal year was immediate. Prime Minister Özal announced that the government would defer ratification of the Side Letter to the DECA, which provided for an extension of the agreement, while President Evren cancelled his scheduled visit to the US. These early warning signals which expressed Ankara's dissatisfaction were followed in early autumn by a series of restrictive measures on the number of aircraft allowed to participate in NATO exercises in Turkey as well as on US aircraft flights in Turkish airspace.[52] So Özal and the Turkish military resurrected the aggressive bargaining that had been used in the 1970s by refusing to provide services.[53]

Domestic political considerations certainly also had a big role to play. Özal and his government were accused by political opposition of having agreed to renew the DECA before securing binding commitments from the US.[54] This criticism might not have mattered much had Özal and his party not been on the political offensive. In the September 1986 by-elections, the Motherland Party did less well than predicted and got only 32 per cent of the vote, a big decline when compared with 45 per cent in the 1983 general elections. With parliamentary elections coming up in November 1987 Özal must have felt a pressing need to silence his opponents on every front, even though dissatisfaction was mainly related to his economic reform programme.[55] In the end, Ankara's reaction proved to be more symbolic than real. Despite the furor over the reduction of US assistance the Turks remained eager to accommodate US strategic interests. Although they pressed hard to maintain the high level of assistance they had been used to, clearly they were prepared to continue their strategic co-operation with the Americans for less. As has been noted elsewhere, refusing to provide services is a time-honoured important pressure tactic employed by weaker states, when favoured by geopolitical reality, in their dealings with a great power. But it can only last for a limited period.[56] Eventually, after intense negotiations, Ankara ratified the Side Letter in late February 1988, three months after Özal's electoral victory in the national elections. All the restrictive measures were also lifted even though the Turks had not received any concrete rewards and instead had to be satisfied with promises. For example the Democratic senator and majority leader in the Senate, Robert C. Byrd, who had been on a two-day visit to Turkey in mid-February 1988 with a high-level Senate delegation, declared on the Senate floor that he would work to put together an assistance package that 'responded positively' to Turkey's stance 'as a staunch and loyal' ally who made a 'maximum effort within its limited financial resources' to modernize its military forces. Byrd commented that Congress should also reward Özal's efforts for 'forward-looking diplomacy' when it came to relations with Greece. It was a reference to the initiative by the Turkish prime minister for two-day high-level talks with his Greek counterpart, Andreas Papandreou, in Davos, Switzerland, in January 1988 with the aim of finding ways to diffuse tension between the two countries, which had suffered a big crisis the previous year.[57]

Ankara's pressure tactics in 1987/8 bore mixed immediate results. Total US assistance for fiscal year 1989 grew only very slightly, from $522 million (FY 1988) to $560 million. However, a compensating factor was that the amount of aid in the form of grants increased from $344 million (FY 1988) to $470 million. Yet such tactics were successful in the sense that they pressed upon the US administration the oft-repeated underlying message that US assistance was 'central' to Turkey's security co-operation;[58] hence aid levels continued to remain high, relatively speaking. Washington fully understood this message first during the embargo years. Since then the Turks consistently made sure that it was not forgotten. Very often congressional decisions unfavourable to Turkish interests were followed not only by the Turks' official reaction but also by caustic commentaries in the Turkish press that the Americans knew very well were orchestrated by the Turkish government.[59] These invariably questioned the value the US placed on its relationship with Turkey and doubted the future of the bilateral relationship.[60]

In reality, the Turkish stance led only to temporary frustration of certain aspects of security co-operation. Essentially Ankara was using pressure tactics as a bargaining card: it kept tension in the bilateral dialogue under control while it never failed to emphasize its keen interest in the continuation of the strategic co-operation.[61] Yet the Turks' behaviour raised within the US administration the question of the sustainability of the security relationship in the future, for it seemed clear that although the US had invested quite a substantial amount in Turkey it had not won the Turks' unfailing co-operation. Back in 1985 a briefing paper for President Reagan, prepared jointly by the National Security Council staff and the State Department on the occasion of Prime Minister Özal's visit to Washington, pointed out that the argument that the Turks had no alternative to alliance with the US

> underestimates their national pride and overestimates their degree of commitment to the West. Should Turkey conclude the advantages it offers the West are not sufficiently valued and reciprocated, it could resume the neutral policy it pursued in World War II or seek to shift its orientation to the Islamic bloc. Our task is to make Turkey feel wanted and to keep her as a valued ally.[62]

Nonetheless, in the latter part of the 1980s, although the Turks became more openly aggressive in their demands, they were not ready to seriously question their co-operation with the US. Whether this was the case because they had no political/military alternative to the alliance with the US, as some at least argued in Washington, is a moot point. But it was clear that the Turkish ruling elites had no alternative source that might offer the financial and military rewards the US extended in return for Turkey's collaboration. There was no obvious alternative to US military assistance and industrial defence co-operation, if Turkey was going to modernize its military forces and build its own defence industry. Between 1980 and 1988 Turkey received on average around $726 million per year in total security (military and economic) assistance, of which almost one-third was in the form of grants. Even when the Reagan administration failed to maintain the dizzying levels of assistance that were the hallmark of the period from 1982 to 1986 Turkey continued to receive half a billion dollars per year, of which almost two-thirds were in grant form or on concessional terms.[63]

There were also other forces at work. Prime Minister Özal's political future was tied to the success of his economic programme. He had won the election in 1983 partly on account of his promise that he would revive the Turkish economy, which was faltering following its remarkable recovery from the abysmal crisis of the late 1970s. His pledge was that he would revive the 1980 economic stabilization programme, he would make the economy respond more to market forces and strengthen Turkey's balance of payments. The immediate results of his policy, however, were mixed. On the one hand, there was a marked improvement in economic growth and the balance of payments. But, on the other, inflation (35–40 per cent annually) and unemployment, which could brew dissatisfaction and extremism, still remained very high.[64] Özal's party was a coalition of various forces that to a large extent were kept together as a result of his popularity with the party's rank and file and the public. In the final analysis the cohesion of his party depended on his popularity and in order to remain popular he had to show results on the economic front. In the mid 1980s the State Department and the CIA assessed that the failure of Özal's programme would cause defections in his party and a viable challenge from his political opponents. The CIA even pointed out that pressure would be brought upon him not only from the public but also from the military, which had allowed him a free hand in running the economy. At the time the agency was of the view that Özal was not in immediate danger. Nevertheless, it underlined, like the State Department, that his economic programme was far from yielding the results which would keep his critics at bay any time soon. Therefore, the CIA contended that he would need to use all his 'tactical skills to fend off critics and keep his programme on track.' If the economy failed to show progress under his direction, concluded the agency, he ran the risk that the military might step in and replace him.[65] By the late 1980s Özal was not in any stronger position. The performance of the Turkish economy still remained mixed. In the period from 1981 to 1988 Turkey experienced an impressive 5.8 per cent average annual growth rate of real gross domestic product (GDP) and the external deficit to GDP ratio fell from

7 per cent in 1980 to negative 1 per cent (surplus) in 1988. The downside was that rampant inflation (running between 60 and 65 per cent annually in the late 1980s) and the high unemployment rate (of about 20 per cent) persisted. The end – essentially in 1984 – of Ankara's grace period on rescheduled foreign debt resulted in the sharp rise of principal repayments and so added to the problematic picture. In addition, defence expenditure accounted for some 25 per cent of the budget. Turkey found itself particularly squeezed.[66] Total service costs on medium and long-term debt remained high throughout the 1980s. Özal's liberalization efforts had not succeeded in attracting actual direct foreign investment to the extent that had been hoped.[67] By the end of the 1980s Turkey was becoming a 'super debtor'[68] country in order to generate growth. In 1989 the country's external debt would rise to almost $45 billion from around $15 billion in 1979 and $25.6 billion in 1985. Hence, Turkey continued to be heavily dependent on aid from the West as well as on borrowing in international financial markets in order to meet the over $7 billion per year debt payments.[69]

Under the circumstances Özal needed US help in order to deal with his economic and political problems as tensions at home were high. The Reagan administration wished to strengthen Özal because the US in its turn needed him. The US interest in bases, military facilities and a strong, modernized Turkish army was linked to the necessity of re-orientating the economy away from its traditional centrally controlled and highly protected model to one that was more responsive to market forces. The State Department, the CIA and the National Security Council regarded Özal as the most 'influential champion' of the 'badly needed' economic reforms and by extension to the stability and even the success of the democratic process in Turkey.[70]

Ankara's pressure tactics were not solely motivated by the desire for high levels of assistance and/or no further reductions, at least: to see the Turkish stance only in this light would be an oversimplification. It is reasonable to assume that a parallel aim was to remind the Americans that Turkey was not at their beck and call. We know that Ankara craved foreign policy independence and in fact was concerned at, and even resented its dependence on, US security assistance.[71] Even though, on the whole, the Turks were able to achieve most of their objectives based on the idea of reciprocity, the truth of the matter was that the relationship between Turkey, a weak state in the international system, and the US was an unequal one. As students of international politics know, often the relationship between a weak state and a great power can assume a less favourable form from the weak state's point of view. In other words, despite the reciprocity that may exist, the imbalance, if it is too big, may result in a command relationship in which the great power dominates the weak state.[72] Ankara's aggressive pressure-tactics should also be seen as a strong reminder to Washington of the *conditional* character upon which Turkey's co-operation was based. In brief, they reflected the Turks' resistance to the establishment of a patron-client relationship which would allow the US to impose its own terms and to show lack of respect to Turkey.[73]

Essentially Turkish leaders were up against a problem that has been identified as often being central for the weaker states in the international system: how not to allow the much stronger power to exploit their weakness, but instead to benefit themselves the most from their relationship with it, while at the same time making sure that they do not upset too much the great power whose support they need.[74] But there was an important inherent contradiction in Turkey's approach, assuming that it was informed by this kind of thinking. The bigger the assistance sums Ankara was after, the greater its dependence on the US and consequently the greater its vulnerability to Washington's manipulation or even coercion.

The above analysis is not enough to fully explain Ankara's tactical manoeuvers. It is worth bearing in mind that in unequal relationships the position of the weaker party is also determined by the degree to which the great power is dependent (or perceived to be dependent) on the weaker power's services.[75] Undoubtedly Ankara's approach to a large extent mirrored the Turks' conviction that Turkish bases were indispensable to the US.[76] As a former Turkish prime minister put it rather bluntly, 'you [the Americans] must pay our bills because you need us'.[77] In brief, the Turks were convinced that Washington would not wish to alienate its strategically positioned ally. Consequently, Ankara kept the price of its strategic co-operation high, like the bazaar seller who does not lower his price when he senses that the buyer is not going to turn his back and leave. The Turks' conviction that Washington needed Turkey to a large extent was the result of the sincere efforts by the Ford and later the Carter administrations to lift the embargo.[78] In the early 1980s the staggering amounts of security assistance requested by the Reagan administration and authorized by Congress further strengthened this conviction. But there was also a psychological element affecting Ankara's behaviour. This was reflected in the view that the rich Americans *could afford* to give Turkey, a poor country, much more than what they were already giving in order to secure their interests.[79]

Bases and Turkish approaches to the Middle East

Despite continuing co-operation it was clear in the latter part of the decade that bilateral relations left a lot to be desired for each side. After 1986 it became increasingly difficult for the Turks to get the full compensating benefits they judged they should be receiving for accommodating US strategic needs. The US executive feared that as a result the Turks' trend of resistance to security co-operation might be reinforced, but it had no way of effectively dealing with congressional aid cuts. While the aid battle between Washington and Ankara was going on apparently the Reagan administration had only partly satisfied – through the COB agreement – its plans to use Turkey as a staging base for military operations in the Gulf.

Ankara's stance on this matter had been rather consistent for two decades. Since the 1960s every Turkish government had held the same line: bases on Turkish soil could be used by the Americans only in support of (a) NATO operations; and/or (b) operations that served Turkish security interests as judged by the Turks themselves.[80] Characteristically, during the 1967 and 1973 Arab-Israeli wars Süleyman Demirel's government and the caretaker government of Naim Talu respectively refused to allow the use of Turkish military installations for US operations in support of Israel. In the 1980s it was still inconceivable for the Turks to waive their independence on foreign and security issues and to commit themselves in favour of a bases agreement that could serve US interests and offer Turkey short-term rewards but might jeopardize its interests in the Middle East. For any Turkish government it would have been extremely difficult to justify such a decision. In the final analysis the Turkish-US co-operation did not reflect a convergence of security interests which might make Turkish flexibility over the bases acceptable. In fact the Turks had a different view from the US of how Turkey's strategic value within the context of Middle East security should be employed to best advantage. While the Americans wished to commit Turkey to military responsibility for the defence of the Gulf, Turkish leaders argued that 'Turkish approval for use of these bases by the United States in a Middle Eastern or Gulf contingency would be incompatible with Turkey's security concept as well as with its self-defined role in the area', as Ali Karaosmanoğlu, the eminent Turkish security analyst, noted at the time.[81] The Turks insisted that Turkey's role in the area should be limited to deterrence, unless conditions dictated otherwise. They believed, Karaosmanoğlu pointed out, that the upgrading of Turkey's armed forces and the improvement of its bases with a view to effective reinforcement capability already would serve to 'heighten deterrence' and would 'affect the regional balance of power in the Middle East/Persian Gulf area in favor of the West, even without an advance Turkish commitment beyond NATO's zone of responsibility'.[82] They also underscored, noted Karaosmanoğlu, that they regarded their 'subtle' policy in the Middle East, which took into consideration both global and regional aspects of Gulf security, to be 'in the best interests' not only of Turkey but also of the Western alliance. By contrast, as they openly admitted, they did not feel 'confident' about the effectiveness of US strategy, which focused on military intervention in the area in response to security problems that in Turkey's view were more political than military. From a Turkish perspective, although the danger of a 'direct Soviet intrusion' could not be dismissed, the 'centerpiece of security concerns' in the area was the Arab-Israeli conflict.[83] In addition, the Turkish position was that the regional countries themselves were better able to deal with low-level conflicts whether or not indirect Soviet action was involved, while the US should limit its role to 'arms transfers and other security programs'.[84] In sum, for the Turks their low-key, non-interventionist policy in the Middle East, in combination with Turkey's membership of NATO, was a means for Turkey to play a bridging role between the West and the Middle East.[85]

Karaosmanoğlu pointed out that it would not 'be easy' for the Turks 'to keep a harmonious balance between the main course of Turkey's policies and its regional policies in a period of East-West tension.'[86] This was particularly so as greater flexibility by the Turks' concerning the use of the bases would clearly contribute to the better management of the politics of their relationship with the US, including enhancing prospects for receiving more aid, as a number of US officials argued.[87] In response to the challenge Turkish leaders sought to perform a delicate balancing act by employing an ambiguous stance. So they agreed to consult with the Americans – and their other NATO allies – on issues concerning Gulf security. Even more importantly they prepared the military infrastructure for the event of a Gulf contingency. But while they stressed that they were not prepared to make any military commitment outside the NATO framework they did not exclude the possibility of Turkey's military involvement on an ad hoc basis in the event of an actual threat to the Gulf.[88]

The Turks' preference for an ad hoc approach, in other words for maximum flexibility, in their co-operation with the US in the security of the Middle East was again not something new. For some time Ankara's tactical approach was on the one hand to avoid as much as possible a close identification with US policies in the area, while on the other hand keeping possibilities for co-operation open. For instance, in late November 1979, when the issue of the use of Turkish bases emerged within the context of possible military action in Iran for the liberation of the American hostages, the Turkish government initially left the Turkish position completely open.[89] The picture that emerges from the little we know is that in the 1980s the Turks were ready to accommodate – but out of the limelight – US strategic objectives in the Middle East as long as the risks involved for Turkey were judged to be low. So, they permitted the Americans to use installations on Turkish soil to collect intelligence information about the Gulf for non-NATO related activities.[90] They also offered, albeit reluctantly and with minimum publicity, support to the Multinational Force in Beirut, which at some point included about 1,800 US marines.[91] Ankara's understated policy of support was designed to keep Washington satisfied – in recognition and expectation of further rewards to Turkey – while at the same time to avoid complications and reactions adverse to Turkish interests in the Arab world.

The Turks' stance reflected the evolution of Turkish foreign policy towards the Middle East in the course of the previous two decades, which is worth discussing at some length. Since the 1960s it had become clear to the majority of Turkish leaders that US strategic interests and Turkey's political, security and economic interests in the Middle East did not always coincide.[92] So Turkish governments – assisted by the ebbing of tension between the superpowers – ceased to formulate their policy in the Middle East through the one-dimensional lens of the Cold War as they did in the 1950s when they automatically aligned with the US. Instead, the Turks recognized that they had to take into consideration the dynamics of the Middle-East sub-system, of which Turkey was a part and where the country had significant security, political[93] and – as it gradually transpired – economic interests. It has been remarked that the need for a pro-Arab policy was perhaps the only foreign policy issue upon which all Turkish political forces across the spectrum agreed, 'albeit for different and even conflicting reasons.'[94] In concrete terms this meant that the Turks tended to side more with the Arab viewpoint with respect to the Palestinian issue;[95] they adopted a policy of non-interference in intra-Arab relations while they pursued an active role in the Islamic Conference and the development of relations with every country in the area. In essence, Ankara made a substantial effort to change Turkey's negative image as a surrogate of the US, which had been developed in the region mainly as the result of the Menderes government's foreign policy. Turkey's initial rapprochement with the Arabs in the 1960s was not informed by economic considerations. But from the mid to late 1970s the development of political ties with the Arab world led to the development of economic relations that accrued significant benefits to Turkey. These benefits were particularly noticeable in the field of Turkish exports to the oil-producing Arab states, as Turkey was making an effort to balance its increased imported-oil bills. In 1977 Turkey's exports to the Middle East countries accounted for 10.9 per cent of its total exports. In 1982 this share had climbed to 37.6 per cent, while during the same period the share of Turkish exports to the OECD countries had declined from 70.4 to 44.5 per cent. In 1982 the total value of Turkish exports to the Middle East amounted to $2.5 billion and in 1985 it would rise to almost $3.2 billion. The Turkish construction sector also benefited substantially through the award of construction projects to Turkish companies in the Gulf Arab states, Iraq and Libya. By the end of 1982 the total value of contracts by Turkish companies in Saudi Arabia, Libya and Iraq alone was estimated at around $10 billion and in 1985 it would reach $14.9 billion. As a result of this boom the Turkish workforce in the Middle East grew rapidly. By the middle of the 1980s Turkish expatriates in the Arab countries represented 9.1 per cent of all Turkish expatriates, and Saudi Arabia had emerged as the second country in the world with the largest number of Turkish expatriates after West Germany.[96]

The resurfacing of the 'Soviet threat' after 1979 did not cause the Turks to reconsider their policy toward the Middle East – another piece of evidence that they were not alarmed by it. Even though by and large it became more difficult to reconcile Turkey's regional policies and US strategic interests in the Middle East, Turkish leaders were convinced that any strong support for US policies particularly in the military field would harm Turkish interests in the region.[97]

The Turks took a long view of their interests. Although their co-operation with the US offered significant security and economic benefits they continued to resist linking their interests exclusively with their mighty ally. Their caution was also informed by lessons of history. It has been observed that the experience small states have of their participation in alliances significantly influences future decisions as to whether they should assume commitments in the international system.[98] This was certainly the case with Turkey. Its enthusiastic participation in the American-inspired Baghdad Pact (1955) had far more adverse consequences than Ankara had expected for Turkey's relations with most Arab states. On top of this, the pact did not succeed in advancing

Western security interests as it failed to prevent the military coup that overthrew the Iraqi pro-Western monarchy in 1958[99] or the expansion of Soviet influence in the area. This negative experience taught the Turkish political, military and bureaucratic elites the lesson that Turkey would best promote its interests by not getting involved in conflicts between the states of the area and external powers.[100] Furthermore, the Turks remained suspicious of the US. In fact they were convinced that Turkey's accommodation of US strategic interests in the Middle East would not at all prevent the Americans from abandoning Turkey in the future once they no longer needed its co-operation.[101] Although in the early 1980s this was not very openly discussed it was always there under the surface, rooted in the Turks' historical experience of the bilateral relationship and particularly in the embargo years.[102] Actually, Ankara had every reason to remain suspicious. From a Turkish perspective it was clear that after the mid 1980s the US executive yet again was unable to prevail over Congress and 'alien influences' in order to honour its pledges of assistance to Turkey. Therefore, in short, the consensus among Turkish leaders was that policy in the Middle East would be determined solely by Turkey.[103] In addition to the Turks' fears and justified lack of trust in the US, their lack of confidence in the US military approach to the security problems in the Middle East, which was mentioned earlier, strengthened their determination to maintain as much as possible a safe distance from US strategic initiatives in the area. Furthermore, the stance of the European allies who did not succumb to US pressures to involve NATO in Middle East security made the Turks even more cautious. European NATO members did not share the Reagan administration's perception of the Soviet threat in the Middle East. They were far more concerned about the risks of US overreaction that might lead to a conflict between the two superpowers.[104] Their reluctance to commit the alliance to the security of the Gulf and to engage in military programmes which might in the end destabilize the region meant for the Turks that 'the advantage expected from the linkage between Persian Gulf security, Turkey and NATO' became 'highly problematic', as Karaosmanoğlu noted.[105] Besides, as far as one can judge, the Turks must have also been apprehensive about the risk of finding themselves involved in a regional conflict as a result of an ill-thought-out US strategy if they supported US action in the Middle East.

The realities of the regional security context at the time could not but also enhance the Turks' apprehension about possible negative consequences for Turkey if it openly supported US strategic objectives in the area. Radical political forces in the Arab world were on the rise following the Iranian Revolution and Egypt's ostracization because of its peace treaty with Israel. Throughout 1979 and 1980 Saddam Hussein's regime in Iraq, the most powerful of the Arab regimes, was leading the radicals' efforts to isolate Egypt. In 1980 Hussein proposed the Pan-Arab Charter that aimed to define the rules of conduct of the Arab states. On paper Iraq, which was already behaving like a hegemonic power in the Gulf, was charting the course for a non-aligned Arab world and rejected the military presence of either superpower. Jordan and

Kuwait endorsed the plan. Developments in Iran had also led to the rise of radical Islam in the area. Anti-Americanism was the meeting point for all these forces.[106] Besides, most Arab Gulf states already viewed with suspicion the hegemonic presence of both superpowers. And the emphasis given by the US to the defence of the oil fields by the RDF made the Arabs regard the Rapid Force as a threat to their sovereignty of the oil resources.[107] When Oman participated in late 1981 in the US Bright Star military exercises it was criticized by Saudi Arabia, the close ally of the US, for not abiding by the non-alignment principle that all Gulf Cooperation Council states agreed upon. Actually the conservative Arab regimes of the Gulf needed US protection 'more than ever before'. But even so, they welcomed the US security umbrella as long as it remained 'over the horizon' and did not require basing American arms and military personnel in their countries.[108] Under the circumstances the Turks must have come to the conclusion that open co-operation with the Americans through the stationing of American troops or granting access to bases on their soil for US military operations was simply calling for trouble. The heart of the matter was that Ankara's improved relations with most states in the region had yielded benefits principally in the economic field but on the other hand they had made Turkey more vulnerable to pressures from regional regimes.

In the greater scheme of things the Turks' reluctance to commit Turkey's contribution to a US military intervention in the Gulf outside a NATO framework reflected the influence of two other interrelated parameters. The first was the relative decline of the structural power of the US: in other words, a decline in its ability to define and shape the frameworks within which it related to other states and to adapt these frameworks according to changes in the international system in order to satisfy its interests through the satisfaction of the needs of its allies.[109]

The second parameter was the difference of perspective between Ankara and Washington regarding the Soviet threat. Clearly, Turkish leaders worried more about the implications of getting involved in US operations in the Middle East than the wider security implications in the Gulf following the Soviet invasion in Afghanistan. Although the Turks favoured strengthening NATO's southern flank, hoping, as a US Senate delegation visiting Turkey in 1980 remarked, for substantial US military assistance to strengthen Turkey's military forces and for economic benefits,[110] the idea of closer military co-operation with the US in the region outside the NATO framework was resisted because it raised the stakes for Turkey. Not only would it be a provocative act in the eyes of Moscow, but also it threatened to implicate Turkey in a conflict with the Soviet Union (or with a Middle East country) outside the protection of the North Atlantic Treaty.[111] There is another piece of evidence that the Turks were not apprehensive of an immediate Soviet threat to Turkey's security. Had they felt in danger one would expect that they would have been less concerned about their economic and political interests in the Middle East and more willing to fully co-operate with the US. For as it has been observed, when there is a serious crisis in the international system the members of an alliance tend to put aside their narrow national interests and to accept without resistance the guidance of the stronger member upon which they depend for their security.[112]

In sum, the Turks' preference for a flexible ad hoc approach as a response to US pressure for a firm commitment was a reflection of the Turkish leaders' intense dilemmas at the time. The first one was how to accommodate US strategic interests – an approach that carried benefits – while at the same time preserving Turkey's foreign policy independence towards the Middle East. The second one was how to accommodate the strategic requirements of the US – whose enhanced interest in Turkey was due to the perception of the resurgence of the Soviet threat – without causing damage to Turkey's relations with Moscow and in the final analysis how to rescue the fruits of détente without undermining Western security and by extension the security of Turkey. Carving out a position that balanced these interests demanded skill, resolve and a clear idea of Turkey's interests. In the end Ankara managed to perform this delicate balancing act. Had the international environment in the 1980s been different this might not have been the case. As it was, Washington did not push the Turks too far in order to impose its goals in relation to the security of the Middle East. The main reason was that the Reagan administration did not find itself under the pressure of a strategic emergency but rather planned primarily within the context of hypothetical scenarios. The absence of a serious crisis in the Middle East allowed the Turks the luxury of maintaining their ambiguity for they were not truly forced to decide.[113]

The bilateral relationship under a microscope

Students of US–Turkey relations consider the 1980s as a period of when the bilateral relationship was revived. This was undoubtedly true, particularly when seen against the tensions of the previous decade. Nonetheless, Washington's enhanced interest in Turkey and the enthusiastic support extended to it by US officials in the Reagan administration by all accounts did not suggest that Turkey had been placed on a higher level of attention on US's foreign policy agenda than it had previously been. In other words, relations with Ankara were not given a place among those prominent issues that engrossed US foreign policy and therefore demanded the regular attention of the US president.[114]

Bilateral relations, like a plethora of other US foreign policy issues, remained the responsibility of middle-rank officials within the foreign policy bureaucracy (Perle himself was one of them) and continued to be given only middle/low-level attention. Even more importantly, the renewal of strategic ties did not lead to the expansion of bilateral co-operation into other fields. Both sides still looked at the relationship through the same very narrow lens that had been employed since the Truman doctrine. The Americans were interested in military facilities and a strong Turkish army and the Turks desired to maximize military and economic benefits by accommodating US strategic needs.

This is not to say that all Turkish leaders were happy with this state of affairs. Özal for one, as well as foreign ministry officials, resented this well-established parochialism. They apparently thought that it both enhanced the asymmetry of the relationship and undermined its future sustainability.[115] In fact they were keen to develop a multifaceted relationship that they hoped would help bridge the existing asymmetry. So Özal, whose economic stabilization programme gave emphasis to export-led growth, eagerly sought to expand the scope of the economic aspect of relations through trade. He wanted the US to lift restrictions on Turkish textile products – which were the leading commodity among Turkey's exports – and for Turkey 'to be a genuine partner of the US'.[116] But while the Turks emphasized export growth the Americans were interested in reduced Turkish trade barriers.[117]

Towards the end of the first Reagan administration there was discussion about expanding the narrow scope of the bilateral relationship through the development of closer trade and cultural relations. The rationale was that a relationship which was not solely focused on military interests would be more able to withstand pressures borne as a result of congressional actions.[118] But this discussion remained mostly confined among State and Defense officials who were dealing with Turkey and thought that the US should pay more attention to this country. In the end there was no serious push for broadening relations with Turkey beyond the strategic co-operation framework for the simple reason that Washington's interest in Turkey was essentially based on hard security considerations, not on economic ones. But also the Turks themselves worked against the realization of a broader relationship for they unfailingly made Turkish military priorities the focus of the dialogue with Washington.[119] Nor there was a big interest in Turkey by US private investors. Although after 1980 American banks and oil companies made new investments in Turkey and American business showed interest in investments in mining, the growth of major US investment remained slow despite Özal's efforts to court foreign investors.[120] In 1986 the Turks sought to link trade issues with the negotiations for a new DECA and pressed for a larger Turkish textile quota.[121] Özal's efforts to achieve a more favourable treatment of Turkish exports to the US did not bear any significant results. And while the volume of bilateral trade almost quadrupled during the 1980s (from $846.4 million in 1981 to $3.25 billion in 1990) Turkey's trade balance with the US remained in the red.[122]

As the decade was coming to a close it was clear that the scope of the bilateral relationship was going to remain narrow in the foreseeable future. If anything, the great energy that characterized relations in the beginning of the decade was no longer there. One of the main reasons was the inability of the US government to secure the high levels of military assistance it had promised the Turks at the beginning of the 1980s. This was due to the increasing US deficit but also to the gradual evolution of US strategic needs after 1985.

Throughout the Cold War the American interest in Turkey was primarily shaped by US strategic needs in accordance to the dynamics between the two superpowers. The height of the Cold War was the best environment for the US–Turkey strategic relationship to grow. Washington viewed Turkey as an important ally and consequently extended to it significant military and economic assistance, though the amounts did not always satisfy Ankara. At the turn of the 1970s the emphasis with which the Pentagon advocated the need to renew and strengthen strategic ties with Turkey reflected yet again the renewal of tension between Washington and Moscow. From a Turkish point of view the renewal of Cold War tension was a fortuitous event, and it was rather unfortunate that it did not last longer. It was only natural that Washington's focus on Turkey would ease off following the relaxation of tension between the two big powers after 1985. By contrast, the Turks' persistence for the continuation of high levels of US assistance did not make sense under the international security circumstances. Towards the end of the 1980s, much of the substance of US policy still remained, but the intensity that characterized Washington's approach to Turkey from 1979 until the mid 1980s had gone.

A decade is indeed a long time in international politics. In the 1980s bilateral relations had been through the subsequent phases of renewal, strengthening and finally of mutual frustration and irritation towards the end of the decade against the backdrop of the big systemic change that was under way. American officials refused to take seriously Ankara's grievances, which they no longer regarded as critical but rather as an everyday nuisance.[123] These grievances mainly revolved around the amounts of aid allocated to Turkey, which Ankara found inadequate, even though Turkey continued to receive on average half a billion dollars annually.[124] Therefore, at the end of the 1980s the US officials' growing perception was that the Turks visited Washington only to ask for money. Actually, senior officials refused to meet with Turkish delegations because they knew that the requests for assistance would be the focal point of discussion.[125] The Turks' key argument was that contrary to the initial understanding between the two countries the level of assistance that the Americans were giving to Turkey could not meet the military modernization needs of the country. However, this argument could no longer find much support even among Turkey's keen supporters. Amidst the changed international environment and the relaxation of tension with Moscow the Americans no longer felt the urgent need to carry on striking bargains with Ankara regarding base rights and access to military facilities. On top of this Turkey's military modernization programme was as a matter of fact in progress thanks to the US assistance that had been received and continued to be received. So inevitably under the circumstances the US–Turkey dialogue became typical of one between a big power with global foreign policy responsibilities and a much smaller power who needs the benefits the big power can provide but realises that the latter does not place relations with the smaller power high on its list of priorities. Before the decade was out the pattern of interaction had almost crystallized in an exchange of US rhetoric favourable to Turkey, on the one hand, and Turkish complaints and disappointment on the other. Essentially the bilateral dialogue had degenerated to what David Vital describes as 'a *dialogue de sourds* in which minds cannot meet, not necessarily because of ill-will, but because the attention of each side is fastened on matters and interests which are largely or entirely unrelated.'[126]

Washington's new tone was particularly felt during the first year of the George H. W. Bush administration. One of the main reasons, setting aside the systemic change, was that the foreign policy of the Bush administration was not characterized by the ideological zeal that was the hallmark of the foreign policy of its predecessor. In addition, Bush's foreign policy did not pay much attention to the eastern Mediterranean.[127] It was shortly after Bush's accession to office that relations became tense.[128] In addition to the Turks' usual displeasure about reduced aid levels and trade issues there was deep concern in Ankara over the stance that the new president might take towards the Armenian issue, discussion of which had flared up again in Congress. US Vice President George Bush during his electoral campaign – contrary to the Reagan administration policy – had characterized as genocide the death of a million Armenians under the Young Turks' regime. Bush's pronouncements had raised fears in Ankara that he might approve of a joint resolution to commemorate 24 April 1990 as the seventy-fifth anniversary of the Armenian Genocide that was introduced by the Republican Senator Bob Dole.[129] Such was the importance the Turks attached to the issue that Prime Minister Özal called President Bush to warn him that the resolution would 'damage' bilateral relations.[130] As soon as the judiciary committee voted to forward the resolution to the Senate floor the Turks adopted a confrontational attitude. Ankara limited US aerial operations in Turkey while threatening more reprisals if the Senate adopted the resolution. Eventually it became clear that Bush was going to continue the Reagan administration policy on the issue and normalcy prevailed.[131] Nonetheless, both sides were aware that there was no real force to carry the bilateral relationship forward.

In the early days after the end of the Cold War and as relations between Washington and Moscow warmed up the future pattern of the US Turkey relationship was not easily identifiable, although it was clear that strategic co-operation would carry on, at least in the foreseeable future, for each side had good reasons to keep it alive. The US strategic interest in Turkey continued – albeit with less fervour – because the Soviet Union was still in existence. Also because US officials thought that Turkey was useful as far as US strategic interests in the Middle East were concerned.[132] The Turks, too, still considered the relationship with the US to be at the centre of their foreign policy for reasons of security and military modernization.[133]

However, there had been no settlement of questions relating to levels of assistance, which was a central issue for the Turks. The only certainty was that Washington was not going to compensate them with the amounts of military and economic aid that Ankara sought as a quid pro quo for accommodating US strategic needs. Relations between the US and its European allies were going to rely more and more on burden sharing, which involved the shifting of a significant amount of the cost of collective security from the US on to the allies. Both the Republican Party and the Democratic Party had emphatically supported the idea during the 1988 presidential campaign.[134] Of course, it was primarily relevant to the allies of the US who were stronger economically; nevertheless it was a sign that the US was seeking to reduce its international commitments.

More importantly the goals and terms of the strategic relationship in the post-Cold War period were far from clear while Washington's policy towards Turkey was becoming tougher. According to Morton Abramowitz, the American ambassador to Ankara (1989–91), US officials increasingly thought that the Turks' steadfast position as Cold War allies was not enough to place them in a strong position with regard to their future bargaining with the US. Rather, they would have to prove again their value as US allies.[135] So, the Turks and Turkey's supporters in Washington – to the extent that they were interested in maintaining the strength of the relationship – had to think hard about how Turkey could recapture the dwindling US attention.

Notes

1 J.W. Spain, *American Diplomacy in Turkey: Memoirs of an Ambassador Extraordinary and Plenipotentiary*, New York: Praeger Publishers, 1984, pp. 44–6 offers a good account of the Turks' financial expectations.

2 United States General Accounting Office, *The Defense and Economic Cooperation Agreement – U.S. Interests and Turkish Needs: Report by the Comptroller General of the United States*, Washington DC and Gaithersburg, MD: US General Accounting Office, 1982, pp. 2–3. 'Talking Points for President's Meeting with Prime Minister Ozal', 23/3/85, European & Soviet Affairs Directorate, NSC Records, 1983–89, series IV, file folder: Ozal visit – 2 April 1985, (1) RAC Box 15, p. 2. Ronald Reagan Presidential Library.

3 'Security Assistance', [n.d.], Department of State, Briefing Paper, European & Soviet Affairs Directorate, NSC Records, 1983–89, series IV, file folder: Ozal visit – 2 April 1985, (4) RAC Box 15, Ronald Reagan Presidential Library; J. Phillips, 'Turkey: An Increasingly Key Strategic Asset for the U.S.', Washington DC: The Heritage Foundation, Backgrounder 609, 1987, pp. 5, 9; B. Kuniholm, 'East or West? The Geopolitics of Turkey and Its NATO Alliance', in A. L. Karaosmanoğlu and S. Taşhan (eds), *Middle East, Turkey and the Atlantic Alliance*, Ankara: Foreign Policy Institute, 1987, pp. 134–9.

4 E. B. Laipson, 'Turkey and the U.S. Congress', in G. S. Harris (ed.), *The Middle East in Turkish-American Relations*, Washington, DC: The Heritage Foundation, 1985, pp. 31–2.

5 Amnesty International, *Turkey: Testimony on Torture*, London: Amnesty International Publications, 1985; Helsinki Watch, *Human Rights in Turkey's 'Transition to Democracy': A Helsinki Watch Report*, New York and Washington, DC: US Helsinki Watch Committee, 1983; Helsinki Watch, *State of Flux: Human Rights in Turkey, December 1987 Update*, New York: Helsinki Watch, 1987.

6 Helsinki Watch, *'Transition to Democracy'*, pp. 66–75.

7 For a concise account of political developments in Turkey during the period, see H. Bozarslan, *Istoria tis Syhronis Tourkias*: Apo tin Epanastasi ton Neotourkon

Mehri Simera, Athens: Savvalas, 2008, pp. 88–95; E. J. Zürcher, *Turkey: A Modern History*, London: I. B. Tauris, 1993, pp. 292–302; William Hale, *Turkish Politics and the Military*, London: Routledge, 1994, pp. 246–71.

8 B. Newman, 'At the Crossroads: Turkey Seems to Be on the Road to Democracy, but Its Route There Appears Very Undemocratic', *The Wall Street Journal,* 15 June 1982; E. Walsh, 'Turkey Tests "Controlled Democracy"', *The Washington Post*, 6 November 1983.

9 Laipson, 'Turkey and U.S. Congress', pp. 31–2.

10 For some insight into the administration's way of thinking, see N. S. Ludington J. W. Spain, 'Dateline Turkey: The Case for Patience', *Foreign Policy*, no. 50, 1983, pp. 167–8 and passim.

11 Laipson, 'Turkey and U.S. Congress', pp. 27–31.

12 'Security Assistance' [n.d.], Department of State, Briefing Paper, European & Soviet Affairs Directorate, NSC Records, 1983–89, series IV, file folder: Ozal visit – 2 April 1985 (4), RAC Box 15, Ronald Reagan Presidential Library.

13 Quoted in C. Migdalovitz, *Greece and Turkey: Current Foreign Aid Issues*, Washington, DC: CRS, Issue Brief, 1996, available online at http://www.fas.org/man/crs/86–065.htm#summ (accessed 16 June 2006). Economic aid was not affected by the 7/10 ratio.

14 Laipson, 'Turkey and U.S. Congress', pp. 27–31. For an interesting account of the efforts by the Reagan government to offset any actions by Congress that were negative to Turkey, see M. L. Evriviades, 'The U.S. and Cyprus: The Politics of Manipulation in the 1985 U.N. Cyprus High Level Meeting', Athens: Institute of International Relations, Occasional Research Paper, no. 3, Oct. 1992, pp. 7–10.

15 The figures include assistance (around $3 million per year) received by Turkey under the U.S. International Military Education and Training Programme: T. Gabelnick, W. D. Hartung, and J. Washburn, with research assistance by M. Ciarrocca, *Arming Repression: U.S. Arms Sales to Turkey during the Clinton Administration*, a joint report of the World Policy Institute and the Federation of American Scientists, October 1999, tables II and IV, available online at http://www.fas.org/asmp/library/reports/turkeyrep.htm (accessed 4 March 2000).

16 Laipson, 'Turkey and U.S. Congress', p. 27; Evriviades, 'Politics of Manipulation', p. 8.

17 R. Perle, 'Turkey and US Military Assistance', in G. S. Harris (ed.), *The Middle East in Turkish-American Relations*, Washington, DC: The Heritage Foundation, 1985; Kuniholm, 'East or West', p. 140.

18 'Suggested Talking Points for the President's Meeting with Prime Minister Ozal', 23 March 1985, [prepared by the Department of State], European & Soviet Affairs Directorate, NSC Records, 1983–89, series IV, file folder: Ozal visit – 2 April 1985 (3), RAC Box 15, p. 4, Ronald Reagan Presidential Library.

19 Presidential Remarks: Prime Minister Turgut Ozal of Turkey Departure Statement, 2 April 1985, European & Soviet Affairs Directorate, NSC Records, 1983–89, series IV, file folder: Ozal visit – 2 April 1985 (2) RAC Box 15, p. 2; Ronald Reagan Presidential Library.

20 Presidential Remarks: Prime Minister Turgut Ozal of Turkey Departure Statement, 2 April 1985, p. 2.

21 There used to be more of a balance between grants and concessionary loans.

22 'Turkish Economy at a Glance' [n.d.], Department of State, Briefing Papers, file folder: Ozal visit – 2 April 1985 (4), RAC Box 15, Ronald Reagan Presidential Library; and 'Security Assistance' [n.d.], Department of State, Briefing Papers, European & Soviet Affairs Directorate, NSC Records, 1983–89, series IV, file folder: Ozal visit – 2 April 1985 (4), RAC Box 15, Ronald Reagan Presidential Library.

23 The cuts in aid concerned the amounts of subsidized loans, while the amount of aid in the form of grants was maintained at the level of the previous years: see Gabelnick *et al.*, *Arming Repression*, table II.

24 The Armenian genocide referred to the treatment of Armenian subjects of the Ottoman Empire by the government of the Young Turks during the First World War, which led to the death of over a million people, according to estimations. The Turkish state refused to accept that the genocide ever took place. This standpoint was also shared by Turkish historians, who maintained that the Young Turks had employed a policy of deportation but not of genocide. The first, to my knowledge, Turkish book that took the view (although not substantiated by archival material) that genocide of the Armenians was committed was published in 1992. Its author, Taner Akçam, who belonged to the far left was not a historian. Taner Akçam, *Türk Ulusal Kimliği ve Ermeni Sorunu*, Istanbul: Iletişım Yayınları, 1992.

25 On Ankara's displeasure regarding these developments, see Laipson, 'Turkey and U.S. Congress', pp. 32–3; Perle, 'Turkey and US Military Assistance', p. 26; B. R. Kuniholm, 'Turkey in the World', in G. S. Harris (ed.), *The Middle East in Turkish-American Relations*, Washington, DC: The Heritage Foundation, 1985, p. 12; Y. Eralp, 'An Insider's View of Turkey's Foreign Policy and Its American Connection', in M. Abramowitz (ed.), *The United States and Turkey: Allies in Need*, New York: The Century Foundation Press, 2003, p. 114.

26 A reference to President Johnson's 1964 letter, which caused a big uproar in Turkey, see Chapter 1 in this book.

27 'Turkey: A Bridge between East and West', 29/3/85 [briefing paper for the president prepared jointly by the State Department and the staff of Robert McFarlane, Reagan's National Security Advisor, on the occasion of Özal's visit], European & Soviet Affairs Directorate, NSC Records, 1983–89, series IV, file folder: Ozal visit – 2 April 1985 (3), RAC Box 15, p. 4; Ronald Reagan Presidential Library, 'Armenian Resolutions', Department of State, Briefing Paper [n.d.], European & Soviet Affairs Directorate, NSC Records, 1983–89, series IV, file folder: Ozal Vvsit – 2 April 1985 (4), RAC Box 15, Ronald Reagan Presidential Library.

28 Laipson, 'Turkey and U.S. Congress', p. 33.

29 Perle, 'Turkey and US Military Assistance', p. 26

30 Laipson, 'Turkey and U.S. Congress', p. 33; Perle, 'Turkey and US Military Assistance', in p. 26.

31 'Armenian Resolutions', Department of State, Briefing Paper, file folder: Ozal Visit – 2 April 1985 (4), RAC Box 15, Ronald Reagan Presidential Library.

32 '[We] may have to consider the option of reducing the number of our armed forces'. Interview by Turkish President General Kenan Evren with the *Wall Street Journal*, 1 July 1988.

33 M. Abramowitz, 'American Policy Making on Turkey', in M. Abramowitz, (ed.), *Turkey's Transformation and American Policy*, New York: The Century Foundation Press, 2000, p. 166.

34 H. J. Barkey, 'The Push and Pull of Strategic Cooperation: The US Relationship with Turkey in the Middle East', in D. W. Lesch (ed.), *The Middle East and the United States: A Historical and Political Reassessment*, Boulder, CO: Westview, 2007, p. 449.

35 D. B. Sezer, 'Turkish Foreign Policy in the Year 2000', *Turkey in the Year 2000*, Ankara: Turkish Political Science Association, 1989, pp. 90–92.

36 The total authorized US assistance for fiscal year 1987 including FMS funds amounted to $590 million; the administration had requested $975 million.

37 United States Congress, House Committee on Foreign Affairs, *United States Political-Military Relations with Allies in Southern Europe: Report of a Staff Study Mission to Portugal, Spain, Greece and Turkey, October 15–30, 1986, to the*

Committee on Foreign Affairs, U.S. House of Representatives, Washington DC: US Government Printing Office, 1987, p.34.

38 House Committee on Foreign Affairs, *United States Political-Military Relations with Allies in Southern Europe*, p. 34.

39 House Committee on Foreign Affairs, *United States Political-Military Relations with Allies in Southern Europe*, p. 34.

40 House Committee on Foreign Affairs, *United States Political-Military Relations with Allies in Southern Europe*, p. 35.

41 For the relevant figures, see House Committee on Foreign Affairs, *United States Political-Military Relations with Allies in Southern Europe*, p. 33; Gabelnick *et al.*, *Arming Repression*, table II.

42 House Committee on Foreign Affairs, *United States Political-Military Relations with Allies in Southern Europe*, p. 35.

43 This was within the context of a broader US plan that aimed to assist recipients of Foreign Military Sales assistance with their interest payments: House Committee on Foreign Affairs, *United States Political-Military Relations with Allies in Southern Europe*, p. 35.

44 House Committee on Foreign Affairs, *United States Political-Military Relations with Allies in Southern Europe*, pp. 35–6.

45 J. Phillips, 'Turkey: Key Strategic Asset', p. 5; 'Weinberger Trying to Reassure Turks on U.S. Arms Help', *The New York Times*, 19 March 1987; 'Washington Talk: Greece and Turkey, the Local War', *The New York Times*, 26 March 1987.

46 The reduction concerned grants under the Economic Support Fund programme, while the level of military assistance was the same as that of the previous year.

47 Gabelnick *et al., Arming Repression*; Phillips 'Turkey: Key Strategic Asset', p. 5

48 'Washington Talk', *The New York Times*, 26 March 1987. Also author's interview with Peter Marudas.

49 See Chapter 5 in this book.

50 US Department of the Treasury, *Historical Debt Outstanding-Annual, 1950–99*, Available online at www.treasurydirect.gov/govt/reports/pd/histdebt/histdebt.htm (accessed 20 March 2006).

51 For the relevant figures, see Gabelnick *et al. Arming Repression.*

52 Phillips, 'Turkey: Key Strategic Asset', p. 5; G. Gruen, 'Turkey between the Middle East and the West', in R. O. Freedman (ed.), *The Middle East from the Iran-Contra Affair to the Intifada*, Syracuse, NY: Syracuse University Press, 1999, p. 406.

53 D. Vital, *The Inequality of States*, Oxford: Clarendon Press, 1967, pp. 147–8.

54 Phillips, 'Turkey: Key Strategic Asset', p. 5

55 For an overview of the main political developments in Turkey during these years, see Zürcher, *Turkey: A Modern History*, pp. 298–302.

56 Vital, *Inequality of States*, pp. 147–8.

57 Gruen, 'Between the Middle East and the West', p. 406. The March 1987 Turkish-Greek crisis that brought the two countries to the brink of war concerned the Aegean continental shelf bilateral dispute. On the crisis and the Davos meeting, see A. Heraclides, *The Greek-Turkish Conflict in the Aegean: Imagined Enemies*, Houndmills, Basingstoke: Palgrave Macmillan, 2010, pp. 120–24. One cannot help but wonder whether the timing of the March 1987 crisis (one month before Congress completed its deliberations over assistance to Turkey for the 1988 fiscal year) was partly related to Ankara's wish to send Congress the implicit message that if Turkey were not satisfied there was the risk of a deterioration of Turkish-Greek relations. As a matter of fact, Ankara used such pressure tactics on Congress by threatening damage to Turkey's relations with Israel unless Ankara was satisfied by Washington: Gruen 'Turkey between the Middle East and the West', pp. 419–20, n. 42. It is also worth asking whether Turkey's supporters within the

Reagan administration had any role at all in Özal's Davos initiative. An improvement in Turkish-Greek relations was likely to positively influence Congress when it came to authorizing assistance for the following fiscal year. Actually, this was the point that Byrd made.

58 'Bridge between East and West', file folder: Ozal visit – 2 April 1985 (3), RAC Box 15, p. 2, Ronald Reagan Presidential Library.

59 Author's interview with a member of the US diplomatic delegation in Ankara at the end of the 1980s, who spoke on condition of anonymity due to active service, July 2007, Washington DC.

60 Perle, 'Turkey and U.S. Military Assistance', p. 26; Gruen, 'Between the Middle East and the West', p. 405.

61 Author's interview with Ian Lesser (a).

62 'Bridge between East and West', file folder: Ozal visit – 2 April 1985 (3), RAC Box 15, p. 4, Ronald Reagan Presidential Library.

63 The figures are drawn from 'Security Assistance', Briefing Paper [n.d.], Department of State, European & Soviet Affairs Directorate, NSC Records, 1983–89, series IV, file folder: Ozal visit – 2 April 1985 (4), RAC Box 15, pp. 1, 6, Ronald Reagan Presidential Library; Gabelnick *et al.*, *Arming Repression*.

64 A. Ertuğrul and F. Selçuk, 'Turkish Economy, 1980–2000', in A. Kibritçioğlu, L. Rittenberg and F. Selçuk (eds), *Inflation and Disinflation in Turkey*, Aldershot, Hampshire: Ashgate, 2002, p. 13.

65 'Turkish Economy at a Glance', file folder: Ozal visit – 2 April 1985 (4), RAC Box 15, Ronald Reagan Presidential Library; 'Internal Turkish Political Stability' [n.d.], Department of State, Briefing Paper, European & Soviet Affairs Directorate, NSC Records, 1983–89, series IV, file folder: Ozal visit – 2 April 1985 (4), RAC Box 15, Ronald Reagan Presidential Library; 'The Turkish Economy under Ozal', 29 March 1985, Central Intelligence Agency, European & Soviet Affairs Directorate, NSC Records, 1983–89, series IV, file folder: Ozal visit – 2 April 1985 (2), RAC Box 15, pp. 1, 6; Ronald Reagan Presidential Library.

66 For a good overall analysis of Turkey's economic performance in the 1980s, see also D. Rodrik, 'Premature Liberalization, Incomplete Stabilization: The Ozal Decade in Turkey', in M. Bruno, S. Fischer, E. Helpman and N. Liviatan (eds), *Lessons of Economic Stabilization and Its Aftermath*, London: MIT Press, 1991.

67 Ertuğrul and Selçuk, 'Turkish Economy', pp. 19, 21–22.

68 S. Gold, 'The Costs of Privatization. Turkey in the 1980s', *The Multinational Monitor*, vol. 10, 1989, available online at http://www.multinationalmonitor.org/hyper/issues/1989/10/gold.html (accessed on 15 February 2005).

69 V. Yilanci and B. Özcan, 'External Debt Sustainability of Turkey: A Nonlinear Approach', *International Research Journal of Finance and Economics*, issue 20, October 2008, p. 92; Gold, 'The Costs of Privatization'.

70 'Turkish Economy under Ozal', Central Intelligence Agency, file folder: Ozal visit – 2 April 1985 (2), RAC Box 15, p. 6, Ronald Reagan Presidential Library, 'Turkish Economy at a Glance', file folder: Ozal visit – 2 April 1985 (4), RAC Box 15, Ronald Reagan Presidential Library; 'Bridge between East and West', file folder: Ozal visit – 2 April 1985 (3), RAC Box 15, pp. 23–4, Ronald Reagan Presidential Library.

71 'Bridge between East and West', file folder: Ozal visit – 2 April 1985 (3), RAC Box 15, p. 3, Ronald Reagan Presidential Library, W. Weiker, *The Modernization of Turkey. From Ataturk to the Present Day*, New York: Holmes & Meier Publishers, 1981, p. 214.

72 M. I. Handel, *Weak States in the International System*, London: Frank Cass, 1981, pp. 131–3.

73 The Turkish leadership was extremely sensitive over the issue of being treated with respect by the US; author's interview with Mehmet Ali Birand (a).
74 Vidal, *Inequality of States*, p. 87. See also Handel, *Weak States*, pp. 121–2.
75 Handel, *Weak States*, p. 133.
76 Richard Perle, 'A Turkish Story'; Eralp, 'An Insider's View', p. 114; C. Çandar, 'The Post-September 11 United States through Turkish Lenses', in M. Abramowitz (ed.), *The United States and Turkey: Allies in Need*, New York: The Century Foundation Press, 2003, p. 158.
77 Quoted in D. A. Rustow, 'Turkey's Travails', *Foreign Affairs*, vol. 58, 1979, p. 102.
78 Harris, 'Turkey between Alliance and Alienation', p. 120; author's interview with a Turkish diplomat who spoke on condition of anonymity due to active service, December 2006, Istanbul.
79 Author's interviews with Morton Abramowitz, US ambassador to Ankara (1989–91) (a), and with Ian Lesser (a).
80 Congressional Research Service, Foreign Affairs and National Defense Division, *Turkey's Problems and Prospects: Implications for US Interests*, report prepared for the Subcommittee on Europe and the Middle East of the Committee on Foreign Affairs, US House of Representatives, by the Foreign Affairs and National Defense Division, Congressional Research Service, Library of Congress, Washington DC: US Government Printing Office, 1980, p. 21; *The New York Times*, 20 January 1981.
81 A. L. Karaosmanoğlu, 'Turkey's Security and the Middle East', *Foreign Affairs*, vol. 62, 1983, p. 161. Karaosmanoğlu, in a number of articles written at the time offered a clear and comprehensive account of the security and foreign policy perspectives of Turkey's leaders concerning how to reconcile Turkey's security co-operation with the West on the one hand and with Turkey's regional security interests on the other.
82 A. L. Karaosmanoğlu, 'Turkey's Discreet Foreign Policy between Western Europe and the Middle East', in A. L. Karaosmanoğlu and S. Taşhan (eds), *Middle East, Turkey and the Atlantic Alliance*, Ankara: Foreign Policy Institute, 1987, p. 93; Karaosmanoğlu, 'Turkey's Security and the Middle East', p. 175. Also B. Rubin, 'U.S. Middle East Policy in the Turkish Context', in G. S. Harris (ed.), *The Middle East in Turkish-American Relations*, Washington DC: The Heritage Foundation, 1985, p. 79.
83 Karaosmanoğlu, 'Turkey's Security and the Middle East', pp. 170–72.
84 Karaosmanoğlu, 'Turkey's Security and the Middle East', p. 170; I. Barutçuoğlu, 'Evolution of Turkey's Security Role in the Middle East', in G. S. Harris (ed.), *The Middle East in Turkish-American Relations*, Washington DC: The Heritage Foundation, 1985, p. 66; Gruen, 'Turkey between Middle East and West', p. 410.
85 Karaosmanoğlu, 'Turkey's Security and the Middle East', pp. 164–70; Karaosmanoğlu, 'Turkey's Discreet Foreign Policy', pp. 93–4. Also, Rubin, 'U.S. Middle East Policy in the Turkish Context', pp. 78–9; I. Barutçuoğlu, 'Evolution of Turkey's Security Role in the Middle East', p. 67; J. C. Campbell, 'The Superpowers and Turkey: An American View', in A. L. Karaosmanoğlu and S. Taşhan (eds), *Middle East, Turkey and the Atlantic Alliance*, Ankara: Foreign Policy Institute, 1987, p. 72.
86 Karaosmanoğlu, 'Turkey's Security and the Middle East', p. 167.
87 G. F. Treverton, 'Managing Alliance Politics', in A. L. Karaosmanoğlu and S. Taşhan (eds), *Middle East, Turkey and the Atlantic Alliance*, Ankara: Foreign Policy Institute, 1987, p. 176; Kuniholm, 'Turkey in the World', p. 15.
88 Karaosmanoğlu, 'Turkey's Security and the Middle East', p. 168; Rubin, 'U.S. Middle East Policy in the Turkish Context', p. 168; Barutçuoğlu, 'Evolution of Turkey's Security Role in the Middle East', p. 66.

89 Congressional Research Service, *Turkey's Problems and Prospects*, p. 49.
90 Barutçuoğlu, 'Evolution of Turkey's Security Role in the Middle East', p. 66.
91 The Turkish government insisted in its public statements that the support offered to the US marines was purely humanitarian in nature and that Turkey was not involved militarily in the Lebanon crisis, H. Hubel, 'Turkey and the Crisis in the Middle East', in A. L. Karaosmanoğlu and S. Taşhan (eds), *Middle East, Turkey and the Atlantic Alliance*, Ankara: Foreign Policy Institute, 1987, p. 112.
92 S. Taşhan, 'Turkey's Relations with the U.S.A. and Possible Future Developments', *Diş Politika* (Foreign Policy), vol. 8, 1979, p. 27.
93 The Kurdish issue was one of the most pressing security concerns that necessitated good relations with Syria, Iraq and Iran so that they would not encourage subversive Kurdish activities in Turkey. On the political front Turkey hoped to enlist the support of the regional states in the international fora over the Cyprus issue. For a semi-official account of Turkey's foreign policy in the Middle East during the same period, see I. Türkmen, *The Middle East Policy of the Republic of Turkey*, Istanbul: Bilgesam, 2010, vol. 4, pp. 15–19. Ambassador Türkmen served as Turkey's minister of foreign affairs between 1980 and 1983. See also M. M. Bishku, 'Turkey and Its Middle Eastern Neighbours since 1945', *Journal of South Asian and Middle Eastern Studies*, vol. 15, 1992; W. Hale, *Turkish Foreign Policy, 1774–2000*, London: Frank Cass, 2000, pp. 169–70; M. H. Yavuz, 'O Diismos stis Tourkoaravikes Sxesis ke to Palestiniako Zitima', in F. Sönmezoğlu (ed.), *Mythos ke Pragmatikotita: Analysi tis Tourkikis Exoterikis Politikis*, Athens: Infognomon, 2001, tomos B, pp. 191–3.
94 O. Kurkçuoğlu, 'The Evolution of Turkish-Arab Relations', in G. S. Harris (ed.), *The Middle East in Turkish-American Relations*, Washington DC: The Heritage Foundation, 1985, pp. 46–7.
95 For an overview of Ankara's policy concerning the Palestinian question, see Ö. Kürkçüoğlu, 'Turkey's Attitude towards the Middle East Conflict', *Foreign Policy*, vol. 5, no. 4, 1976; Ö. Kürkçüoğlu, 'Development of Turkish-Arab Relations: A Historical Appraisal', in A. L. Karaosmanoğlu and S. Taşhan (eds), *Middle East, Turkey and the Atlantic Alliance*, pp. 18–20; M. B. Aykan, 'The Palestinian Question in Turkish Foreign Policy from the 1950s to the 1980s', *International Journal of Middle East Studies*, vol. 25, 1993.
96 Karaosmanoğlu, 'Turkey's Security and the Middle East', pp. 164–6; H. Akder, 'Turkey's Export Expansion In the Middle East 1980–85', *Middle East Journal*, vol. 41, 1987; Kürkçüoğlu, 'Development of Turkish-Arab Relations', p. 21; A. Mango, 'Turkey and the Middle Eastern Market', in E. Manisalı (ed.), *Turkey's Place in the Middle East*, Istanbul: Middle East Business and Banking Publications, 1989; P. Robins, *Turkey and the Middle East*, London: Pinter Publishers, 1991, pp. 100–107.
97 Barutçuoğlu, 'Evolution of Turkey's Security Role in the Middle East', pp. 66–7. Also author's interview with Mehmet Ali Birand (b).
98 D. Reiter, 'Learning, Realism, and Alliances: The Weight of the Shadow of the Past', *World Politics*, vol. 46, 1994.
99 The Baghdad Pact was renamed CENTO after Iraq left it following the 1958 coup.
100 Author's discussion with Ali Karaosmanoğlu and interviews with Cengiz Çandar, columnist and Özal's advisor (a), and Hasan Köni, professor of international relations.
101 'Discussion on "Turkey between Alliance and Alienation", comments by the Turkish participants: Dr. Duygu Sezer, Seyfi Taşhan [director of Foreign Policy Institute, Ankara], Professor Kemal Karpat, Ilter Türkmen [Turkey's representative at the U.N. secretariat], Mehmet Ali Birand [correspondent of the daily *Milliyet* in Washington]', *Foreign Policy*, vol. 8, 1980, pp. 125–33 and passim.

102 Treverton, 'Managing Alliance Politics', p. 178; Harris, *Coping with Crisis*, p. 200.
103 Author's interview with Mehmet Ali Birand (a).
104 On the difference of perspective between the European and the Americans concerning the strategic objectives of the alliance and of the Soviet threat, see among others H. Schmidt, 'A Policy of Reliable Partnership', *Foreign Affairs*, vol. 59, 1981, p. 747; J. Joffe, 'European-American Relations: The Enduring Crisis', *Foreign Affairs*, vol. 59, 1981, pp.843–44 and passim; C. Bertram, 'Introduction', *America's Security in the 1980s*, London: IISS, Adelphi Paper, 1982, vol. 22, part I, passim; Congressional Research Service, *The Persian Gulf: Are We committed? At What Cost? A Dialogue with the Reagan Administration on U.S. Policy*, prepared for the use of the Joint Economic Committee, Congress of the United States with the assistance of the Congressional Research Service, Library of Congress, Washington DC: US Government Printing Office, 1981, pp. 26–7, 32.
105 Karaosmanoğlu, 'Turkey's Security and the Middle East', p. 169.
106 S. T. Hunter, 'The Gulf Cooperation Council. Security in the Era Following the Iran-Contra Affair', in R. O. Freedman (ed.), *The Middle East from the Iran-Contra Affair to the Intifada*, Syracuse, NY: Syracuse University Press, 1999, pp. 146–8.
107 Congressional Research Service, *Persian Gulf. Are We Committed?*, pp. 22–4; Karaosmanoğlu, 'Turkey's Security Policy in the Middle East', p. 16. Of course, there were exceptions to this general approach as the interests of the Gulf states differed. Oman for instance agreed to allow the use of its territory for US military operations: Congressional Research Service, *Persian Gulf. Are We Committed?*, p. 22.
108 Hunter, 'Gulf Cooperation Council', pp. 147–8.
109 S. Strange, *States and Markets: An Introduction to International Political Economy*, London: Pinter Publishers, 1988, p. 25. According to Strange, structural power is the power to decide how things shall be done and to shape frameworks within which states relate to each other, to people or to corporate enterprises.
110 United States Senate, *Perspectives on NATO's Southern Flank, Senate Delegation Report, April 3–13, 1980*, a report to the Committee on Foreign Relations, United States Senate, Washington DC: US Government Printing Office, 1980, p. 11.
111 Karaosmanoğlu, 'Turkey's Discreet Foreign Policy' p. 80; Karaosmanoğlu, 'Turkey's Security and the Middle East', pp. 159–60; Rubin, 'U.S. Middle East Policy in the Turkish Context', p. 78; Kuniholm, 'East or West?', p. 146.
112 D. Vital, *The Inequality of States*, Oxford: Clarendon Press, 1967, p. 187.
113 We do not know whether the Americans asked to use Turkish bases in support of the US Operation Earnest Will (July 1987–Sept 1988), which offered military protection to Kuwait's oil tankers from Iranian attacks. In any event, the nature of the operation was such that it did not necessitate major Turkish involvement. Therefore it was perfectly possible for Turkey to help the US logistically while expecting that its contribution would remain out of the public eye. According to contemporary press reports Turkey maintained its neutrality, A. Cowell, 'Turkey Tries to Stay Aloof on War', *New York Times*, 10 July 1987.
114 M. Halperin and P. A. Clapp with A. Kanter, *Bureaucratic Politics and Foreign Policy*, Washington DC: Brookings Institution Press, 2006, pp. 16–17.
115 Author's interview with Mehmet Ali Birand (b). On this subject see also the interesting comments by Duygu Sezer, *Foreign Policy*, vol. 8, 1979, p. 127.
116 Eralp, 'An Insider's View', p. 114. 'Turkish Economy under Ozal', Central Intelligence Agency, file folder: Ozal visit – 2 April 1985 (2), RAC Box 15, p. 63, Ronald Reagan Presidential Library.
117 'Economic/commercial Relations', Department of State Briefing Paper [n.d.], European & Soviet Affairs Directorate, NSC Records, 1983–89, series IV, file

folder: Ozal visit – 2 April 1985 (5), RAC Box 15, Ronald Reagan Presidential Library.

118 See reference to comments by Richard Haas, deputy assistant secretary of state responsible for the Eastern Mediterranean, in H. Laipson, 'US Policy towards Greece and Turkey since 1974', in D. Constas (ed.), *The Greek-Turkish Conflict in the 1990s: Domestic and External Influences*, Houndmills, Basingstoke: Macmillan, 1991, p. 172. Also comments by Richard Burt, assistant secretary of state for European and Canadian affairs (1983–5), R. Burt, 'Turkey and the Reagan Administration', in G. S. Harris (ed.), *The Middle East in Turkish-American Relations*, Washington, DC: The Heritage Foundation, 1985, p. 20. Before assuming this position Burt was director of the Military-Political Affairs Bureau at the State Department (1981–3) and hence in close co-operation with Perle's office at Defense.

119 Author's interview with Ian Lesser (a).

120 'Economic/commercial Relations', Department of State Briefing Paper, file folder: Ozal visit – 2 April 1985 (5), RAC Box 15, Ronald Reagan Presidential Library.

121 N. Uslu, *The Turkish-American Relationship between 1947 and 2003: The History of a Distinctive Alliance*, New York: Nova Science Publishers, Inc., 2003, p. 262.

122 I. O. Lesser, *Bridge or Barrier? Turkey and the West After the Cold War*, Santa Monica, CA: RAND, 1992, p. 38.

123 Author's interviews with Morton Abramowitz (a) and Ian Lesser (a).

124 US security assistance for FY 1988 and FY 1999 totalled $522 million and $560 million respectively, Gabelnick et al., *Arming Repression*, table II.

125 Author's interviews with Morton Abramowitz (a) and Ian Lesser (a).

126 Vital, *Inequality of States*, p. 29.

127 Laipson, 'US Policy towards Greece and Turkey', p. 174.

128 Author's interviews with Mehmet Ali Birand (b) and Morton Abramowitz (a).

129 22 May 1988, *New York Times*; Eralp, 'Insider's View', p. 114.

130 The White House, memorandum of telephone conversation with Turgut Ozal, Prime Minister of Turkey, 2 October 1989, available online at http://bushlibrary.tamu.edu/research/pdfs/memcons_telcons/1989-10-02–Ozal.pdf (accessed 20 February 2010).

131 Author's interview with Mehmet Ali Birand (b).

132 Author's interview with Morton Abramowitz (a).

133 Author's interview with Mehmet Ali Birand (a) and discussion with Ali. K. Karaosmanoğlu.

134 The American Presidency Project, 'An American Vision: For Our Children and Our Future', Republican Party Platform of 1988, 16 August 1988, and Democratic Party Platform of 1988, 18 July 1988, in J. T. Woolley and G. Peters, The American Presidency Project, Santa Barbara, CA, [n.d], available online at http://www.presidency.ucsb.edu (accessed 20 February 2010).

135 Author's interview with Morton Abramowitz (b).

Part II

1991

Facing up to reality

4 The Gulf War

The Turkish position revisited

A critical matter

At the dawn of the post-Cold War decade perhaps the biggest foreign policy challenge for Turkish rulers was the future course of relations with the US following the rapid decline of Turkey's value as a strategic asset against the Soviet threat. As the Turks were struggling to adjust their foreign policy to the changes in the international environment the question of Turkey's involvement in the defence of the Gulf resurfaced with intensity in Washington as a result of Saddam Hussein's invasion of Kuwait on 2 August 1990. On 16 January 1991, upon the expiration of the UN deadline for the withdrawal of all Iraqi forces from Kuwait, the US-led coalition forces for its liberation began a massive military assault targeting Iraqi military sites and Iraqi forces in Kuwait. On 17 January, in the wee hours of the morning, the US ambassador to Ankara, Morton Abramowitz, called Turgut Özal, who was at the centre of the decision-making process during the Gulf crisis.[1]

In 1989 Özal was elected president of the Turkish Republic. Upon assuming office he managed to shift the centre of political power from the office of the prime minister, where it had resided up until his election, to the presidency. Moreover, he sought to contain the military's overwhelming power within the state structure.[2] According to Abramowitz, the telephone conversation with Özal was brief. The ambassador informed the Turkish president that the US bombers had left a few hours earlier from Spain on their way to Baghdad and the US government was in urgent need of over-flight rights over Turkey. 'Can they fly over Syria?' was the only question the Turkish president asked, and once Abramowitz responded negatively Özal said he would call back. A short while later the President called back and gave his approval while he requested that the B-52s fly close to Turkey's border with Syria so that the over-flight could be 'plausibly' denied by Ankara.

Abramowitz did not hang up once Turkish approval for the over-flight had been secured. The ambassador reminded Özal that they had already discussed many times during the crisis the need to use Turkish air bases to bomb targets in Northern Iraq. The matter was now 'critical', stressed Abramowitz. Washington 'urgently needed' the government's permission. 'When can we get an answer?' was his final question? 'Today', said Özal.[3] The same day the Turkish parliament voted that the Incirlik base as well as other Turkish air bases could be used by the coalition air forces to bomb Iraq. The opposition was against it but Özal's Motherland Party – which he controlled behind the scenes – was in the majority.[4]

The established view

The 1991 Gulf War and Turkey's participation in it represented a turning point for Turkish foreign policy toward the Middle East. So it is not surprising that students of Turkish foreign policy have primarily focused their attention on this aspect. Of course, it was also a critical turning point within the context of US–Turkey relations but *not only* for the reasons that were discussed at the time of the war and subsequently. These reasons could be summarized as follows. The close US–Turkey co-operation during the war 'succeeded in strengthening relations between the two countries in the aftermath of the crisis'[5] and 'yielded speedy and positive results at the strategic, trade, military, diplomatic and even personal levels.'[6] Also, Turkey's contribution to the war underscored Turkey's continuous, although changing, geopolitical importance to the US,[7] and its value as an ally;[8] it gave Turkey an important role in US policy in the Middle East, which had been 'in abeyance since the collapse of the Baghdad Pact.'[9]

According to Abramowitz, while the Gulf crisis was underway Ankara was faced with the urgent need to respond to three American requests. The first was that Turkey send a battalion to join the allied forces stationed in Saudi Arabia. The second was that Turkey deploy troops along the Turkey-Iraq border in order to help pin down Iraqi forces which otherwise would move south to the Kuwait front. The third thing Washington asked for was permission to use Turkish bases for a sustained air campaign against Northern Iraq.[10] It should be mentioned here that there is an important variation in the content of the second request. Hale states that the second question which Turkey had to answer was whether it would 'open a second front against Saddam Hussein in the event of a general war against Iraq.'[11] But Hale does not make clear whether the US had asked specifically for the opening of a second front (rather than for a major reinforcement of troops along the border) or whether it was Özal's idea.[12] When I discussed this point with Ambassador Abramowitz, he said that Washington only asked for the deployment of Turkish troops to the border with Iraq. This is confirmed by the memorandum of a conversation between President Özal and President Bush on 20 November 1990.[13] Abramowitz also underlined that there was no point for the US to ask Turkey to open a second war front against Iraq because the Turks would not be expected to agree to that.[14] To the extent that one can guess it is likely that Özal with an eye to the Mosul oil fields proposed the opening of a second front to the Americans. Özal's interest in Mosul is mentioned by the then general chief of staff in his memoirs.[15] Allegedly the Americans supported the idea.[16] However, it should be said that Washington's endorsement would have run contrary to US objectives at the time because Turkey's active involvement in Northern Iraq would certainly cause a reaction by its Kurdish population, whose support against Saddam Hussein the Bush administration was seeking.[17]

Students of Ankara's stance who relied primarily on contemporary press reports (mainly Turkish) describe how Özal was very eager to co-operate with the Americans on all fronts and took the initiative to this effect. They argue that his stance was the result of a number of calculations based on the belief that the US would defeat Saddam Hussein, whom Özal considered very dangerous even before the crisis. Primarily, it is maintained, the Turkish president saw the war as an opportunity to re-establish Turkey's strategic importance for the US. He essentially wished to 're-invent' Turkey's strategic value to the West.[18] It is also stated that Özal was a visionary who wished to place Turkey in a position to benefit from future economic and other opportunities that would emerge in a transformed post-Saddam Hussein Middle East.[19] Put differently, by collaborating with the US Özal wanted to make sure that Turkey would not be left out of negotiations when the Americans decided on the new security and economic arrangements for the area once Saddam Hussein was defeated.[20] But, as the same studies maintain, Özal's willingness to accommodate US interests by responding positively to all three issues Washington raised was faced with serious domestic criticism. The opposition but also a significant number of his own party members, the military establishment and the public were all opposed to Turkey's direct involvement in the war effort. The basic standpoint of the opponents was that Turkey should maintain its long-established policy of neutrality towards conflicts in the Middle East and not sacrifice it in the name of far-from-certain future benefits. Eventually, in early September 1990, Özal succeeded in achieving a majority vote in parliament that authorized the use of Turkey's air bases for operations against Iraq, the deployment of foreign troops on Turkish soil and the dispatch of Turkish troops abroad. (The latter, however, were never deployed due to 'determined opposition in Parliament and the cabinet', according to Hale[21] or, according to Abramowitz, due to the 'strong opposition by the Turkish general staff.'[22]) In its vote on 17 January 1991 the parliament made clear that the authorization also included permission for the allied air forces to use Turkish air bases. In the meantime, Turkish forces amounting to around 120,000 troops supported also by air had been deployed along the border with Iraq.[23]

In sum the mainstream analysis of Turkish foreign policy during the Gulf War maintains that Turkey's decision to co-operate with the US should be attributed almost exclusively to President Özal, who as has been remarked 'dominated Turkish policy-making during the Gulf crisis and thus himself alone deserved any credit or criticism derived from it.'[24] The idea that Ankara's policy was a reflection of the strategic vision of Özal, who 'took matters into his own hands and placed the country squarely behind President Bush's policy',[25] is disputed only by one analyst. Hale points out that two aspects on the president's agenda, the deployment of Turkish forces to the

Gulf and the opening of a second front, did not materialize. Therefore, he concludes, Turkish policy at the time rather reflected a compromise between Özal's ambitions and 'stiff domestic opposition from the public, parliament and the army'.[26] All the same, he also maintains that the decision on Turkey's co-operation with the US was Özal's – albeit not to the degree that he wished.

The analysis outlined above suggests that had Özal not been in office Turkey's policy would have been different because the Turkish parliament and the military would not have accommodated US requests. In other words, as the deployment of Turkish troops to Saudi Arabia had already been refused, the Turks would have also refused to accommodate the US request concerning the use of Turkish air bases by the coalition forces. (The deployment of troops along the Iraqi border would have to be ordered anyway but for defensive purposes in case Saddam decided to launch attacks against Turkey.[27]) But how likely was this to happen given the Turks' interests and concerns at the time?

For a start it should be stressed that there is very little information about the thinking and the particular viewpoints of any of the Turkish leaders, including Özal. We know what they chose to say in their public statements, in rhetorical pronouncements and in statements made in Parliament. We know what press reports, and rumors, often contradictory, said about what the leadership thought. But this cloud of phrases tells us very little about the Turkish decision-makers' inner thinking, the details of their views and calculations. Unfortunately, we do not know what was really discussed at the meetings of the National Security Council, the cabinet or the general staff. And we do not know, the details of what was discussed between Washington and Ankara. Hence, the mainstream analysis of Ankara's foreign policy during the Gulf crisis constitutes more or less a conjecture. So, before we accept its conclusion that Turkey's co-operation with the US in the Gulf War has to be attributed to Özal we need first to identify the hard realities beneath the surface that influenced US–Turkey relations at the time.

Reconstruction

Mainstream studies of Turkey's policy during the Gulf crisis focus their analysis on Özal's view of Turkey's future relations with the US and overlook the dynamics of the bilateral relationship as they evolved during the 1980s. It is not difficult to understand the reasons that account for this oversight. To start with, Özal in his public statements repeatedly aligned Turkey's future strategic significance to the US with the choices that Ankara would make during the crisis. Also, the Gulf crisis erupted after the end of the Cold War and as the international system was entering a fluid period. The interest of political analysts was focused on the future of the bilateral relationship, while the elements that shaped the bilateral relationship in the 1980s were overlooked. Yet, but for a change of cosmic proportions historical experience does not abruptly end and then begins again; it rather evolves and, more often than not, evolves slowly. Assuredly the measure of Ankara's co-operation with

Washington during the crisis would affect future relations, at least in the short term. But its significance equally lay in what it conveyed about the evolution of the relationship in the near past.

Essentially, the crisis was for the Turks the moment of truth within the context of their strategic co-operation with the Americans. In the 1980s Turkey's potential role in the security of the Gulf had become increasingly important to US strategic planners and had influenced the administrations' approach to Turkey, including the commitment in maintaining high levels of assistance. The signing of the 1982 COB agreement, which resulted in the modernization and construction of air bases in Eastern Turkey that now could accommodate allied reinforcements, underscored the country's role in US strategic plans for the protection of the West's access to the oil in the Gulf. Even though the use of these bases had to be authorized by the Turks, their purpose was clear. Following Saddam Hussein's invasion of Kuwait the American's need for access to the bases was no longer related to a hypothetical contingency in the Gulf but to a real unfolding crisis. In fact, the three things that Washington wanted from the Turks essentially boiled down to one: permission to use the bases for operations against Iraq. Although the Cold War was over US security requirements in the Gulf remained the same and the Americans now needed the 1982 COB agreement to be put in action outside a NATO framework. And it was this agreement, as its architect on the US side, Richard Perle, observed, that enabled the US-led coalition air forces to attack Iraq from Turkey during Operation Desert Storm.[28]

The hard side of interdependence

According to Morton Abramowitz, Secretary of State James Baker communicated to President Özal all three things that Washington wanted from Turkey during the course of four meetings between August and December 1990.[29] Abramowitz also recalls that he discussed these issues with Özal a number of times during the same period and up until the outbreak of the war. According to the American ambassador, these three issues did not carry the same importance for the US. In reality, the deployment of 1,500 Turkish soldiers to the Gulf was only of symbolic value to the Americans. Also, the movement of more troops to the border with Iraq though important was not considered as crucial in Washington. According to Abramowitz, the most 'essential' requirement for the US was the permission to use the bases, and it was to this end that a major diplomatic effort was exercised by James Baker and himself.[30]

It can be reasonably assumed that the Americans' pressure on the Turks to use the bases increased once the Bush administration focused its attention on the use of military means for the liberation of Kuwait. That must have happened in early November 1990 when Baker visited Ankara to discuss with Özal both political and military matters, including Washington's three requests.[31] Did the Turks expect a US request for Turkey's military co-operation after the invasion had taken place? Most likely they did, as the US president and

President Özal discussed on the phone the possibility of resort to military means if sanctions failed. Actually, the day after the invasion of Kuwait Özal suggested to President Bush that the NATO allies should get together.[32] And in early September he urged Bush to try and secure Moscow's agreement for a UN resolution enabling military intervention.[33] It is reasonable to assume that Özal's suggestions reflected at least to some extent an anxiety to invoke a broader framework within which Turkey's potential military involvement could be justified. In any case, what is clear is that the Turks had to respond under the pressure of 'too rapid' developments[34] that left no room for much reflection, let alone for tactical maneuvering.

As has been pointed out elsewhere,[35] early on Turkish leadership showed that it preferred to maintain its longstanding policy of non-interference in the crisis, which was seen as an inter-Arab affair. Had this been possible without Turkey incurring any significant costs when it came to its relations with the US, probably the Turks would have tried to maintain a policy of neutrality throughout the crisis. However, the adoption of a policy of neutrality in a crisis which also involved Turkey's Western allies and mainly the US required room for maneuvering. As we know Turkey was not allowed such room for three reasons: because Saddam refused to withdraw his troops from Kuwait; because the George W. Bush administration decided that it was not enough to defend Saudi Arabia but also Kuwait had to be liberated; and finally because the US secured a UN resolution authorizing the US-led coalition to use 'all necessary means' against Iraq to liberate Kuwait if Iraqi troops did not withdraw by 15 January 1991. Therefore Turkey's involvement could not be helped. Not because the Turkish president viewed the crisis as an opportunity for Turkey to reinvent its strategic value for the US, as the conventional accounts maintain, but because the US had decided that the war effort demanded Turkey's contribution. A refusal by the Turks to co-operate would incur costs that not just Özal,[36] but the Turkish military establishment and presumably at least a good number of political leaders too were not truly ready or willing to face at this point in time. In short, only a Turkey that was stronger domestically and internationally might have said 'no'.

In the final analysis the Gulf crisis brought back home to the Turks the hard side of their relationship of interdependence with the US. This was a most difficult moment for Turkish leaders. It must have been the moment they wished would never happen throughout the previous decade. For it must have been clear to them – unless they underestimated the realities of their relationship with the Americans, which is hard to imagine – that their 'flexible', ambiguous approach concerning their military contribution to Gulf contingencies could not be maintained at a time of crisis. Turkey's co-operation cannot be properly explained on the basis of Özal's wish to revamp Turkey's strategic value for the US in the post-Cold War environment,[37] as Özal claimed in his public statements, although undoubtedly the Turkish president naturally calculated how Turkey's loyalty to US strategic needs might strengthen bilateral ties. Public rhetoric can sometimes be confused with hard political reality. In this case, the political reality was that Turkey had to pay its dues to the US or otherwise seriously undermine bilateral relations and consequently sacrifice the significant benefits that its co-operation with the US yielded. The Turks' concern over Iraq's growing military machine and aggressive posture in the area[38] and Özal's belief that Turkey's co-operation with the US for the defeat of Saddam would allow Turkey to benefit from the changed post-Saddam security environment in the Middle East, may have made it easier for the Turkish leaders to bite the bullet and offer the Turkish bases to the US-led allied war effort, but these were not the decisive factors.

Turkey benefited as a result of its independent foreign policy in the Middle East, but its relationship with the US was by now at the heart of Turkish foreign policy considerations. One of the main reasons was that Turkish leaders desired Turkey's military modernization and a self-sufficient national defence industry. To this effect since 1979 the Turks sought and received on an annual basis US military assistance, military equipment, training programmes worth millions of dollars for Turkish military officers, modern fighter aircrafts, as well as support in the development of the Turkish defence industry. In Washington's eyes this was the best way to protect the US strategic stake in Turkey.[39] As the decade of the 1980s was coming to a close, Turkey still received over half a billion dollars in US assistance, of which over $400 million was in the form of grants.[40] This had been the 'primary means of financial support for the purchase of hardware in Turkey's military modernization program'[41] and still was.[42] Only Israel and Egypt were receiving more US security assistance than Turkey per year (although the Turks complained that the overall assistance was not enough for the country's military needs). The net result was that the Turkish leaders' military modernization plans became fully dependent on the US. Had there been a change of political/military leadership in Turkey for one that was ready to seriously question the relationship with the US, or had there been a scaling down of Turkish military modernization goals following the end of the Cold War, the story of Turkey's interaction with the US during the Gulf crisis might have been different. But neither took place. Actually, as late as 1989 Prime Minister Özal in a meeting with President Bush underlined that Turkey was 'at a critical state economically' and sought to impress upon him the need for continuous US security assistance, which the Turks 'preferred' to receive in the form of grants. Özal of course understood, said he, the constraints of the US deficit, but as he pointed out US military assistance was insufficient for the modernization of Turkey's forces.[43] In short, permission to the US-led coalition to use Turkish bases – which was the central point of Turkey's military contribution – was not dictated by Özal's choices, against the wishes of the military, as the established analysis would have us believe. On the contrary, it was primarily dictated by the goals set by the military in particular, but which also met with the approval of some of Turkey's political leaders in the 1980s.[44] These were to build up Turkey's military strength to a very serious level. The success of this objective relied on maintaining close military co-operation with the US, in return for which

Turkey received on average over half a billion dollars in annual security assistance (between 1984 and 1990), state-of-the-art military equipment and technological support for its defence industry. From an American perspective Turkey's potential role in the defence of the Gulf lay at the heart of this co-operation.

Turkish foreign policy makers were pragmatic, not idealistic. Ali Karaosmanoğlu describes the historical evolution of the Turkish leaders' national security culture as a rather consistent combination of *realpolitik* and the desire to modernize through a policy of Westernization.[45] Ankara's policy of co-operation with its Western allies during the crisis was a testament to that. But at the same time it revealed Turkey's weakness. At the end of the 1980s the Turks had made significant steps in the realization of their military goals with US assistance and support. Nonetheless, as the post-Cold War decade began these were still far from being fully realized while US assistance levels were dropping. Moreover, Turkey had accumulated over $2 billion in debt to the US from the purchase of weapons.[46] Turkish political and military leaders may have been inspired by ideas of an independent foreign policy, but the truth was that they were totally dependent on the US for the strengthening of their military machine upon which the pursuit of an independent policy rested to a large extent. Essentially, Turkey was faced with the problem (and eventually the dilemma) that confronts many small states. The heart of this problem is that the small state feels the need for an effective military as 'the pre-condition of independent action and autonomous decision'. But a modern military machine is extremely costly and a small state is unable to build it through its own limited means. So, 'the greater its success in satisfying its purely military requirements the greater will be its subsequent dependence on foreign sources of equipment and technology',[47] and thus its independence will be inevitably compromised and its room for maneuvering will be limited.

In the final analysis, during the Gulf crisis the Americans received the dividends of the Reagan administrations' expensive investment in Turkey, which had led to the growth of dependency ties.

It was mentioned earlier that we know hardly anything about the deliberations that led to the formulation of Ankara's policy during the Gulf crisis. Yet a few years after the end of the Gulf War, a statement made by Kenan Evren regarding US access to Turkish bases revealed a lot about the way Turkey's rulers thought about the matter. Evren, the leader of the 1980 military coup who subsequently became the president of Turkey (November 1982 to November 1989), was one of the major architects of the military co-operation with the US in the 1980s. In 1995 Turkish air bases were still used by US forces (in co-operation with the British and the French) participating in Operation Provide Comfort (alternatively also called Operation Poised Hammer). This was designed to protect the Kurds of Northern Iraq from Saddam Hussein's aggression. The Turkish parliament routinely renewed their stay every year from 1991, although a large section of the political world was against the operation because it was seen as threatening Turkey's national interests.[48] Evren himself was against the deployment of the US-led force,[49] but as he stated in a television interview in March 1995 there was no way for Turkey to stop it. In his words, the US 'put forward some demands. If you give them a finger you cannot free your arm. Whoever is in power cannot cancel Poised Hammer; because we have been too dependent on the United States, both economically and politically.'[50] Naturally, Evren failed to mention that Turkey's dependence grew when he was in power, and that the 'finger' was given to the Americans by the 1982 COB agreement, which was negotiated by the Turkish military under his leadership. But, on the other hand, perhaps his statement contained a small dose of subtle self-criticism. All the same, what he said was the plain truth about the nature of the bilateral relationship, a truth which Özal did not dare publicly state in January 1991 when he was faced with strong political opposition (also from within his own party) that was supported by public opinion against any kind of co-operation with the US over Iraq.[51]

Ambassador Morton Abramowitz and Cengiz Çandar, one of Turkey's well informed political commentators and one of Özal's special advisers on the issue of Northern Iraq, in their interviews with me confirmed the analysis outlined in the preceding pages. Ambassador Abramowitz underlined that the Turkish military was not against the granting of permission to the US to use the Turkish bases during the Gulf War. 'They did not oppose the US request to use the bases. This does not mean that they were happy about it', recalls Abramowitz, but primarily, he adds, they were not happy about Turkey's involvement in the war. Their main but not very serious concern was that Saddam Hussein might launch missile attacks against Turkey in retaliation. All the same, 'they knew that they *had* to allow the use of the bases'; this was one of the key elements in the bilateral security co-operation.[52] Actually, Abramowitz recalls that the Turkish leaders had decided early on during the crisis that they would allow the US to use the bases, despite press reports and government statements.[53] This is also confirmed by a senior official at the time in the Turkish Ministry of Foreign Affairs.[54] Due to the declassification of most of Özal's conversations with Bush, now we are at least in the position to know that on 20 November 1990 Özal in his meeting with George W. Bush stated that Turkish airfields could be used.[55] However, as Özal first tried in early August 1990 to have parliament authorize him to send Turkish troops abroad or receive foreign troops in Turkey, the decision must have been taken earlier than November.[56] According to Abramowitz, the reason that Özal did not lobby hard for parliament's approval before war was actually declared was that he feared the domestic political cost as well as Baghdad's hostile reaction in case the US decided not to go to war against Iraq in the end.[57] Özal in the same November meeting made it clear to Bush that Turkey and particularly the Incirlik base could be 'used only as a staging area ... '. 'If a war breaks out, you can use Incirlik for support', said Özal and added, 'we can use a Turkish NATO ACE mobile force exercise as a cover for moving 50 or 60 planes into Incirlik. … We would want to know in advance if you expected hostilities to begin. We would then decide whether you could use Incirlik not only for support but for offensive operations within one or two days after hostilities begin. Saddam Hussein must go.' Bush and Baker, who was also present at the meeting, commented that they were satisfied with Turkey's decisions.[58] Not surprisingly Turkish leadership preferred to keep Turkey's military involvement as limited as possible. Also, they chose a stage-by-stage approach, which allowed them to preserve control over the bases even though they had most likely come to the conclusion that the bases could be used in the event of war not only for staging purposes. This was all very consistent with the Turks' longstanding attitude over base rights, and there is no reason to assume that Özal was in favour of a clear commitment in advance as Turkey would have nothing to gain. Certainly the Americans were satisfied with this approach and apparently did not press for more. According to the senior Foreign Ministry official mentioned earlier, Turkish foreign policy makers were prepared to allow the use of bases for offensive operations, if necessary, but they remained undecided for some time as to whether Turkey would allow the bases to be used to support full- or only limited-scale military operations against Iraq in the event of war.[59] How did the Turks' thinking on this matter evolve? Was there actually a major difference of opinion concerning this between the Turkish president and the military? What were the pressure tactics employed by the Americans? Only when more relevant material from Turkey becomes available shall we be able to answer these questions.

Abramowitz dismisses the proposition that the US–Turkey dialogue during the crisis was essentially shaped by Özal as far as the Turkish side was concerned. A considerable amount of discussion was taking place between President Bush and James Baker with the Turkish president for two reasons, Abramowitz points out. For one, Özal was at the top of the decision-making pyramid. Also, he was open to the Americans and wanted to offer a helping hand within the context of their regional diplomacy. However, says the American ambassador, there was at the same time and out of the public eye a continuous and substantial dialogue between the Americans and the Turkish military.[60]

Cengiz Çandar also confirms Abramowitz's account concerning the position of the Turkish military over the use of the bases. As Çandar puts it, the army was not enthusiastic about letting the Americans use the bases 'but they knew they had no alternative. The whole relationship with the Americans was about the bases.'[61] The military leadership, says Çandar, was concerned that Turkey risked getting involved in a major way in the Middle East, but even this fear was eased by Özal's argument that Turkey would be on the winning side and so it would be well placed to reap the benefits at the end of the war.[62]

It has to be stressed that General Necip Torumtay, chief of the Turkish General Staff (July 1987–Dec 1990), in his memoirs does not mention that there was a breach between the president and the military leadership concerning the use of the bases by the US. Torumtay resigned his position before the outbreak of war in early December 1990. At the time it was widely thought and reported in the press that he had resigned because he disagreed with Özal's policy over the crisis, that is, the extent of military support he was willing to give the Americans and more specifically whether the Turkish bases would be used by the US for attacks against Iraq including in the event of a war.[63] These press reports and pervasive rumours were reflected in some of the almost contemporary analysis of Ankara's policy.[64] However, Torumtay's memoirs, which were published in 1994, challenged the accuracy of these rumours. In his account Torumtay let it to be understood that he had resigned because he resented Özal's tendency to dominate the decision-making process during the crisis and in the final analysis to bypass him, not because there was a disagreement over the substance of policy during the crisis.[65]

It is true that General Torumtay does not offer a detailed analysis of his own views or those of his colleagues over what policy Turkey should have followed over the Gulf crisis. But it is not unreasonable to assume that had there been a significant divergence of views as to the use of the bases he might have mentioned something. For sure, as discussed earlier, he does not conceal that he and the other Turkish generals objected to the idea of Turkey opening a second front against Iraq.[66]

Morton Abramowitz and Cengiz Çandar sum up rather aptly the issue of Torumtay's resignation. According to them, during the crisis Özal wished to conduct the high-level political/military discussions with the US, which until then had been handled by the Turkish military. Özal wished to bypass the military leadership, which resulted in Torumtay's intense resentment. This might have caused a serious crisis had Özal not been able to isolate him within senior military circles, even though the other generals shared Torumtay's feelings and there was no difference of opinion concerning Turkey's policy during the crisis.[67] In short, the Turkish president skilfully exploited the jealousies and personal rivalries among senior military officers. After Torumtay resigned, General Doğan Güreş, commander of the Turkish Land Forces, was only too happy to take his position.[68]

Fears of a security vacuum

Explaining Ankara's policy during the Gulf crisis only on the basis of Özal's choices and calculations also raises questions for other reasons which have to do with the intense security concerns of Turkish rulers at the time, borne as a result of new post-Cold War security challenges. As discussed earlier, since the mid 1960s Turkey's ability to maintain a policy in the Middle East that was independent of the US was to a very large extent the result of reduced West-East tension. In the 1980s the Turks, although they renewed their co-operation with the US, could maintain an ambiguous posture concerning their military involvement in a Gulf contingency for two reasons. First, no security crisis burst in the area. Second, they were not exposed to any serious security threats or pressures producing the desire to close ranks with the US. But at the end of the 1980s the Turks' analysis of the security challenges facing

Turkey changed. Turkish leaders grew deeply concerned about the security implications for their country of the end of the Cold War. The majority did not consider this systemic change to Turkey's advantage. On the contrary they feared that it could cause the country many problems.

For sure, Turkey like every state in the international system benefited from the reduction of Soviet power because the danger of a conflict between the two opposing camps was significantly diminished. However, Turkey like all other states, big or small, still had to rely on military power, diplomacy and alliances in order to protect its security and national interests. Most Turkish rulers sided with the view that the collapse of bipolarity and its replacement by regional rivalries and loose alliances increased the possibilities for the eruption of local and regional armed conflicts.[69] For them, the contemporary reality in the Middle East sub-system was a good case in point, so at the end of the 1980s this area was at the centre of their immediate security concerns.[70] The Turks were particularly alarmed by the disruption of the balance of power between Turkey and its neighbours on the southeast, Syria, Iraq and Iran. All three possessed significant conventional weapons but also chemical weapons and were interested in building stronger military machines, with Iraq leading the way.[71] Had Turkey's relations with her three neighbours been normal the Turks might have paid less heed to their militarization. As has been pointed out, states feel the need to balance themselves against threats rather than against power alone.[72] But Turkey's relations primarily with Syria but also with Iraq and Iran caused apprehension in Ankara.[73] Turkey's security concerns in relation to Syria had mainly to do with the support Damascus gave to the Kurdish rebels of the PKK in Turkey. Assad used support for the PKK to a large extent as a pressure tactic on Turkey mainly on account of another issue bedevilling bilateral relations: management of the waters of the sources of the Euphrates in Turkey. The water issue was also causing Turkey tension with Iraq. Relations between Turkey and Iran were also sensitive, again because of the Kurdish issue but also for ideological reasons.[74] Turkish elites regarded the ideas exported by the Islamic republic as a challenge and a threat to the Kemalist ideology that constructed an identity based on the Western model. Following the Iranian Revolution, Ankara sought with some success to cultivate non-competitive relations with Tehran and to avail itself of opportunities for the development of economic relations. Ankara's policy towards Iran was largely dictated by the wish to discourage the new regime in Tehran from exploiting the Kurdish card in the region against Turkey's interests. For Turkey it was a delicate and complex balancing game as the Kurds were spread out in Iran, Northern Iraq, Syria and the Lebanon. In fact, in the 1980s Ankara's growing concern that Baghdad was losing control over the Kurdish-inhabited areas in Northern Iraq and the Turks' fears concerning Iran's designs in the area led them to intensify their co-operation with the Iranian regime. Their growing suspicions of Tehran in relation to the rising power of Islam in Turkey also made them seek out a normal pace of relations with Iran.

The Turks were not only apprehensive about the security of the country along the southeastern border. At the turn of the 1990s the power of the Soviet Union still cast a heavy shadow on their minds. They were particularly anxious about the consequences of the Conventional Armed Forces Treaty for Turkey. Their main fear was that the treaty while promoting stability in central Europe might change other regional balances at the expense of Turkey's security, i.e. with the Soviet forces stationed across from eastern Anatolia. Furthermore, they were afraid that strong secessionist national movements in the Soviet Union, particularly in the south like in Azerbaijan, where there were predominately Turkic populations, might cause unwelcome complications for Turkish foreign policy because of the growth of a more vocal Turkish public opinion. In addition, the possibility of an independent Armenia with territorial claims against Turkey was considered a major problem because it threatened to complicate Turkey's relations with both Washington and Moscow.[75]

These security concerns were intensified because of the prevailing uncertainly felt in Ankara concerning the terms of Turkey's relationship with the West in the post-Cold War international system. For almost half a century Turkish foreign and security policy was primarily shaped according to the requirements of Turkey's NATO membership and influenced by its bilateral strategic relationship with the US as well as its relations with its European allies. In short, it was shaped to a very large degree, although not exclusively, by Turkey's Western orientation. Since 1945 the Turkish elites sought integration with the West not only in search of security in the traditional sense but also for economic and ideological reasons. However, these efforts had not fully yielded the results Turkey's leaders desired.[76] At the end of the 1980s Turkey's most important institutional link with the West continued to be the North Atlantic Alliance. But as the Cold War receded into the past and NATO's importance diminished the future shape of Turkey's relationship with the West became unclear, much to the distress of Turkish political and security elites.[77] The Turks feared most a gradual marginalization of the country within the context of Western strategic interests and subsequently its international isolation, as Turkey's postwar relations with the West were essentially built within the context of its role as a bulwark against the Soviet threat.[78] Therefore, the 1989 rejection of Turkey's application to become a member of the European Community (EC) was received in Ankara as a major blow and reinforced the palpable sense of anxiety.[79] In a sense, Turkey's leaders were experiencing a similar distress to the one they felt in the 1940s and up until the accession of the country to NATO in 1952, when they were deeply disturbed about the risk of the West leaving Turkey out if its orbit.[80] In sum, in the short period between the fall of the Berlin Wall and the Gulf War Turkey seriously felt the pressure of new major security challenges, even threats. These are not so much visible to us today. Yet at the dawn of the 1990s they were very clear to the Turkish leaders, even though they had no ready or sure solutions for them.

Ankara's security concerns at the time are not understudied. In fact, they have been adequately presented and analyzed by students of Turkish foreign policy.[81] Yet, rather surprisingly, in describing Turkish foreign policy during the Gulf crisis analysts have focused on the impact that some of these concerns had only on Özal's calculations.[82] However, there can be no doubt that these concerns, which tantalized Turkey's political and security leadership at large, did not affect just the president and influence his decisions alone. As far as one can judge, a significant number of Turkish foreign policy decision-makers, like Özal, must have felt compelled, under the pressure of these concerns, to rekindle the strategic relationship with Washington rather than undermine it by refusing Turkey's co-operation in the Middle East. 'In the prevailing atmosphere of uncertainty Turkish officials are anxious to reassert the value of the United States-Turkish strategic relationship',[83] a perceptive analyst of US–Turkey relations noted following his visit to Ankara just three months before the Gulf crisis erupted.[84] Actually, the same analyst remarked that many Turkish politicians and strategists favoured the idea of closer co-operation with the US in out-of-NATO operations, although this was a very sensitive issue with Turkish public opinion.[85]

While growing security concerns also induced Turkish political leaders and strategic planners to closely co-operate with the US, arguments about economic prospects must have added a positive element into the calculus. These were present in the mind of Özal as well as of a number of senior bureaucrats and members of Turkey's economic elite. The latter's influence on foreign policy decisions had began to grow since the late 1980s although not at an institutional level, for the interaction between government and business was mainly taking place at a personal level involving direct meetings of key businessmen with Özal and a small core of ministers and senior bureaucrats.[86] Özal and his close advisers, including members of the business community as well as officials in key bureaucratic agencies, were keen for Turkey to capitalize on the opportunities presented all around its periphery, from Central Asia and the Black Sea to the Middle East, in order to gain economic benefits.[87] Actually the postwar reconstruction of Kuwait was seen by many in Ankara as a big opportunity for lucrative contracts for Turkish construction companies. Of course, this economic optimism was based on relevant American assurances given to the Turks as soon as the crisis erupted.[88] It should be mentioned here that towards the end of the 1980s Iraq remained a major market for Turkish exports, but economic relations had become sticky as Iraq increasingly owed money to Turkey, which actually had to extend credit in order to maintain a trade relationship. At the end of 1988 Iraq's debt to Turkey amounted to almost $2 billion. The emergence of Turkey, which itself was faced with a significant foreign debt, 'as a significant creditor' was indeed 'a costly irony.'[89]

To sum up, when examining Ankara's policy during the Gulf crisis analysts have paid too much attention on Özal's statements and his personality while they have underestimated other parameters. The analysis offered above clearly does not doubt that there was a clash of perspectives between the Turkish president, on the one hand, and mainly the military and the foreign policy bureaucrats, on the other. As General Torumtay points out, there were serious differences, but they had to do rather with the issue of Turkey's broader involvement in the war, either by sending troops to Saudi Arabia or by opening a second front in Iraq.[90] Apparently, they did not concern the use of the bases by the US. This can explain why Özal's wishes did not prevail concerning the two issues on which there was disagreement. In contrast, the use of the Turkish bases was allowed, not because Özal was able to overrule the political/military opposition, or because in the end there was a compromise between the two trends represented by Özal and the more traditional Kemalist elite respectively, but rather because the military did not oppose it.

For sure, the issue of Turkey's involvement in the war must have caused Ankara a lot of angst and raised difficult foreign policy dilemmas, which the dominant literature vaguely touches upon. Their investigation is beyond the confines of this study. Suffice it to say that while security ties with the US had assumed a new weight in Turkish foreign policy the Turks still clung to their idea of an independent policy towards the Middle East. The Gulf War escalated like never before the tension borne of this contradiction. The Turkish political and security elite must have become overwhelmed by the hard decisions they had to take under very difficult circumstances. One thing that clearly emerges from the careful study of their reaction is that Özal and the military were determined to act cautiously, to adopt a step-by-step approach and to offer the US only what could not be avoided, i.e. the use of the bases, if necessary, while preserving the right of final decision over their usage until the very last moment. It has been argued that Özal 'seemed only too eager to take risks in the Gulf for the sake of the enlarged role' he envisaged for Turkey after the crisis.[91] The Turkish president's conversations with President Bush do not support this assessment. On the contrary, they reveal that Özal rather than offering his enthusiastic support to the Americans and taking risks acted with extreme caution and diplomatic dexterity. It is worth illustrating this with one example. On 3 August, one day after the invasion of Kuwait, Bush called Özal to enquire what Turkey intended to do concerning the Iraqi oil pipelines in transit through Turkey. 'I view you as a friend and as an important member of NATO. In your geostrategic location you occupy a key position' because of the Iraqi pipeline, said Bush. 'I wanted to know the conditions under which you might close it.' Özal completely evaded the subject.[92] Bush called again the following day. This time Bush spoke at length, exercising pressure on Özal to close the pipeline.

> Sanctions have failed in the past because countries did not stand together in enforcing them. I have a hopeful feeling that, if we can deny Saddam access to money, he will crumble faster. ... We are preparing military options. ... We must stand together on the economic front. When we go through with the plan, we must close the pipeline and get the Saudis to

> close their pipeline. … I have read the statement issued by your foreign ministry that Turkey does not support closing down the pipeline at present and that it wishes to remain neutral. … I cannot emphasize enough my view that there can be no neutrality in these circumstances and my hope that we can get the plan for the Saudis and you to be prepared to shut down the pipeline. … This is my appeal. What is your view?[93]

At first Özal again avoided addressing the issue directly and he did not agree with Bush's suggestion that he should tell the Iraqis that Turkey would shut down the pipeline unless Saddam withdrew from Kuwait. As Bush insisted on the matter, Özal finally responded that if the UN imposed sanctions on oil then 'it would be easier' for Turkey 'to do something'.[94] This was not only about securing international legitimacy. Özal was careful not to tie Turkey too closely to US policy. According to Cengiz Çandar, the Turkish president found unacceptable Bush's heavy-handed approach on this matter. 'The [impolite expression] expects me to shut down the pipeline like this', Özal commented, 'I told him bring me a UN resolution and then I shall close it down', recalls Çandar.[95] Ankara announced the closure of the pipeline on 7 August, one day after the Security Council had called upon all UN members to prevent the importation into their territories of all commodities and products originating in Iraq or Kuwait.[96] It is worth asking whether similar concerns partly accounted for the Turks' delay in formally granting permission to the US to use the bases until after 15 January 1991, which was the UN deadline for the withdrawal of Iraqi troops from Kuwait.

Aftermath

During the crisis Özal sought to strike bargains with the Bush administration in return for Turkey's support. The Turkish president hoped to earn recognition by the Americans that Turkey was a reliable ally but also hoped to obtain concrete benefits and to receive compensation for the loss of revenue that the Turks incurred as a result of sanctions against Iraq. The outburst of many political leaders and public opinion against any co-operation with the US strengthened Özal's hand at the negotiationing table, and we can safely assume that he used the furor over Turkey's involvement in the war to maximum advantage. Bargaining tactics might possibly further explain why the Turks delayed their formal commitment to the war effort.[97] Unfortunately, we do not know the details of the negotiations, which were kept under a thick veil of secrecy from the moment they began a week after the eruption of the crisis and throughout its duration up until the end of 1990. The bulk of these negotiations took place during private meetings between James Baker and President Özal, who after each meeting limited himself to making only general statements to the press. Nonetheless, we do know most of the rewards Turkey obtained in the end but without knowing how exactly they related to the demands that Özal had put forward.[98] The DECA, which was ready to expire, was prolonged for another year, automatically extending US assistance to Turkey for that period. So, for their part the Americans secured the use of the bases they still needed without any of the usual exasperating negotiations, causing the opposition to criticize the decision as a sacrifice of Turkey's interests. In return, all US bases in Turkey were to remain in place, although the Pentagon had already announced that many military installations overseas were to be closed due to budgetary cuts. (In the end, most US bases in Turkey were to last only for a bit longer.)[99] The Bush administration pledged that the level of annual US assistance to Turkey would not drop below $545 million. It also promised to support the release to Turkey of an American Eximbank credit of $1.4 million (that had been frozen because the Turks had not met the bank's economic criteria), which Turkey was going to use to buy US-made weapons. In addition, the US would finally deliver 40 used F-4 Phantom fighter bombers that had been held up since 1984 due to congressional reaction. And in November 1990 the US government announced a rise in the quotas of Turkish textiles, meeting thus, at least partially, a longstanding Turkish demand. In the wake of the war the Bush administration also recognized that Turkey had incurred a significant cost as a result of closing down the Kirkuk-Yumurtalik oil pipeline and the continuation of the embargo against Iraq. So US assistance to Turkey increased by $282 million for the fiscal year 1991. As a result, the total assistance for that year reached $850 million (of which $750 million were in the form of a grant), an amount similar to what Turkey was receiving in the middle of the 1980s.[100] Furthermore, the Americans orchestrated the purchase by Egypt of 40 F-16s manufactured in Turkey and took the initiative for the creation of a Turkish Defense Fund with the participation of Saudi Arabia, Kuwait, the United Arab Emirates and the US, towards which the Arab states of the Gulf pledged to contribute $2.5 billion. The capstone of Turkey's rewards was the Bush government's promise to lobby in favour of Turkey's application to join the European Community, while apparently the US government was instrumental in the EC's decision to increase the value of the quota of Turkish textiles.

As a result of Turkey's accommodation of US needs in the Gulf the anticipated decrease in economic and military assistance was slowed down, and although the Turks repeatedly argued that the financial rewards they received did not fully compensate for their losses,[101] bilateral ties maintained their forward momentum at least for a while.

Despite the new energy that the war infused into the bilateral relationship, it was already clear that in the longer run it would be difficult for the Turks to obtain from Washington satisfaction of their principal interests, at least to the degree that they desired. There were many reasons for this. At the end of the Cold War the US was faced with a colossal debt and huge budget deficits. It was for a good reason that the Gulf War was financed mainly by the Arab Gulf states, Germany and Japan. (Of the estimated $61 billion that the war cost the US contribution was $7 billion.)[102] Economic realities obliged the US to cope with its financial problems and a reduction of defence expenditure following the transformation of relations with the Soviet Union was inevitable. In addition, the emerging discussion about the new post-Cold War European security architecture and the Europeans' role meant that most of the assumptions and facts that had determined US postwar security policy in Europe, including the eastern Mediterranean, had become redundant.[103] Nobody knew yet what the US approach to this part of the world was going to be, and how Turkey might fit within the context of the post-Cold War US strategic interests was not really clear. While it seemed that Turkey could support US interests in Central Asia, the Caucasus, the Balkans and the Middle East, the exact content of a new US–Turkey strategic co-operation was still vague. Nonetheless it soon became evident that Özal's hopes[104] that Turkey's participation in the Gulf war would allow it to become an essential part of the postwar security arrangement that the US would put in place in the Middle East would not materialize.[105]

Undoubtedly, Turkish bases were an essential element in the war effort against Saddam Hussein and continued to be important to the US for imposing a no-fly zone over Northern Iraq in co-operation with the British and French soon after the war had ended (through Operation Provide Comfort II). But Turkey did not manage to institutionalize its relations with the US, despite Özal's efforts to this effect after the crisis was over. His proposal for an enhanced US–Turkey 'strategic co-operation' (or 'bilateral co-operation over a multitude of issues') through the expansion of bilateral relations, political co-operation in trouble-spot areas and military co-operation in the Gulf and the Middle East in general, which was rather vaguely presented, did not ignite Washington's interest.[106] The lack of interest by the Bush administration in this enhanced 'strategic co-operation with Turkey' has been explained by one analyst as the result of a combination of reasons, including the emergence of new US security priorities and the decrease in US military spending.[107] According to Morton Abramowitz, the Bush administration did not feel inclined to give more attention to Turkey. Besides, in his opinion Özal most likely would not have been able to deliver on his military co-operation offer, an opinion that was shared by other State Department officials.[108] Therefore, in reality, Turkey's participation in the war did not mark, as has been argued, a 'critical turning point' within the context of the bilateral relationship for 'it gave Turkey an actual and potential role in US policy in the Middle East, which had been in abeyance since the collapse of the Baghdad Pact.'[109] Turkey's role as a military base for the projection of US power into the Middle East was already well established in the minds of American strategic planners. Actually, as discussed earlier, this role played an essential part in shaping US policy towards Turkey since the proclamation of the Carter Doctrine. The Gulf War simply confirmed the existing US strategic viewpoint. On the other hand, Turkish policy during the crisis underlined that Turkish military and most political leaders still recoiled from the idea of close open co-operation with the US in the Middle East. This message was clearly sent by the Turks' refusal to send troops to Saudi Arabia because, as Özal explained to Bush, he did not think it was wise for Turks 'to be in an Arab country preparing for conflict with another nation'[110] due to the Ottoman past. The Turks knew that they had to offer their support and so they did, but had the stakes not been so high for Turkey Ankara might have said 'no' to the Americans in the end. For sure the overall instinct of the government was to maintain a low public profile for Turkey's involvement in the actual war effort, bearing in mind critics both at home as well as in the Arab world. Even Özal's public statements were measured during the crisis. It is worth remembering that, when he allowed the US bombers to use Turkey's airspace on their way to bomb Iraqi targets, the Turkish president himself asked Abramowitz whether they could fly close to the border with Syria so that the Turkish government could deny it had any knowledge of the flight. And when the very first flight of the bombers from Incirlik took place the government stated that the fighters were involved in military exercises and refused to acknowledge Turkey's involvement in the war against Iraq.[111] In fact, it was only on the fifth day of the war that the Turkish government publicly acknowledged, while avoiding self-promoting rhetoric, that Turkey's territory was used in the war effort against Iraq.[112] The defeat of Özal's party in the 1991 general elections, which brought to an end his overwhelming political influence from the presidential office, would seem to have cost the US one of the most energetic advocates of US–Turkey co-operation. On the other hand, as the implications of the Gulf War for the Middle East in general and Turkey in particular became clear its involvement with US strategic designs for the Middle East looked more difficult to resist. Had the EC after the Gulf War given Turkey a warm response to its longing for closer economic and political ties the Turks might have felt less urgently the need to seek satisfaction of many of their interests by assisting US strategic aims in the Middle East. But the Europeans, who were trying to develop their own common foreign and security policy, made it crystal clear that they were even less keen than before the crisis to develop closer relations with Turkey. One of the main reasons was that they did not wish to run the risk of exposing themselves to the heavy security demands of the Middle East.[113] So inevitably the Turks continued to rely heavily on their relationship with the US.

Notes

1 The account is based on M. Abramowitz, 'The Complexities of American Policymaking on Turkey', in M. Abramowitz (ed.), *Turkey's Transformation and American Policy*, New York: The Century Foundation Press, 2000, pp. 153–4.
2 W. Hale, *Turkish Politics and the Military*, London: Routledge, 1994, pp. 283, 292–3.
3 Abramowitz, 'Complexities of American Policymaking on Turkey', pp. 153–4.
4 W. Hale, *Turkish Foreign Policy, 1774–2000*, London: Frank Cass, 2000, p. 221.
5 Y. Çelik, *Contemporary Turkish Foreign Policy*, Westport, CT: Praeger, 1999, p. 78;
6 P. Robins, *Turkey and the Middle East*, London: The Royal Institute of International Affairs, 1991, p. 71.

7 B. R. Kuniholm, 'Turkey and the West since World War II', in V. Mastny and R. Craig Nation (eds), *Turkey between East and West: New Challenegs for a Rising Regional Power,* Boulder, CO: Westview Press, 1996, p. 62; also, Çelik, *Contemporary Turkish Foreign Policy,* p. 78.
8 Kuniholm, 'Turkey and the West', p.62; Çelik, *Contemporary Turkish Foreign Policy,* p. 78.
9 Hale, *Turkish Foreign Policy,* pp. 219–20, 223.
10 Abramowitz, 'Complexities of American Policymaking on Turkey', p. 155.
11 W. Hale, 'Turkey, the Middle East and the Gulf Crisis', *International Affairs,* vol. 68, 1992, p. 684; and Hale, *Turkish Foreign Policy,* pp. 220, 222.
12 Hale's statement is repeated by Mustafa Aydin, *Turkish Foreign Policy during the Gulf War of 1990–1991,* Cairo: Cairo Papers in Social Science, 1998, p. 28, who uses Hale as his source.
13 The White House, memorandum of conversation with President Ozal of Turkey, 20 November 1990, Kleber Center, Paris, France, available online at http://bushlibrary.tamu.edu/research/pdfs/memcons_telcons/1990-11-20-Ozal.pdf (accessed 20 February 2010). This material was declassified in late August 2009.
14 Author's interview with Morton Abramowitz (b).
15 N. Torumtay, *Orgeneral Torumtay'ın Anıları,* Istanbul: Milliyet Yayınları, 1994, p. 116; also see Hale, *Turkish Foreign Policy,* p. 246, n. 15.
16 Hale, *Turkish Foreign Policy,* p. 246, n. 15.
17 On the efforts of the Bush administration to involve the Kurds' support, see Peter Malanczuk, 'The Kurdish Crisis and Allied Intervention in the Aftermath of the Second Gulf War', *European Journal of International Law,* vol. 2, 1991, p. 117.
18 Hale, *Turkish Foreign Policy,* p. 223.
19 This vision enjoyed mostly the support of technocrats within the administration, according to Robins, *Turkey and the Middle East,* p. 73. But support was also to be found among Turkish businessmen, according to the author's interview with Selim Egeli, member of the board of directors of Turkey's Foreign Economic Relations Board (DEIK) and Turgut Özal's adviser.
20 Hale, 'Turkey, the Middle East and the Gulf Crisis', pp. 683–7; Robins, *Turkey and the Middle East,* pp. 70–72, 73; S. Sayari, 'Turkey: The Changing European Security Environment and the Gulf Crisis', *Middle East Journal,* vol. 46, 1992, pp.13–14, 16–20; Aydin, *Turkish Foreign Policy,* pp. 14–48, 73 and passim; Çelik, *Contemporary Turkish Foreign Policy,* pp. 77–8; Hale, *Turkish Foreign Policy,* pp. 220–21, 223; S. Laciner, 'Turgut Özal Period in Turkish Foreign Policy: Özalism', Ankara: *USAK Yearbook of International Politics and Law,* 2009, vol.2, pp. 177, 197–200. For a detailed account of Turkey's gradual involvement in the war and the opposing viewpoints in Turkey, see the sources already mentioned in this footnote.
21 Hale, 'Turkey, the Middle East and the Gulf Crisis', pp. 685, 686.
22 Abramowitz 'Complexities of American Policymaking on Turkey', pp. 155–6.
23 According to the memoirs of the then Turkish chief of staff, the deployment was mostly defensive in nature, although there was also preparation for a counter-attack in the event that Saddam Hussein attacked Turkey, Torumtay, *Torumtay'ın Anıları,* pp. 109, 113. Apparently, Özal also entertained ideas of invasive operations into Northern Iraq once the war had began, but the military strongly opposed the idea and it seems that there were no coherent military plans to this end: Torumtay, *Anıları,* pp. 109, 115–16, 126; Hale, *Turkish Foreign Policy,* p. 246, n. 15; M. Mufti, *Daring and Caution in Turkish Strategic Culture: Republic at Sea,* Houndmills, Basingstoke: Palgrave, Macmillan, 2009, pp. 72–5; author's interview with Mehmet Ali Birand (a).
24 Aydin, *Turkish Foreign Policy,* p. 3.
25 F. Ahmad, *The Making of Modern Turkey,* London: Routledge, 1993, p. 200.

26 Hale, *Turkish Foreign Policy*, p. 224; Hale, 'Turkey, the Middle East and the Gulf Crisis', p. 684.
27 Hale, 'Turkey, the Middle East and the Gulf Crisis', p. 684 also makes the point that the Turks had to deploy troops along the border for their defence.
28 R. Perle, 'A Turkish Story', the First Annual Robert Strausz-Hupé Lecture, Foreign Policy Research Institute, FPRI Wire, September 1999, vol. 7, p. 3, available online at http://fpri.org/fpriwire/0711.19909.perle.turkishstory.html (accessed 20 June 2000).
29 Author's interview with Morton Abramowitz (b).
30 Author's interviews with Morton Abramowitz, (a) and (b). Also Abramowitz, 'Complexities of American Policymaking on Turkey', p. 155, 278, n. 2. We do not know whether the issue of the bases was also discussed between the Turkish and the US presidents in some of their telephone conversations, which occurred frequently during the crisis, as some of them are still classified.
31 The White House, memorandum of telephone conversation with President Turgut Ozal of Turkey, 31 October 1990, available online at http://bushlibrary.tamu.edu/research/pdfs/memcons_telcons/1990-10-31–Ozal.pdf (accessed 20 February 2010); The White House, memorandum of conversation with President Ozal of Turkey, 20 November 1990, Kleber Center, Paris.
32 The White House, memorandum of telephone conversation, telephone call to President Turgut Ozal of Turkey, 3 August 1990, available online at http://bushlibrary.tamu.edu/research/pdfs/memcons_telcons/1990-08-03–Ozal.pdf (accessed 20 February 2010).
33 The White House, memorandum of telephone conversation, 6 September 1990, available online at http://bushlibrary.tamu.edu/research/pdfs/memcons_telcons/1990-09-06–Ozal.pdf (accessed 20 February 2010). Özal argued that a UN resolution for military action would not have to be used; its value would be that it would hang over Saddam's head like the sword of Damocles.
34 H. Batu, 'Turkish Foreign Policy in a Changing World', *Studies on Turkish-Arab Relations: Special Issue on Turkey and the Gulf Crisis*, Istanbul: Foundation for the Study of Turkish-Arab Relations (TAIV), vol. 6, 1991, p. 85.
35 Hale, 'Turkey, the Middle East and the Gulf Crisis', p. 683; Robins, *Turkey and the Middle East*, pp. 68–9.
36 For instance, Hale, *Turkish Foreign Policy*, p. 224 makes the point that Turkey's refusal to allow the coalition forces to use the Incirlik base would have 'fatally undermined' Özal's claims that Turkey continued to be a valuable ally of the West in the post–Cold War era.
37 Robins, *Turkey and the Middle East*, p. 71; Hale, *Turkish Foreign Policy*, p. 223.
38 Author's interviews with Mehmet Ali Birand (a) and with Morton Abramowitz (a); Robins, *Turkey and the Middle East*, p. 71.
39 For an overview of how US administrations from Truman to Reagan considered US foreign assistance programmes as a powerful means of promoting US national interests, see D. L. Clarke, D. B. O'Connor and J. D. Ellis, *Send Guns and Money: Security Assistance and U.S. Foreign Policy*, Westport, CT: Praeger, 1997.
40 T. Gabelnick, W. D. Hartung, and J. Washburn, with research assistance by M. Ciarrocca, *Arming Repression: U.S. Arms Sales to Turkey during the Clinton Administration*, a joint report of the World Policy Institute and the Federation of American Scientists, October 1999, table II, available online at http://www.fas.org/asmp/library/reports/turkeyrep.htm (accessed 4 March 2000).
41 United States Congress, House Committee on Foreign Affairs, *United States Political-Military Relations with Allies in Southern Europe: Report of a Staff Study Mission to Portugal, Spain, Greece and Turkey, October 15–30, 1986, to the Committee on Foreign Affairs, U.S. House of Representatives*, Washington DC: US Government Printing Office, 1987, p. 32.

42 Author's interview with Lale Sarıibrahimoğlu.
43 The White House, memo of conversation, president's meeting with Prime Minister Turgut Ozal of Turkey, 24 February 1989, American ambassador's residence, Tokyo, available online at http://bushlibrary.tamu.edu/research/pdfs/memcons_telcons/1989-02-24–Ozal.pdf (accessed 20 February 2010).
44 Author's discussion with Ali Karaosmanoğlu; author's interview with Mehmet Ali Birand (a).
45 A. Karaosmanoğlu, 'The Evolution of the National Security Culture and the Military in Turkey', *Journal of International Affairs*, vol. 54, 2000.
46 By the end of September 1991: J. E. Sanford, *Debt Owed to the United States by Foreign Countries: Recent Rescheduling and Forgiveness*, CRS report for Congress, Washington DC: Congressional Research Service, the Library of Congress, 19 November 1993, p. 5, n. 7, 11.
47 D. Vital, *The Inequality of States*, Oxford: Clarendon Press, 1967, pp. 60–61.
48 On the operation and Turkey's role and objections see for instance R. Gözen, 'Operation Provide Comfort: Origins and Objectives', *Ankara Üniversitesi Siyasal Bilgiler Fakültesi Dergisi*, vol. 50, 1995, available online at http://dergiler.ankara.edu.tr/search.php (accessed 20 October 2007).
49 C. Çandar, 'Some Turkish Perspectives on the United States and American Policy Toward Turkey', in M. Abramowitz (ed.), *Turkey's Transformation and American Policy*, New York: The Century Foundation Press, 2000, p. 139.
50 Quoted in Çandar, 'Turkish Perspectives', p. 139.
51 The opposition from within the governing party, according to C. Çandar, an astute observer of Turkish politics, to a large extent was inspired by third-worldism ideas. In other words, it reflected a genuine opposition to Western aggression against Iraq, a neighbouring Muslim country: author's interview with Cengiz Çandar (a). But the reaction both within the governing party and within the opposition was also a protest to the imperial way Özal was conducting foreign policy, ibid; Aydin, *Turkish Foreign Policy*, pp. 31–3.
52 Author's interviews with Morton Abramowitz.
53 On these, see Aydin, *Turkish Foreign Policy*, pp. 40–41.
54 Mr K. spoke to the author about this subject on condition of anonymity, December 2006, Istanbul.
55 The White House, memorandum of conversation with President Ozal of Turkey, 20 November 1990, Kleber Center, Paris.
56 Hale, *Turkish Foreign Policy*, p. 221,
57 Author's interview with Morton Abramowitz (b). See also Abramowitz, 'Complexities of American Policymaking on Turkey', p. 155.
58 The White House, memorandum of conversation with President Ozal of Turkey, 20 November 1990, Kleber Center, Paris.
59 Author's interview with Mr. K., December, 2006, Istanbul. *The New York Times*, 6 December 1990.
60 Author's interviews with Morton Abramowitz.
61 Author's interviews with Cengiz Çandar (b) and (c).
62 Author's interviews with Cengiz Çandar (b) and (c).
63 *Los Angeles Times*, 4 December 1990; *MEI*, 7 December 1990; *Turkey Briefing*, 10 December 1990; see also Hale, 'Turkey, the Middle East and the Gulf Crisis', p. 686; Aydin, *Turkish Foreign Policy*, pp. 38–9.
64 Hale, 'Turkey, the Middle East and the Gulf Crisis', p. 686 mentions that it was believed that there had been a disagreement over the use of the bases for offensive attacks by the US against Iraq, Robins, *Turkey and the Middle East*, p. 72 noted that the resignation of the chief of the Turkish armed forces was the result of 'a personal snub' by Özal. However, he also pointed out that the personal tension derived from differences over Gulf policy but 'notably the possible use of Turkish

military power against Iraq. President Özal seemed to support Washington's plan of early recourse to military solution, with Turkey figuring in its execution. General Torumtay together with the military and bureaucratic establishment, appeared to have greater reservations.'

65 Torumtay, *Torumtay'ın Anıları*, pp. 109–13, 116, 119, 125–6, 130.

66 General Sabri Yirmibeşoğlu was also laconic – although critical of Özal's policy during the Gulf crisis – in his memoirs, which were published nine years after the war: S. Yirmibeşoğlu, *Askeri ve Siyasi Anıları*, Istanbul: Nisan, 1999, p. 140. Yirmibeşoğlu held the important position of secretary general of the National Security Council during the very early stage of the Gulf crisis (until the end of August 1990). A short while later Özal forced him into early retirement.

67 Author's interviews with Morton Abramowitz and with Cengiz Çandar (b) and (c).

68 Author's interviews with Cengiz Çandar (b) and (c); also with Mr. K., December 2006, Istanbul.

69 On this wider perspective, see among others S. Brown, *The Causes and Prevention of War*, New York: St Martin's Press, 1994, p. 224.

70 For an excellent, succinct presentation of the Turkish leadership's overall security concerns in this period, see among others I. O. Lesser, *Southern Region Perspectives on Security and International Affairs*, Santa Monica, CA: RAND, 1991, pp. 27–30; also Sayari, 'Changing European Security Environment and Gulf Crisis', pp. 10–14; S. Hunter, 'Bridge or Frontier? Turkey's Post-Cold War Geopolitical Posture', *The International Spectator*, Vol. XXXIV, 1999, pp.67–8.

71 On the military capabilities and defense expenditures of Syria, Iran and Iraq in the years 1988 to 1990, see A. H. Cordesman, *The Military Balance in the Middle East: An Executive Summary*, Institute on Global Conflict and Cooperation, University of California, Policy Paper #49, March 1999, pp. 24, 57.

72 S. Walt, *The Origins of Alliances*, Ithaca, NY: Cornell University Press, 1987, p. 5.

73 S. Bölükbaşı, 'Turkey Challenges Iraq and Syria: The Euphrates Dispute', *Journal of South Asian and Middle Eastern Studies*, vol. 16, 1993; author's interviews with Mehmet Ali Birand (a) and with Morton Abramowitz (a).

74 R. Olson, *Turkey's Relations with Iran, Syria, Israel, and Russia, 1991–2000. The Kurdish and Islamist Questions*, Costa Mesa, CA: Mazda Publishers, 2001, pp. 11–13; S. Bölükbaşı, 'Turkey Copes with Revolutionary Iran', *Journal of South Asian and Middle Eastern Studies*, vol. 13, 1989.

75 Lesser, *Southern Region Perspectives*, pp. 28, 29, 33.

76 A. L. Karaosmanoğlu, 'European Security and Turkey in a Changing Strategic Environment', *Year Book 1989*, Athens: Hellenic Foundation for Defense and Foreign Policy, 1990.

77 Author's interview with Ambassador Özdem Sanberk, permanent undersecretary at the Turkish Ministry of Foreign Affairs (1991–95), foreign policy chief adviser (1985–7) to Prime Minister Turgut Özal.

78 Ian O. Lesser, *Changes in the Character of East-West Relations: Implications for NATO's Southern Region*, Santa Monica, CA: RAND, June 1990, p. vi and *passim*.

79 Lesser, *Changes in the Character of East-West Relations*. Also statement by Hikmet Çetin, foreign minister of Turkey (1991–3), quoted in S. Ilkin, 'Les tentatives de coopération économique en mer Noire', *Cahiers d'Études sur la Méditerranée orientale et le Monde Turco-Iranien*, vol. 15, 1993, p. 53.

80 On Ankara's fears that Turkey might become isolated in the periphery of the Western world in the late 1940s and how these fears made the Turkish governments energetically seek Turkey's accession to the North Atlantic Treaty, see E. Athanassopoulou, *Turkey: Anglo American Security Interests, 1945–1952. The First Enlargement of NATO*, London: Frank Cass, 1999, p. 120.

81 For the relevant literature see n. 70 in this chapter.

82 See, among others, Sayari, 'Changing European Security Environment and Gulf Crisis', pp. 13–14; Aydin, *Turkish Foreigh Policy.*
83 Lesser, *Southern Region Perspectives*, p. 31.
84 Lesser, *Southern Region Perspectives*, p. 31
85 Lesser, *Southern Region Perspectives*, p. 31
86 Z. Öniş and S. B. Webb, *Political Economy of Policy Reform in Turkey in the 1980s*, Washington DC: The World Bank, Policy Research Working Papers, WPS 1059, 1992, pp. 15–16.
87 Author's interview with Selim Egeli. Ankara's initiative to launch the Black Sea Economic Co-operation (1992) was a good example of the economic and political ambitions of many a member of the Turkish political and business elites in the beginning of the post–Cold War decade, E. Athanassopoulou, 'Turkey and the Black Sea Initiative', in R. Gillespie (ed.), *Mediterranean Politics*, London: Pinter Publishers, vol. 1, 1994, p. 131.
88 Author's interview with Selim Egeli. On the economic promises made by the Americans, see later on in this chapter.
89 Robins, *Turkey and the Middle East*, p. 110.
90 Author's interviews with Morton Abramowitz and Cengiz Çandar (b) and (c);
91 Aydin, *Turkish Foreign Policy*, p. 25.
92 The White House, memorandum of telephone conversation, telephone call to President Turgut Ozal of Turkey, 3 August 1990.
93 The White House, memorandum of telephone conversation, telephone call to President Turgut Ozal of Turkey, 4 August 1990, available online at http://bushlibrary.tamu.edu/research/pdfs/memcons_telcons/1990-08-04–Ozal.pdf (accessed 30 March 2010).
94 The White House, memorandum of telephone conversation, telephone call to President Turgut Ozal of Turkey, 4 August 1990.
95 Author's interviews with Cengiz Çandar (b) and (c).
96 When the United Nations Security Council adopted resolution SCR-661 (6 August 1990), which imposed international sanctions on Iraq, the Turkish government announced its decision to implement it and on the same day banned the loading of Iraqi oil from its Mediterranean port at the end of the pipelines, although it did not actually shut the pipelines, Aydin, *Turkish Foreign Policy*, pp. 21–2.
97 According to Morton Abramowitz, although the delay was primarily related to Özal's fear of political cost, in the event that the war did not happen there were also bargaining tactics involved. Author's interview with Morton Abramowitz (b).
98 On a more detailed presentation of the rewards Turkey reaped, see *Wall Street Journal*, 3 August 1990; *The Independent*, 16 August 1990; *Middle East International* (*MEI*), 28 September, 12 October 1990, 25 January 1991; J. Bulloch and H. Morris, *Saddam's War*, London: Faber and Faber, 1991, pp. 154–5; Robins, *Turkey and the Middle East*, p. 71; Sayari, 'Changing European Security Environment and Gulf Crisis', p. 19; Aydin, *Turkish Foreign Policy*, p. 36. Aydin also offers an account of the items on Özal's wish list, p. 73.
99 See Chapter 5 in this book.
100 Gabelnick *et al.*, *Arming Repression*.
101 Author's interview with Hasan Köni; also, H. Köni, 'Gulf Savaşı Sonrasında Orta Doğunun Durumu' in *Değişen Dünyada Türkiye ve Türk Dünyası Sempozyumu*, Ankara: Hacettepe Üniversitesi Atatürk İlkeleri ve İnkılap Tarihi Enstitüsü, 1993, pp. 48–9.
102 United States Department of Defense, *Conduct of the Persian Gulf War: Final Report to Congress, 1991*, Responsibility Sharing, Appendix P, Washington, DC: US Government Printing Office, 1992.
103 E. Laipson, 'Thinking About the Mediterranean', *Mediterranean Quarterly*, vol. 1. 1990; D. Ruiz Palmer, 'Paradigms Lost: A Retrospective Assessment of the

NATO-Warsaw Pact Military Competition in the Alliance's Southern Region', *Comparative Strategy*, vol. 9, 1990.

104 Robins, *Turkey and the Middle East*, pp. 71, 73; Sayari, 'Changing European Security Environment and Gulf Crisis', p. 14; Aydin, *Turkish Foreign Policy*, pp. 25, 75; Hale, *Turkish Foreign Policy*, p. 224.

105 Aydin, *Turkish Foreign Policy*, p. 75.

106 *Info Türk*, 15th Year – No. 176, June 1991, available online at http://www.info-turk.be/176.E.htm (accessed 23 August 2006); M. B. Aykan, 'Turkish Perspectives on Turkish-US Relations Concerning Persian Gulf Security in the Post-Cold War Era', *Middle East Journal*, vol. 50, 1996, p. 148.

107 Lesser, *Bridge or Barrier?*, pp.34–6.

108 Author's interview with Morton Abramowitz (a); also, M. I. Abramowitz, 'Dateline Ankara: Turkey After Özal', *Foreign Policy*, no. 91, 1993, p. 179.

109 Hale, *Turkish Foreign Policy*, pp. 219–20; Aydin, *Turkish Foreign Policy*, pp. 69–70.

110 The White House, memorandum of conversation with President Ozal of Turkey, 20 November 1990, Kleber Center, Paris. Özal also provided another strategic reason: he argued that the deployment of Turkish troops to Saudi Arabia would make Saddam doubt that Turkey would attack from the North, ibid. It is not clear to what extent Özal personally accepted these arguments, for it has been pointed out that he was keen to deploy the troops and apparently it was only after he realised that Turkish forces would make no 'meaningful difference in the build up' that he changed his mind, Aydin, *Turkish Foreign Policy*, pp. 31, 35, n. 62.

111 *Milliyet*, 18 January 1991; *The Independent*, 18 January 1991.

112 Aydin, *Turkish Foreign Policy*, p. 45, n. 5.

113 I. O. Lesser, 'Turkey and the West after the Gulf War', *International Spectator*, vol. 72, 1992, p. 35.

Part III

The 1990s

New strategic games, old ideas

5 Period of uncertainty

An 'enhanced partnership'?

The last Bush administration security assistance request for Turkey for fiscal year 1992 amounted to $725 million in military aid and $74.5 million in economic aid.[1] The request, which did not essentially deviate from the levels of the 1991 fiscal year, in the words of the administration was designed 'to assist the Turks in continuing the multi-year program to modernize their air defence forces, and also in offsetting part of their military costs and economic losses [due to the Gulf War and the sanctions regime], thereby deepening our relationship with a key partner for regional stability.'[2] However, under the immense pressures of a huge federal budget deficit and a slow-moving US economy that showed no signs of recovery Congress authorized $575 million in total security assistance (of which $520 million were in the form of a grant).[3] So the promise Bush gave Özal while the Gulf crisis was unfolding that the annual security assistance to Turkey would not fall below $545 million was honoured. Nonetheless, for the Turks it was the first big disappointment within the context of the bilateral relationship and a sure sign that the Turkey-US honeymoon that followed the Gulf War was over.

In early February 1992 Süleyman Demirel, Turkey's new prime minister, paid an official visit to Washington. On the occasion of his departure ceremony President Bush referred to an 'enhanced partnership' between Turkey and the US.[4] But even though Turkey was still receiving significant security assistance, primarily for its role in the enforcement of the no-fly zone over Northern Iraq via Operation Provide Comfort II, Bush's rhetoric was unmatched by reality.

Studies of US–Turkey relations in the post-post-Cold War decade argue that Ankara's co-operation in the Gulf War revived the US strategic interest in Turkey and strengthened the relationship. They point out that at the end of the 1990s the alliance remained strong and relations grew very warm, despite tensions and problems that arose in the middle of the decade. These were mainly due to differing perspectives over Northern Iraq and to the fact that the Clinton administration initially gave more attention to human rights than to hard strategic issues.[5] But the history of the renewal of US interest in Turkey needs a more careful analysis than it has been given until now. The revived interest has been explained almost solely in broad terms of Turkey's geopolitics, while other important elements generally have been overlooked. So it is worth looking at the evolution of the US interest in Turkey in some detail, in order to bring to life these elements, which most studies of US–Turkey relations of this period leave unexplored.[6]

In the early 1990s, despite the appearance of close relations, US and Turkish interests were seriously diverging, while the US strategic stake in Turkey, although still there, was growing thinner not stronger. In fact, as Alan Makovsky, a well-informed analyst of US–Turkey relations, points out, during the first two years of the Clinton administration many US officials considered Turkey 'a declining asset.'[7] Özal's proposal for a free-trade agreement, which he had made during his Washington visit just a few months after the end of the Gulf War, had fallen on deaf ears.[8] Nor did his effort to convince the Bush administration to institutionalize and expand the bilateral relationship meet with any success.[9] On top of this, already by the end of 1991 US–Turkey military co-operation had begun to decrease. The US had unilaterally decided to withdraw their military personnel and nuclear weapons from two airbases in Turkey and in December 1991 it was announced that eight of the twelve US bases in Turkey were going to close down by the end of 1993.[10] It has been noted that the closing down of bases that a strong power holds in the territory of a weaker state, as long as the latter does not mind their presence, more often than not is viewed by the weak state as a relaxation of the security commitment offered by the stronger power. Furthermore, the relinquishing of strategic bases also means that the bargaining power of the weak state within the context of its relationship with the stronger power has decreased.[11] It was certainly in this light that the Turkish political and military elites viewed the reduction of the permanent US presence in their country.[12] Under these circumstances, in 1993 the Turks decided to renegotiate with the new US administration the framework of the bilateral security co-operation, in other words the Defense and Economic Co-operation Agreement, which since 1990 had been automatically renewed every year. Inevitably the two allies resumed exhausting negotiations to determine the future terms of their co-operation. Soon it became clear that the Turks sought to secure a US guarantee to their security and were after political pledges of support vis-á-vis Kurdish separatist activities in Turkey, terrorist acts and in the event of aggression from Syria or Iraq.[13] But the Turks' primary goal was the satisfactory continuation of military co-operation, which for the Turks consisted of three things: security assistance; sales of advanced US military equipment and training programmes for the Turkish military; and US co-operation in the field of defence industry.[14] While Turkish political and security elites continued to fix their minds on defence autarky, Turkey still depended heavily on imports to meet needs for basic military equipment, systems and spare parts (79 per cent of these had to be imported) as well as military technology for the development of an indigenous defence industry and the US had the lion's share in Turkey's military line of trade.[15] The Turks were fully aware that Congress's interest in the military support of Turkey was declining,[16] but in spite of this awareness, or rather because of it, they insisted that a commitment concerning the annual levels of security assistance to Turkey should be incorporated in the text of the DECA.[17]

At the end of the day the results of the negotiations were disappointing to the Turks.[18] The US administration was reluctant to offer formal, visible support to Ankara mainly in relation to the Kurdish insurgency, but also when it came to the Turks' regional security concerns vis-à-vis Iraq and Syria.[19] Moreover, in Congress the post-Cold War reassessment of foreign aid and the process of aid cuts (including aid to Turkey) was in full process. For fiscal year 1993 total security assistance to Turkey was maintained at $575 million, although big cuts were anticipated in the future. But there was a change of major significance. The bulk of this assistance ($450 million) was given in the form of loans at interest rates lower than those of the market, but as from fiscal year 1994 market rates were to be introduced.[20] Fiscal year 1993 witnessed the end of outright grants to Turkey under the Pentagon's Foreign Military Financing (FMF) programme, which was designed as a direct subsidy for US military exports and from which Turkey had benefited enormously up until then. Between fiscal years 1988 and 1992 (inclusive) under the FMF programme Turkey received almost $2.4 billion, of which almost $1.8 billion were in the form of grants.[21]

Naturally, these changes were viewed in Ankara with a mixture of indignation and apprehension. It was not only that $450 million were added to Turkey's multi-billion foreign debt, as Morton Abramowitz remarked,[22] and more specifically that they swelled Turkey's debt to the US, which had been accumulated from the purchase of military equipment.[23] It was also a blow for the Turks' ambitious military modernization programme, which essentially depended on broadly defined US security assistance. Turkey was spending 12.4 per cent of its annual budget on this programme even though the Cold War was over. In fact, the push towards modernization that seriously began in 1985 with the reorganization of the defence industry acquired a bigger momentum in the early 1990s. The Gulf War partly contributed to this. According to a number of defence analysts, the allied operations impressed Turkey's military leadership. As a result, they had a major impact on the reassessment of Turkey's military needs after the Gulf War and the dissolution of the Soviet Union. New emphasis was given to the development of advanced weapons, particularly in the field of air defence, including the acquisition of Patriot missiles and additional F-16s, both of which emerged as leading priorities.[24] Turkey's 1990 defence budget was double that of 1989 and stood at $3.4 billion (that was before Saddam Hussein invaded Kuwait). In 1991 it further increased by almost 50 per cent to reach $4.8 billion.[25]

It was a spectacular rise particularly when compared to NATO's defence expenditure trends. In fact, between 1985 and 1996 Turkey's military expenditure annually increased by at least 14 per cent, while that of its European NATO allies annually decreased by 3 per cent during the same period.[26]

The top brass, whose dominating role in the formulation of Turkey's foreign and security policy continued and even grew bigger after the end of the Cold War,[27] gave a host of reasons – albeit some contradictory – in order to justify the huge increases in the defence budget. They pointed to the instability in the Caucasus and the new threats to Turkey's security coming from the Middle East. According to the Turkish general staff, '"Turkey was surrounded by the Bermuda Triangle" of the Balkans, the Caucasus and the Middle East'.[28] Furthermore, although Turkey's NATO allies were in the process of downsizing their military establishments, the Turkish general staff argued that increased defence spending was necessary because Turkey would be called to play a central role within the European pillar of NATO's defence. At the same time they expressed doubts about whether NATO could be relied upon to safeguard Turkey's security against threats that did not fall within the traditional East-West conflict,[29] which in their minds only highlighted the seriousness of the threats surrounding the country.[30]

A lot has been written about the new security challenges facing Turkey in the early post-Gulf War period. Yet a sober examination of Turkish leaders' security concerns at the time would rather agree with Ambassador Abramowitz's conclusion that 'from a security perspective Turkey's situation is the best in its 70-year history. … Turks still love to bemoan their bad neighborhood, but their neighbors look a little threadbare.'[31] In other words, a lot of the security concerns that had distressed the Turks around the time of the Gulf War and while the Soviet Union was still in existence[32] should have subsided after the Gulf War.[33] Iraq's military machine was heavily damaged as a result of the war. Iran was trying to restore its economy and military capabilities, and it would be some time before it could pose a serious military threat to Turkey. Syria was still interfering, like Iran, in Turkey's domestic affairs by supporting the PKK, but despite its military capabilities it did not represent a military threat as it was faced with enormous economic problems and most importantly it was left without its Soviet patron. On top of all this Turkey's traditional threat from the north was becoming a memory. The Turks no longer shared a common border with Russia while at the same time bilateral relations with Moscow were developing fast. In fact, not only was Turkey importing natural gas from Russia but it was the first NATO country to sign an agreement to purchase military equipment (1992). In short, Turkey was surrounded by troublesome but much weaker states, while one could argue that militarily it had 'become the leading power in the area'.[34]

Turkey's increased defence expenditure clearly was not only related to external security concerns – real, perceived or constructed – but also to the major internal security problem of the country, in other words the Kurdish uprising. This had intensified as a result of the power vacuum that emerged in Northern Iraq in the aftermath of the Gulf War. So, the strengthening of the operational capabilities of the Turkish armed forces that would allow extended operations deeply into Northern Iraq where the Kurdish insurgents found shelter emerged as a top priority.[35] Furthermore, as it's been said, 'perhaps inevitably, improvements and acquisitions generated further appetites that went far beyond the needs of a counter-insurgency land force'[36] into acquiring military capabilities that would allow Turkey to project force as an independent security actor in the area.[37]

Security co-operation

By the time the Clinton administration had been in power for almost a year it was becoming clear that the capital which had been generated by Turkey's participation in the Gulf War had been exhausted in Washington. True, the new administration was against any further security assistance cuts. The main reason was that the US continued to need the Incirlik airbase for the enforcement of the no-fly zone over Northern Iraq.[38] Also, US arms industries were lobbying hard for the flow of arms sales to Turkey to be maintained.[39] However, U.S. officials thought that the need for immediate access to Turkish airbases would not last long as in the early 1990s the prevailing idea in Washington was that it was only a matter of time before Saddam Hussein's regime collapsed.[40] Moreover while the Clinton administration was undoubtedly interested in maintaining an active strategic co-operation with Turkey it was, at the same time, unresponsive to Turkey's concerns and calls for a more diversified strategic relationship. Furthermore, whereas the Bush administration had been sympathetic towards the Turks, the early Clinton administration adopted a posture of reluctance which at times would even turn confrontational. When President Özal died (17 April 1993) neither President Clinton nor any other senior US government official attended the funeral, although for those Americans who knew Turkey and the Middle East Özal was perhaps the best friend that the US had in the Muslim world.[41] In fact, the US was represented by a middle-ranking official, Clifton Wharton, undersecretary of state, and a *former* secretary of state, James Baker. It was an omission that deeply insulted the Turks.[42] But it was not the only one. Warren Christopher, secretary of state in the first Clinton administration, officially visited Turkey once in June 1993 and never again, although he was regularly travelling to the region because of the peace process negotiations.

The lukewarm stance toward Turkey during the first two years of the Clinton administration was due to a combination of reasons. For one it reflected the uncertainty of the new US government's foreign policy in the face of a fluid and complex post-Cold World international environment. As the emphasis of US security policy shifted from global ideological confrontation to the need to respond to many diverse threats, the US foreign and security policy was formulated very slowly and often lacked conviction.[43] But there were also elements specifically related to Turkey that accounted for the non-engaged stance of the administration.[44] Following the dissolution of the Soviet Union many US officials believed that Turkey could offer a counter model to that of Iran for the post-Soviet independent Turkic states in Central Asia and the Caucasus and could emerge as a pole of Western influence in the area. But already by the end of 1992 this idea had collapsed. There were many reasons accounting for this.[45] First, Moscow's influence over the new states remained strong. Second, the Turks lacked the necessary resources that would have enabled them to successfully perform this role. Third, it was quickly realized that the advancement of Western interests in the area did not depend on mediators. While Washington surrendered hopes that Turkey could become an influential force in the post-Soviet countries, Clinton's administration grew steadily vexed at the Turks' increasing lack of co-operation over Northern Iraq. US officials had felt confident that they could coerce the Turks into unambiguously endorsing the continuation of the presence of Operation Provide Comfort. But to their great annoyance they did not get exactly what they wanted. The Turks refused to reassure the Americans by assuming an open-ended commitment to the continuation of the Operation. Instead, they offered their co-operation only begrudgingly and according to a formula which provided that the continuation of the operation had to be renewed every six months.[46] Essentially, the alliance that the Bush administration had put together on the eve of the war was collapsing. So, in Turkey, as in Jordan, Russia and also France, reservations regarding the US policy in Northern Iraq were on the rise.[47] The Turkish state, which was confronted with a rising Kurdish insurgency, was deeply concerned because Iraq's Kurds showed solidarity to Turkey's Kurdish insurgents. This meant that Kurdish rebels could hide in Northern Iraq when they had to flee with the Turkish armed forces in hot pursuit, and basically they were using Northern Iraq as a base to launch attacks against Turkish targets. Even worse the de facto autonomy of the Kurds in Northern Iraq was seen in Ankara as a dangerous precedent given Turkey's big Kurdish population. Ankara's apprehension was magnified following the October 1992 declaration for the creation of a federated state of Kurdistan in the liberated part of the Iraq. So, the Turks endeavoured to better seal their border with Northern Iraq, while at the same time they sought to develop political and economic ties with Saddam Hussein's regime and began to favour the return of his control over Northern Iraq. Turkey's efforts to build bridges with the regime in Bagdad took place exactly at the moment when the Clinton administration was resisting European, Russian and Arab pressure to moderate Iraq's international isolation.[48] Under these circumstances the renewal by the Turkish parliament of the mandate for Operation Provide Comfort became 'one of the more contentious issues in the bilateral relations with the US.'[49] The Turks overall resented the Operation because it was thought to facilitate the creation of a Kurdish state. But this was not the only reason that inhibited smooth co-operation between Ankara and Washington over this issue. The Turkish military was using the issue of the continuation of the Operation as a bargaining chip. Hence it preferred 'to let the mission hang in the balance until the parliamentary vote, thereby increasing its own leverage with Washington to extract more concessions for further extensions of the operation.'[50] These bargaining tactics, of which the Americans were only too aware, debased the bilateral dialogue and turned it into a mutual blackmailing exercise.[51] In the end apparently it was found that progress could be made on the basis of a rather general agreement. Apparently in return for the Turks' hosting the Operation the US would allow the Turkish military to launch operations in Northern Iraq against Kurdish insurgents who found shelter there. It would also support Turkey's efforts to join the European Union.[52]

The escalation of human rights violations by the Turkish state as the Kurdish uprising flared up again in 1992 and the conflict grew in intensity added another thorny issue to bilateral relations.[53] The US media chronicled Ankara's human rights violations and harshly criticized the Turkish government. Human rights violations in Turkey resonated primarily with a number of congressmen but a number of State Department officials also became concerned.[54] Cascading news of bombing of Kurdish villages and the accumulation of reports of human rights violations and the laws of war mobilized members of Congress who sought to reduce credits to Turkey and ban sales of certain weapons to the Turks. In May 1994 the House initially adopted a resolution calling for the withholding of 25 per cent of aid to Turkey for fiscal 1995 until the secretary of state reported on allegations of human rights violations by the Turkish state. On 4 July a caustic opinion piece in the *New York Times* under the title 'The Kurdish Killing Fields' drew attention to that fact that the US was arming Turkey and providing it with economic assistance.[55] In early August 1994 Congress decided that 10 per cent of the $364.5 million of FMF loans to Turkey for fiscal year 1995 be withheld until the secretary of state in consultation with the secretary of defense reported to the committees on appropriations about allegations of abuses against civilians as well as on the situation on Cyprus. Furthermore, concern was expressed over the use of US-supplied weapons in the war against the Kurds. Congress required that any agreement for the sale or provision of any weapons to Turkey or grants of any excess defence articles should be subject to the condition that they would not be used in violation of international law. On 23 August President Clinton signed the bill.[56] The human rights issue to some extent conditioned the Clinton administration's relations with Turkey, although the US government preferred to follow a cautious, conservative i.e. non-confrontational policy.[57]

The question of banning the sales of certain weapons (cluster bombs and attack helicopters later on) on Turkey's shopping list due to concerns that they might be used against Kurdish civilians led to a debate within the State Department and between State and Defense. A number of State Department officials mainly in the Office of Humanitarian Affairs and Human Rights argued that US policy towards Turkey ought to set some limits until the Kurdish issue was resolved. Opponents of the ban advanced the argument that if the sales did not go ahead the strategic relationship would suffer and the effect on the Operation Provide Comfort mandate would be detrimental.[58] Efforts to link military sales and human rights concerns resulted in delays in the delivery of military equipment to Turkey from 1994. Apparently these were due to the fact that 'the State Department had not submitted arms transfers for congressional approval, having been discouraged by Members who intend to disapprove.'[59]

Naturally, Ankara was greatly annoyed as human rights concerns stirred congressional action and affected governmental decisions. But Turkish leaders were also furious because their Kurdish policy, which they considered strictly internal, was exposed to public scrutiny and criticism in the US.[60] For example in December 1994 the *New York Times* reported that the Turkish 'government has turned its Kurdish policy over to the army which is seeking a purely military solution. In its war on Kurdish separatists it has turned southeastern Turkey into a killing field, destroying villages and driving out the civilian population.'[61]

Furthermore, efforts to link human rights with the sales of advanced military equipment raised new concerns over the future of the Turkish military modernization programme. For the Turks this linkage and the subsequent delays in the export of specified military articles amounted to a de facto mini embargo that undermined their military modernization efforts.[62] The State Department refused to accept that a mini embargo existed, but it did acknowledge that human rights concerns influenced all decisions.[63] For sure the Turkish military was determined to turn to alternative arms exporters like China, Russia and even South Korea to overcome the limits on the use of arms imposed by the US (but also by Germany in many instances).[64] But the Turkish general staff had a clear preference for US systems and believed that the success of the military modernization programme greatly depended on US advanced weapons.[65] On top of all this Ankara regarded limits on the use of weapons as directly undermining the war effort against the Kurdish insurgency in the southeast.[66]

In the mid 1990s as tension over these issues built the Turks 'raised the question of whether Turkey was regarded as "an ally or a rogue state"'.[67] The question underscored the displeasure and surprise they felt because of Washington's less accommodating stance. Three years after the Gulf War only relations between the US and the Turkish military remained close and warm.[68] In the final analysis the days of the Turks' easy success in Washington were over. In the new international security environment Turkey's strategic importance was not clearly defined in Washington (with the exception of hosting Operation Provide Comfort). Therefore in a sense it was up to Turkey to show the US where its strategic value lay.[69]

The present in the past

Had it not been for the interplay of a number of new factors the tension in the bilateral relationship might not have been reversed. But at the end of 1994 the Clinton administration's new increasing emphasis on 'the security components of foreign policy' that 'had the ring of traditional American foreign policy goals' and also resulted in a greater interest and involvement in regional affairs cleared the way for a new beginning.[70] Of equal, perhaps greater, importance was the entry of new personnel into the bureaucratic mix.[71] One other crucial factor was the Turks' decision to deepen relations and develop strategic ties with Israel. But to better understand the latter point we need to first turn our attention to the 1980s.

In the 1970s Richard Perle created a name for himself in Washington not only as a brilliant young security analyst with neoconservative leanings, but also as a very dynamic presence within the context of congressional operations. As an aide (1969–80) to Democratic Senator Henry Jackson he played an essential role in the campaign to build support within Congress in favour of the 1974 Jackson-Vanik amendment,[72] which passed to almost everyone's surprise. 'No one expected Jackson to succeed in such a blatant revival of the Cold War' for the passage of the amendment was viewed as threatening Nixon's delicate programme of détente.[73]

This success was not due to luck. It was produced by the hard work of Perle and Morris Amitay (another Senate aide who shared Perle's views), their excellent understanding of the internal workings of Congress and eventually their mobilization of the Jewish-American community leadership, which exercised pressure on undecided legislators.[74] According to James Goldberg

> the campaign for the amendment was the first of a series of American-Jewish legislative initiatives that transformed the Jewish lobby into a Washington powerhouse during the 1970s. … The Jewish lobby, for years a central element in coalitions of the liberal left, now became an important factor on the national-security-minded right.[75]

When Perle assumed the office of assistant secretary of defense in the Reagan administration, the clout of Jewish lobbyists over foreign policy issues was recognized in Washington and during the course of the 1980s it would grow much more. As the US–Turkey relationship was bedevilled due to congressional actions, particularly because of cuts in the amounts of aid requested by the executive, Perle saw the US administration and Turkey as allies 'in the long-term effort to prevail with the Congress.'[76] So the Turks, with the objective of increasing Turkey's leverage with Congress in mind, turned their attention towards the pro-Israel lobby in the mid 1980s.[77] In fact, soon after Özal became prime minister leading members of the Jewish community in Turkey were instructed to regularly travel to Washington and ask the Jewish-American lobby groups 'to be kind to Turkey.'[78] Before long the idea that Turkey should develop relations with Israel was spawned in Washington apparently through the synergy of Perle and Şükrü Elekdağ,[79] Turkey's dynamic ambassador to Washington (1979–89), who was eagerly looking for ways to strengthen Turkey's voice in the US capital.[80] It was a strategy which could contribute to strengthening the US administration and Turkey vis-à-vis Congress but would also benefit Israel. This was in accordance with the longstanding idea within US foreign policy circles that co-operation between the two countries in the Middle East that were friendly to the US could only be beneficial to US interests.[81] For their part, the Israeli governments since Ben-Gurion were keen to develop relations with Turkey in order to strengthen their security, for Turkey was a non-Arab country in the perimeter of their Arab enemies. But since the 1960s all Turkish governments had kept co-operation with Israel at a minimum as they wished to advance relations with the Arab regimes.[82] So, for over twenty years relations between the two states were sustained through a low-key bilateral dialogue conducted away from the light of publicity.

Prime Minister Özal was quick to realize that a way to reach Congress was to use Turkey's relations with Israel to influence 'the "powerful" (as the Turks see it) Jewish lobby in the United States'.[83] So, the decision to gradually develop ties with the Israelis was made around the mid 1980s and as a result the bilateral relationship began to grow, slowly but steadily. Undoubtedly the new Turkish policy was facilitated by changes in the Middle East. Already some contact between Egypt, Jordan, Morocco and Israel was registered. Even more important, the Iran-Iraq war had diverted the attention of Turkey's two radical neighbours away from the Arab-Israeli conflict. Furthermore, as George Gruen aptly points out, the low oil prices made Turkey less vulnerable to Arab pressures.[84]

As part of Turkey's new policy toward Israel it was established that Özal should meet with the leaders of the Jewish community every time he visited the US.[85] In September 1986 the Turkish government, responding to personal calls made by the American-Jewish community to Özal,[86] de facto upgraded the level of its diplomatic mission from the lowest level when Ekrem Güvendiren, a diplomat with ambassadorial rank, was appointed second secretary to Tel Aviv. It was an important step because it reinstated relations to the level existing before 1981 when the Turkish government downgraded the level of its representation in protest at Israel's annexation of East Jerusalem and the decision of the Knesset to declare Jerusalem the capital of the state. The action of the Turkish government clearly demonstrated to Israel and the American-Jewish community the Turks' commitment to turn a new page in their relations with Israel, even though they still preferred to move cautiously (hence the upgrading was not de jure). Turkish politicians began to officially visit Israel, and in late September 1987 the first diplomatic meeting between Turkey's and Israel's foreign ministers took place, but not in Turkey or Israel as one would have expected. It took place in New York. The meeting between Foreign Ministers Shimon Peres and Vahit Malih Halefoğlu was organized on the sidelines of the 42nd annual session of the UN General Assembly. As far as one can reasonably judge, the Turkish government aimed to achieve maximum publicity among the American-Jewish community by choosing New York for the 'unprecedented meeting'.[87] The Turkish government was so anxious to make sure that the meeting would send the right message to the Jewish community that at the press conference that followed Turkey's ambassador to the UN stated his government's position without beating about the bush. Peres, he said, wanted Turkey to assist Israel to improve its ties with the Islamic world. The Turks, for their part, wanted Israel to say a good word about Turkey to the Jewish-American community.[88] Actually, there was no need for the Turks to say half as much. At the first news of the scheduled meeting the reaction of Thomas Dine, staff director at AIPAC, was appropriately cynical. 'What is it that the Turks want from us?' was his first thought.[89] After the meeting, in an interview with the Jewish Telegraphic Agency, Inal Batu, the Turkish foreign ministry spokesman, underlined the significance that Turkey's shift in policy had for Israel: 'We demonstrated to the whole Moslem world that Israel is no longer taboo'.[90] In the months and years to come sometimes the Turks would also resort to a veiled threat concerning the damage that could be done to Turkish-Israeli relations if Turkey did not get the right response from the United States.[91]

Organizing Turkey's lobby

At the end of Reagan's second term in office the political clout of Jewish-American lobby groups continued to rise. It was a reflection of the continuous transformation of the US foreign policy–making system that had already begun in the early 1970s – and was going to carry on into the post-Cold War era – 'from the relatively closed and presidentially dominated system of the early cold war into a more open, contentious and pluralistic system'[92] that offered organized interest groups more opportunities to influence the process. It was at this moment in time that the Turks decided to organize their representation in the US capital to a different level that would better fit these changes. The initiative for action again came from Washington, not Ankara. It was Richard Perle who in May 1988 during a meeting with Özal in New York sold him the idea of the need for a registered agent that could officially lobby for Turkey in Washington.[93] For Perle it was crystal clear that the Turkish government ought to modernize the methods it used in order to advance its interests in the US. He recalls that he told Özal:

> There's something else you really need that you don't have. You're not well represented in Washington. You send over ambassadors who are trained in the old school, probably unchanged since Ottoman times, and their narrow focus is on government-to-government relations. They don't communicate well with the American people. And Americans are largely ignorant of Turkey. You need people who can explain Turkey a lot better than your ambassador. And it's not just the current ambassador; it's going to be every ambassador. They're not change orientated.[94]

Perle did not only offer general advice. He specifically suggested to Özal not to hire the services of a big public relations firm, which would be expensive but would not be very effective. Instead, said he, the Turks should go for a small firm that represented only Turkey. By all accounts this was sound advice. But also as Weisman remarks it was obvious that Perle, who had recently resigned from his position in the Reagan government, 'was pitching himself as Turkey's man in Washington'.[95] Perle recalls that Özal loved the idea.[96] So International Advisors Inc. (IAI) (1989–94) was established by Douglas Feith as a foreign registered agency of Turkey. Its stated objective according to the *Wall Street Journal* was to assist in the efforts for the appropriation of US military and economic assistance to Turkey.[97]

The establishment of IAI was essentially another move within the context of the design to register the assistance of the American-Jewish lobby. Actually IAI was more than a registered agency. It became a link between Turkey and conservative members of Congress and the pro-Israel lobby.[98] Perle himself was careful not to have his name directly linked with IAI's activities as federal regulations prohibit former US government employees from representing foreign governments as soon as they leave government service. So he did not have any shares in it but he offered his services as a consultant, reportedly for a handsome fee.[99] But Douglas Feith,[100] a lawyer, who formed IAI had worked with Perle in the past and was along with Perle part of the same network of like-minded individuals. Feith belonged to the group of neoconservatives that was spawned in Senator Jackson's office in the 1970s and which revolved around Perle, the senator's aide.[101] When Perle became assistant secretary of defense Faith served as a special counsel to him (1982–84) before he was named deputy assistant secretary of defense for negotiations policy, a position he held until he left the Pentagon in 1986. When Perle recruited him to establish IAI Feith was already a partner of the Faith and Zell law firm, which represented high-profile customers including big arms exporting companies like Lockheed Martin. At the time it was widely believed in Washington that Feith's interest in Turkey had more to do with its importance to Israel's security interests rather than those of the US.[102] Noticeably, one of the first members of the IAI board of consultants was Morris Amitay,[103] one of the architects of the Jackson-Vanik amendment.[104] Amitay was an important player inside the world of the pro-Israel lobby. As executive director of the American Israeli Public Affairs Committee (AIPAC) in the second half of the 1970s, Amitay was responsible for its transformation 'beyond recognition' from a small, unsophisticated pro-Israel lobbying organization to a modern, extremely effective lobbying machine that would emerge as one of the major forces in Washington power politics, according to Goldberg.[105]

In 1989, just a few months after its establishment, IAI joined forces with activists of the American-Jewish community and the Israeli embassy in order to kill a proposed Senate resolution that called for 24 April to be declared the date officially commemorating the Armenian genocide.[106] It was the first visible (and eventually successful) co-operation between Turkey and Israel in Washington at a time when a growing number of American-Jewish legislators were becoming particularly active in Congress in support of Israel.

What was perhaps more important was that, to a large extent as a result of Perle's initiatives, a Turkey-supporting network was gradually being formed. In time it would grow bigger and would include a large number of former senior

US officials and 'many prominent American Jews – mostly conservatives' (many of them ex-government officials), who lobbied on Turkey's behalf emphasizing Turkey's strategic importance to the US and Israel.[107] The number of the latter would grow significantly in the 1990s as Turkey moved even closer to Israel. Alan Weisman notes that the stated reason for all the attention they began to give to Turkey was that while the Armenian and Greek lobbies in the US were organized and effective, Turkey had nothing similar to compete with. Therefore, the argument went, the US interest demanded that power circles were more and better informed about Turkey. But according to Weisman the backstory was that the advancement of Turkish interests yielded a lot of financial rewards for the 'consultants, lobbyists and defense contractors'.[108] For sure Weisman's view is in line with the reality of the lobbying industry in Washington. The large amounts of aid for Turkey that the executive had to request Congress to authorise every year meant that helping to secure congressional support was a very profitable enterprise. And of course the bigger the amounts approved the more came back to those involved in Turkey's support. Yet this entirely cynical view oversimplifies the motives that guided a lot of Turkey's supporters. At least a number of them, and Perle was a good example, considered Turkey an important strategic asset for the US, while others considered Turkey also a strategic asset for Israel.

Notes

1 *Info Türk*, 15th year – no. 176, June 1991, available online at www.info-turk.be/176.E.htm (accessed 23 August 2006).

2 'Fiscal Year 1992 Security Assistance Budget Request by the Honorable Regibald Bartholomew, Under Secretary of State for International Security Affairs', *The DISAM Journal*, Spring 1991, p. 40.

3 D. J. Wamsted, 'Supplemental Funding Requested for Desert Storm and Aid to Israel', *Washington Report on Middle East Affairs*, 26 March 1991, p. 37, available online at www.wrmea.com/backissues/0391/9103037.htm (accessed 14 April 2007); T. Gabelnick, W. D. Hartung, and J. Washburn, with research assistance by M. Ciarrocca, *Arming Repression: U.S. Arms Sales to Turkey during the Clinton Administration*, a joint report of the World Policy Institute and the Federation of American Scientists, October 1999, available online at www.fas.org/asmp/library/reports/turkeyrep.htm (accessed, 4 March 2000), table II.

4 George Bush Public Papers, 'Remarks at the Departure Ceremony for Prime Minister Suleyman Demirel of Turkey', South Lawn, White House, 11 February 1992, George Bush Presidential Library and Museum, available online at www.bushlibrary.tamu.edu (accessed, 10 January 2008).

5 See, among others, Y. Çelik, *Contemporary Turkish Foreign Policy,* Westport, CO: Preager, 1999, p. 78; W. Hale, *Turkish Foreign Policy, 1774–2000*, London: Frank Cass, 2000, pp. 219, 223, 228; K. Kirişci, 'U.S.-Turkish Relations: New Uncertainties in a Renewed Partnership', in B. Rubin and K. Kirişci (eds), *Turkey in World Politics: An Emerging Multiregional Power*, Boulder, CO: Lynne Rienner Publishers, 2001, pp. 129–30, 132 and passim.

6 For a notable exception, see A. Makovsky, 'U.S. Policy toward Turkey: Progress and Problems', in M. Abramowitz (ed.), *Turkey's Transformation and American Policy,* New York: The Century Foundation Press, 2000.

7 Makovsky, 'U.S. Policy toward Turkey', p. 223; O. Kesic, 'American-Turkish Relations at a Crossroads', *Mediterranean Quarterly*, vol. 6, 1995 also suggests that in the early 1990s Turkey's inability to perform the role Washington expected created uncertainty about the future of the bilateral relationship. However, Kesic's analysis lacks a clear time frame.

8 I. O. Lesser, *Bridge or Barrier? Turkey and the West after the Cold War*, Santa Monica, CA: RAND, 1992, p. 38.

9 Author's interview with Morton Abramowitz (a). Also see, M. I. Abramowitz, 'Dateline Ankara: Turkey after Özal', *Foreign Policy*, no. 91, 1993, p. 179.

10 L. Sariibrahimoglu, 'Turkey Seeks Review of US Defence Agreement', *Jane's Defence Weekly*, 30 January 1993, p. 9; M. B. Aykan, 'Turkish Perspectives on Turkish-US Relations Concerning Persian Gulf Security in the Post-Cold War Era', *Middle East Journal*, vol. 50, 1996, pp. 345–6.

11 M. I. Handel, *Weak States in the International System*, London: Frank Cass, 1981, pp. 126–8.

12 *Milliyet*, 22 January 1992, p. 10, quoted in 'General Staff Chief Views Terrorism, U.S. Aid', Foreign Broadcast Information Service, Daily Report, Western Europe [FBIS-WEU], 92–020, 30 January 1992, p. 28. Also author's interviews with Özdem Sanberk, Alan Makovsky (a) and Ian Lesser (a).

13 Aykan, 'Turkish Perspectives', p. 347.

14 Author's interview with Lale Sarıibrahimoğlu; Aykan, 'Turkish Perspectives', p. 347.

15 G. G. Şenesen, 'Mia Axiologisi tou Programmatos Eksyhronismou ton Tourkikon Enoplon Dynameon', in F. Sönmezoğlu (ed.), *Mythos ke Pragmatikotita: Analysi tis Tourkikis Exoterikis Politikis*, Athens: Infognomon, 2001, tomos B, pp. 220, 232, table 4.

16 Lesser, *Bridge or Barrier?*, p. 36.

17 Author's interview with Lale Sarıibrahimoğlu.

18 *Milliyet*, 29 July 1993, quoted in 'U.S. Military Aid, Washington's Approach Viewed', FBIS-WEU, 93-149, 5 August 1993, p. 44; Author's interviews with Lale Sarıibrahimoğlu and Özdem Sanberk. From 1993 DECA was renewed every year automatically, Aykan, 'Turkish Perspectives', p. 345.

19 Aykan, 'Turkish Perspectives', pp. 349–50; Lesser, *Bridge or Barrier?*, pp. 34–5, 39; S. J. Blank, S. C. Pelletiere, W. T. Johnsen, *Turkey's Strategic Position at the Crossroads of World Affairs*, 3 December 1993, Carlisle Barracks, PA: US Army War College, Strategic Studies Institute, passim.

20 *Milliyet*, 2 May 1993; *The New York Times*, 20 May 1993; Gabelnick *et al.*, *Arming Repression*, table II.

21 Gabelnick, *et al.*, *Arming Repression*, table II. In the same period Turkey also received \$.2 billion in grants under the Economic Support Fund (ESF), another US security assistance programme, ibid. Under the ESF programme Turkey continued to receive grants until fiscal year 1997. Between FY 1993 and FY 1997 their total amount was \$.3 billion dollars, ibid.

22 Abramowitz, 'Dateline Ankara', p. 178.

23 Sariibrahimoglu, 'Review of US defence agreement', p. 9.

24 L. Sariibrahimoglu 'Building an Industry: The Turkish Dimension', *Jane's Defence Weekly*, 9 November 1991; Şenesen, 'Axiologisi tou Programmatos Eksyhronismou', p. 222 and passim; Lesser, *Bridge or Barrier?*, pp. 30–31.

25 Lesser, *Bridge or Barrier?*, p.27.

26 Şenesen, 'Axiologisi tou Programmatos Eksyhronismou', p.210.

27 G. Özcan, 'The Military and the Making of Foreign Policy in Turkey', in B. Rubin and K. Kirişci (eds), *Turkey in World Politics: An Emerging Multiregional Power*, Boulder, CO: Lynne Rienner, 2001, p. 13; M. Mufti, *Daring and Caution in Turkish Strategic Culture: Republic at Sea*, Houndmills, Basingstoke: Palgrave, Macmillan, 2009, pp. 91–2.

28 Statement by Lieutenant-General Çevik Bir, the Turkish general staff director of operations, quoted in Jeffrey Vordermark, 'Security Assistance Mission in the Republic of Turkey', *Defense Institute of Security Assistance Management Journal*, 22 December 2003, available online at www.thefreelibrary.com/Security+assistance+mission+in+the+Republic+of+Turkey.-a0116525416 (accessed 10 March 2007).

29 Lesser, *Bridge or Barrier?*, pp. vi–vii; [*Turkey*] *Briefing*, 20 September 1993, issue 956, p. 15. During the Gulf War it emerged that NATO's assistance was not automatically guaranteed, as one might have expected, in the event of an Iraqi attack on Turkey, *Jane's Defence Weekly*, vol.15, January 1991, p. 43; *The Guardian*, 25 January 1991. Naturally this lesson was internalized by the Turkish military and political leadership.

30 For the arguments of the Turkish military, see Ç. Bir, 'Nato'nun Yeni Stratejisi ve Türkiye', *Savunma ve Havacılık*, vol. 6, no. 2, 1992; S. Elegi, *Taktik Balisti Füzeler ve Türkiye*, Ankara: Milli Savunma Bakanlığı, 1993, pp. 71–76, 84–7. See also Lesser, *Bridge or Barrier?*, pp. 24, 27–31; G. Özcan, 'Politiko Kathestos ke Exoteriki Politiki stin Tourkia (1983–93)', in F. Sönmezoğlu (ed.), *Mythos ke Pragmatikotita: Analysi tis Tourkikis Exoterikis Politikis*, Athens: Infognomon, 2001, tomos B, p. 120; Şenese, 'Axiologisi tou Programmatos Eksyhronismou', p. 212; I. O. Lesser, 'Turkey's Strategic Options', *The International Spectator*, vol. XXXIV, 1999, p. 83.

31 Abramowitz, 'Dateline Ankara', pp. 164–5.

32 On these concerns, see Chapter 4 in this book.

33 For an interesting critical assessment of the security concerns of the Turkish state during this period, see also S. G. Ayman and N. Atefloğlu, 'I Strategiki stis Metavallomenes Diethnis Synthikes: I Tourkia ke oi Gitones tis', in F. Sönmezoğlu (ed.), *Mythos ke Pragmatikotita: Analysi tis Tourkikis Exoterikis Politikis*, Athens: Infognomon, 2001, tomos A, pp. 568–87.

34 Abramowitz, 'Dateline Ankara', p. 165.

35 Ayman, Atefloğlu, 'Tourkia ke Gitones', p. 574.

36 Mufti, *Daring and Caution*, p. 90.

37 M. R. Hickok, 'Hegemon Rising: The Gap between Turkish Strategy and Military Modernization', *Parameters*, vol. XXX, 2000, passim; Özcan, 'The Military and Making of Foreign Policy', pp. 24–5; Mufti, *Daring and Caution*, pp. 90–91; Lesser, *Bridge or Barrier?*, p. 30.

38 Author's interview with Warren Christopher, US secretary of state (1993–97).

39 Gabelnick, *et al., Arming Repression*, passim and appendix table B.

40 Author's interview with Warren Christopher.

41 Author's interviews with Morton Abramowitz (a), Alan Makovsky (a) and Ian Lesser (a).

42 Author's interview with Cengiz Çandar (a).

43 For an interesting early collection of articles on the new challenges facing US foreign policy and its direction, see P. M. Cronin (ed.), *From Globalism to Regionalism: New Perspectives on U.S. Foreign and Defense Policies*, Washington DC: National Defense University Press, 1993. On the foreign and security policy of the first Clinton administration, see among others, J. M. McCormick, 'Assessing Clinton's Foreign Policy at Midterm', *Current History*, November 1995; W. Hyland, 'A Mediocre Record', *Foreign Policy*, 101, Winter 1996; C.-F. David, *Dissecting Clinton's Foreign Policy Making: A First Cut*, Montreal: Center for United States Studies, Université du Quebéc, 2004; J. M. McCormick, *American Foreign Policy and Process*, Boston: Wadsworth, 2010, pp. 179–84; see also L. P. Brady, 'Working with Allies: Clinton's Defense Policy and the Management of Multilateralism', in S. J. Cimbala (ed.), *Clinton and Post-Cold War Defense*, Westport, CO: Praeger, 1996, pp. 71–86.

44 Author's interview with Warren Christopher.
45 'Turkey Loses Its Allure as a Patron in Central Asian Nations', *The New York Times*, 4 August 1993; Makovsky, 'U.S. Policy toward Turkey', p. 223; E. Athanassopoulou, 'American-Turkish Relations since the End of the Cold War', *Middle East Policy,* vol. VIII, 2001, pp.150–51. For a detailed account of the rise and fall of the 'Turkish model' idea in Washington and Ankara, see I. Bal, *Turkey's Relations with the West and the Turkic Republics: The Rise and Fall of the 'Turkish Model'*, Aldershot: Ashgate, 2000.
46 In 1995 the Turkish government decided that the mandate of the operation had to be renewed every three months.
47 W. G. Hyland, *Clinton's World: Remaking American Foreign Policy*, Praeger: Westport, CO: 1999, pp. 174–5.
48 For a good comprehensive account of Ankara's concerns and policy in relation to Northern Iraq at the time, see K. Kirişci and G. M. Winrow, *The Kurdish Question and Turkey: An Example of a Trans-state Ethnic Conflict*, London: Routledge/Curzon, 2004, pp. 157–79; 'Turkey Makes Moves to Limit Kurdish Autonomy Inside Iraq', *Washington Post*, 1 October 1994. On the impact of developments in Northern Iraq on Turkey's relations with the US, see H. J. Barkey and G. E. Fuller, *Turkey's Kurdish Question*, Lanham: Rowman and Littlefield Publishers, 1998, pp. 158–64; H. J. Barkey, 'The Push and Pull of Strategic Cooperation: The US Relationship with Turkey in the Middle East', in D. W. Lesch (ed.), *The Middle East and the United States*, Boulder, CO: Westview, 2007, p. 450.
49 Barkey and Fuller, *Turkey's Kurdish Question*, p. 159; 'No More Comfort', *U.S. News and World Report*, 3 October 1994, p. 24.
50 Barkey and Fuller, *Turkey's Kurdish Question*, p. 160.
51 Blank *et al.*, *Turkey's Strategic Position*, p. iv. Also author's interview with Ian Lesser (a).
52 Author's interview with Mr. P., a State Department official who was still in active service and therefore spoke on condition of anonymity, July 2007, Washington. That the US had promised its tolerance concerning Turkish military operations in Northern Iraq in exchange for the continuation of the Operation is confirmed by a US official quoted in Mufti, *Daring and Caution*, pp. 101–2. Nonetheless, the renewal formula was maintained.
53 'Kurds in Turkey Seem to Be Nearing Full Scale Revolt', 30 March 1992, *The New York Times*; J. Tirman, 'Improving Turkey's "Bad Neighborhood": Pressing Ankara for Rights and Democracy', *World Policy Journal*, vol. 15, 1998, p.4.
54 Barkey and Fuller, *Turkey's Kurdish Question*, pp. 161–2; Author's interviews with Alan Makovsky (a) and Ian Lesser (a).
55 'The Kurdish Killing Fields', *The New York Times*, 4 July 2012.
56 'Fresh Round of Jitters in US Alliance', [*Turkey*] *Briefing*, 30 May 1994, issue 991, p. 3; C. Migdlovitz, *Greece and Turkey: Current Foreign Aid Issues* (CRS, Issue Brief, 1996), available online at www.fas.org/man/crs/86–065.htm#summ (accessed 16 June 2006). Ankara refused to accept the 10 per cent of the loans that were approved with conditions. The total approved amount of security assistance for fiscal year 1995 was $373.8 million; this included $45.75 million in grants under the Economic Security Fund programme.
57 Author's interview with Warren Christopher.
58 Human Rights Watch, *U.S. Cluster Bombs for Turkey?* vol. 6, no. 19, December 1994, available online www.hrw.org/reports/1994/Turkey2 (accessed 12 June 2006); Migdalovitz, *Current Foreign Aid Issues.*
59 Migdalovitz, *Current Foreign Aid Issues.*
60 Author's interview with Cengiz Çandar (a).
61 *The New York Times*, 15 Dec. 1994.

62 S. Atalay, 'ABD Güvenlık Yardımı ABD Türkiye Ilişkileri', *Avrasya Dosyası*, vol. 1, 1994, pp. 246–50; *Milliyet*, 8 April 1994. Also author's interview with Ian Lesser (a).
63 Migdalovitz, *Current Foreign Aid Issues.*
64 Migdalovitz, *Current Foreign Aid Issues.*
65 Aykan, 'Turkish Perspectives', p. 355; Sariibrahimoglu, 'Building an Industry'; author's interview with Ian Lesser (a).
66 Aykan, 'Turkish Perspectives', p. 351.
67 F. S. Larrabee and I. O. Lesser, *Turkish Foreign Policy in an Age of Uncertainty*, Santa Monica, CA: RAND, 2003, p. 172.
68 Author's interview with Ian Lesser (a) and Mr. P., July 2007, Washington.
69 Author's interview with Warren Christopher.
70 McCormick, *American Foreign Policy and Process*, p. 184; Makovsky, 'U.S. Policy toward Turkey', p. 223.
71 On this point, see Chapter 6 in this book.
72 The amendment made US trade relations with communist countries conditional upon the non-restriction of immigration of their citizens. Its intention was to facilitate the exit of Jews from the Soviet Union. Richard Perle was its major drafter.
73 J. J. Goldberg, *Jewish Power: Inside the American Jewish Establishment*, Reading, MA: Addison-Wesley, 1996, pp. 167–9.
74 Goldberg, *Jewish Power*, pp. 168–9.
75 Goldberg, *Jewish* Power, pp.165, 175
76 R. Perle, 'Turkey and US Military Assistance', in G. S. Harris (ed.), *The Middle East in Turkish-American Relations*, Washington, DC: The Heritage Foundation, 1985, p.26 and passim.
77 Barkey, 'Push and Pull', p. 449. Author's interview with Mr J., a leading member of Turkey's Jewish community who spoke on condition of anonymity, December 2006, Istanbul.
78 Author's interview with Mr J., December 2006, Istanbul; author's interview with Mehmet Ali Birand (b).
79 M. L. Evriviades, 'Turkey's Role in United States Strategy during and after the Cold War, *Mediterranean Quarterly*, vol. 9, p. 36, 1998. To the best of my knowledge, Marios Evriviades was the first to write about this co-operation. My interest in Turkey-Israel relations in the late 1980s was spurred by Professor Evriviades' work and our conversations.
80 Author's interviews with Andrew Manatos and Peter Marudas.
81 According to Evriviades, 'Turkey's Role in United States Strategy', p. 44, this strategy reflected Albert Wohlstetter's thinking of Turkey as a valuable strategic base for the US and a strategic ally of Israel.
82 On Turkish policy toward the Arab states and Israel, see among others, K. Karpat, 'Turkish and Arab-Israeli Relations', in K. Karpat *et al.*, *Turkey's Foreign Policy in Transition. 1950–1974*, Leiden: E. J. Brill, 1975; M. H. Yavuz and M. R. Khan, 'Turkish Foreign Policy toward the Arab-Israeli Conflict: Duality and the Development (1950–91)', *Arab Studies Quarterly*, vol. 14, 1992; M. B. Aykan, 'The Palestinian Question in Turkish Foreign Policy from the 1950s to the 1990s', *International Journal of Middle East Studies*, vol. 25, 1993.
83 G. E. Gruen, 'Turkey between Middle East and West', in R. O. Freedman (ed.), *The Middle East from the Iran-Contra Affair to the Intifada*, Syracuse, NY: Syracuse University Press, 1999, pp. 405, 419–20, n. 42; D. B. Sezer, 'Turkish Foreign Policy in the Year 2000', in *Turkey in the Year 2000*, Ankara: Turkish Political Science Association, 1989, p. 89. We do not know whether Elekdağ was instrumental in this regard. According to Yalım Eralp Elekdağ's suggestions may have had an impact on Özal, but the Turkish prime minister was concerned for some

time about how to counter the influence of the Greek and Armenian lobbies and was early on interested in the potential role of the Jewish lobby: author's interview with Yalım Eralp, (a).

84 Gruen, 'Between Middle East and West', p. 414.

85 Y. Eralp, 'An Insider's View of Turkey's Foreign Policy and Its American Connection', in M. Abramowitz (ed.), *The United States and Turkey: Allies in Need*, New York: The Century Foundation Press, 2003, p. 114.

86 Yavuz and Khan, 'Turkish Foreign Policy toward the Arab-Israeli Conflict', p. 81; M. L. Evriviades, 'The Turkish-Israeli Axis: Alliances and Alignments in the Middle East', *ORIENT*, vol. 39, 1998, p. 576.

87 Y. Rabi, 'An Unprecedented Meeting: Foreign Ministers of Israel and Turkey to Meet for the First Time', *Jewish Telegraphic Agency*, 22 September 1987, available online at http://archive.jta.org/article/1987/09/22/3007669/an-unprecedented-meeting-foreign-ministers-of-israel-and-turkey-to-meet-for-the-first-time (accessed 6 March 2010).

88 Goldberg, *Jewish Power*, p. 18; *Jewish Telegraphic Agency*, 1 October 1987, available online at http://archive.jta.org/article/1987/09/22/3005703 (accessed 6 March 2010).

89 Author's interview with Thomas Dine, executive director of the American Israel Public Affairs Committee (AIPAC) (1980–93).

90 *Jewish Telegraphic Agency*, 1 October 1987.

91 Gruen, 'Between Middle East and West', pp. 419–20, n. 42.

92 J. W. Dietrich, 'Interest Groups and Foreign Policy: Clinton and the China MFN Debates', *Presidential Studies Quarterly*, vol. IXXX, 1999, p. 280.

93 J. J. Fialka, 'Former Defense Official Creates Firm to Lobby in Washington for Turkey', *The Wall Street Journal*, 16 February 1989, A16; A. Weisman, *Prince of Darkness: Richard Perle. The Kingdom, the Power and the End of Empire in America*, New York: Union Square Press, 2007, p. 118.

94 Weisman, *Prince of Darkness*, p. 118.

95 Weisman, *Prince of Darkness*, p. 118.

96 Weisman, *Prince of Darkness*, p. 118.

97 Fialka, 'Former Defense Official Creates Firm'.

98 Author's interview with Andreas Manatos.

99 Perle's fee amounted to $48,000 thousand per year according to Weisman, *Prince of Darkness*, p. 118.

100 Douglas Feith served as under-secretary of defense for policy (2001–5) under George W. Bush. Feith resigned his position in 2005. The inspector general of the Department of Defense concluded in a 2007 report that Feith's office manipulated intelligence information relating to Iraq and did not provide accurate intelligence analysis.

101 Perle hired Feith as a summer intern in 1975, Weisman, *Prince of Darkness*, p. 33. On the neoconservative group around Perle see, Weisman, *Prince of Darkness*, passim; J. R. Wedel, *Shadow Elite: How the Wold's New Power Brokers Undermine Democracy, Government, and the Free Market*, New York, Basic Books, 2009, ch. 6.

102 Author's interviews with Andrew Manatos, Peter Marudas and Thomas Dine. See also, Weisman, *Prince of Darkness*, p. 118.

103 *Cumhuriyet*, 10 March 1989, in *Turkish Press Review*, Directorate General of Press and Information, Ankara.

104 Goldberg, *Jewish Power*, p. 167.

105 Goldberg, *Jewish Power*, p. 202. In 1981, after Amitay had left AIPAC, he founded the Washington Political Action Committee, which in the next two decades would contribute a significant amount of money to Israel's supporters in Congress.

106 'Embassy Went Too Far in Armenian Affair' and 'Turkey Seeks Help of Israel and U.S. Jews to Fight U.S. Senate Resolution Marking Armenian Genocide', *The Jerusalem Post*, 24 October 1989; 'Between Ankara and Jerusalem', *The Jerusalem Post*, 25 October 1989; G. Gorenberg, 'Israel Demeans Itself in an Affront to Armenians', *Los Angeles Times*, 30 October 1989. On the resolution see p. 71 in this book.

107 M. Abramowitz, 'The Complexities of American Policy Making on Turkey', in M. Abramowitz (ed.), *Turkey's Transformation and American Policy,* New York: The Century Foundation Press, 2000, p. 168; Weisman, *Prince of Darkness*, pp. 119–20; author's interview with Andrew Manatos.

108 Weisman, *Prince of Darkness*, p. 119.

6 Renewal of US interest

Looking for 'a window of opportunity' in the Middle East

As violence engulfed Palestine when the *intifada* erupted (December 1987) the enemies of Israel, but also its friends, reacted strongly to the way it dealt with the rising.[1] The Turks, always mindful of the Arabs' reaction, slowed down the pace of relations with Israel, which had been steadily increasing since the mid 1980s. But as the decade drew to a close the beginning of the Arab-Israeli peace process led Ankara to eagerly resume the bilateral dialogue. The 1993 Oslo Israeli-Palestinian agreement and the hopes it raised for a peaceful co-existence between the two peoples spurred an even faster pace in the development of bilateral relations, which began to spread into many fields. There were many important considerations that made the Turks seek closer relations with the Israelis in the beginning of the 1990s. A major factor was the desire to acquire advanced weapons and military systems without any hindrances on account of human rights violations. Another was the need for increased sharing of intelligence concerning the activities of the Kurdish guerrillas and the support they received from the Kurds in Northern Iraq and President Assad of Syria. Furthermore, in the wake of the Gulf War the Turks had come to the conclusion that relations with Israel would strengthen their hand when dealing with Assad and the other Arab leaders.[2] Of course, a major goal continued to be Ankara's wish to boost its support in the US.[3] Actually, according to a number of senior Turkish officials, the need to find public allies in Washington who would help advance Turkish interests was the main driving force.[4] In short, the peace process was an unexpected bonus for the Turks, just as the Soviet invasion of Afghanistan had been a decade earlier. The new phase in Arab-Israeli relations greatly helped Turkish rulers to liberate their relations with Israel from self-imposed constraints. These were dictated primarily by Turkish concern not to provoke the Arab regimes, but also at least to some extent by domestic considerations, as Turkish public opinion was very sympathetic toward the plead of the Palestinians.

Against the backdrop of prevailing uncertainty over the future shape of US–Turkey relations it was hardly surprising that Turkey's political and military leaders attached growing importance to strengthening relations with

Israel as a means of enhancing Turkey's leverage in Washington. But by this time the importance given to the relationship with Israel was also related to Ankara's wish to seek for opportunities to enhance Turkey's role in the Middle East. This wish was not an isolated phenomenon. It was part of the larger foreign policy transition that was underway in Ankara – the transition from Turkey being a rather passive international actor to one that was interested in increasing its influence in its adjacent regions (mainly in Central Asia and the Caucasus but also in the Balkans and the Middle East), with US approval.[5]

When the Right Path Party (centre right) of Süleyman Demirel defeated Özal's Motherland Party in the October 1991 parliamentary elections President Özal's personal influence on foreign policy came to an abrupt end, for it had been possible only on the back of the Motherland Party government which he controlled behind the scenes. However, Özal's vision of Turkey as an actor to be reckoned with in the Middle East did not fade away. For good reasons all those involved in the formulation of Turkish foreign policy – the military, the office of the prime minister, the office of the president and the Foreign Affairs ministry[6] – recognized that the Gulf War had created new realities in the Middle East to which Turkish policy needed to adjust swiftly. Although a few officials within the Foreign Ministry bureaucracy emphasized that Turkey should move cautiously in the Middle East, the overall consensus among foreign policy makers was that the 'soft-touch' approach that Turkey had adopted in its dealings with the area since the 1960s had to be revised.[7] A key component of the new thinking was that Turkey should seek to play an enlarged role in the new security and economic arrangements that would emerge in the post-Gulf War era. In short, the new government, part of the bureaucracy and the military, whose influence over foreign policy continued to be very strong, came to advocate what Özal had argued first.[8] So the Turks remained alert for opportunities while claiming that Turkey's security, political and economic role in the region could not be easily dismissed. Within this context Turkey's growing relationship with Israel was considered 'instrumental' in Ankara.[9]

Prime Minister Demirel, who in 1993 became president (1993–2000), and Tansu Çiller, his successor to the leadership of the party and the premiership (1993–96), proved very keen to put into practice the new thinking, although they acted more cautiously and in a less flamboyant style than Özal.[10] When the Turks' intense diplomatic efforts to have Turkey included in the Madrid Peace Conference[11] failed, Demirel – not the prime minister yet – expressed his 'strong regret' at the non-participation of Turkey, 'which is one of the most powerful countries in the Middle East.'[12] The Turks were determined not to be rebuffed. As soon as Demirel's government assumed office, Ankara intensified its diplomatic efforts in Washington, this time in order to have Turkey included in the multilateral track that the peace partners at the Madrid Conference agreed to establish as part of the Arab-Israeli peace process. This parallel track to the bilateral peace negotiations was scheduled to begin in January 1992. Its objective was to promote regional security and co-operation by addressing transnational issues of regional concern, including economic development, arms control and regional security, environmental and water-related issues. The Turks' diplomatic effort was built around the argument that Turkey had an important stabilizing role to play in the region. At the same time, the Turkish government very effectively used as leverage the point that its participation would lead to de jure ambassadorial-level relations with Israel.[13] (Full ambassadorial-level diplomatic relations with the state of Israel were a requirement for participation in the multilaterals.) Turkish diplomacy was successful this time, and having secured a place in the multilaterals,[14] the Turks focused their attention on the deliberations of the Regional Economic Development and Arms Control and Regional Security working groups and proved ready to put significant energy into them.[15] The diplomatic battle for Turkey's participation in the peace process marked the beginning of Ankara's growing determination to have a bigger say on a number of security issues in the Middle East.

It was evident that there was a clash of perspectives in the minds of Turkish foreign policy makers when they approached the region. On the one hand, they did not wish to get really involved in the Middle East, least of all militarily.[16] On the other, they thought it important that Turkey should pursue a number of causes in the Middle East, for the success of which US sanction was necessary. A major cause was to defeat the Kurdish insurgency in the southeast, in full force after 1992, which the Turkish leadership regarded as the principal security threat to Turkey.[17] This led Turkish high brass to conclude that military incursions into Northern Iraq, which had become a safe heaven for the PKK as well, were an absolute necessity in order to eliminate guerrilla bases. But for this they needed tacit US support.[18] Furthermore, the fluid situation in Northern Iraq and Ankara's unease with the de facto autonomous Kurdish entity there created the urgent need for Turkey to become not only militarily but also politically involved in Northern Iraq,[19] and to focus even greater attention on the regional balance-of-power game. This involved the US as well as Iraq, Iran and Syria. Alongside these political/security goals there were also economic ones, which could be given more than a helping hand if Washington's backing were secured. In the wake of the Gulf War, as Heinz Kramer noted, the Turks increasingly viewed their country as the Japan of the area in economic terms[20] and looked at the Middle East with an eye for more and more economic opportunities.

In short, it had become clear to the Turks that in the post-Cold War, post-Gulf War environment US support was necessary if they were to influence developments affecting their national interests in the Middle East.[21] It was also within this context that Turkish rulers regarded relations with Israel as instrumental. To quote Özal, relations with Israel represented 'a window of opportunity' in relation to future developments in the Middle East. This window, he firmly believed, had to remain open were Turkey to have a good chance of playing a larger regional role.[22] Evidently Demirel and Çiller shared these views.[23]

The Bush administration approved and encouraged in a rather general way the tightening of relations between Turkey and Israel but did not show an active interest in it. According to Thomas Dine, the people in Bush's team were rather indifferent.[24] Clearly there was no official policy aimed at deepening co-operation between the two US allies. Apparently, in 1993 State Department officials working on the peace process were surprised when Turkish officials informed them that the Turkish and Israeli governments had initiated talks about a free trade zone.[25] The Clinton administration during its first year in office also remained merely an observer, apparently investing very little energy in Turkey-Israel relations. Nonetheless, US national security officials were fully briefed by the Turks and Israelis over the development of their relations.[26] For good reasons the Americans were watching closely because they wanted to make sure that certain US interests, for example sales of US weapons, would not be adversely affected by the growth of Turkish-Israeli ties.[27]

The initial lack of active interest by the US government in the development of Turkey-Israel ties partly reflected the long-established and widely held perception within US national security circles that it was unlikely for Turkey to co-operate with the US in the Middle East unless its own narrow interests were at stake. Furthermore, after the mid 1980s the Turks' efforts to join the EC were viewed by US officials working on Turkey as a sure sign that Ankara was turning its back to the Middle East.[28] This accounted for why in the wake of the Gulf War Turkey did not figure in the US strategic plans for the area. Turkey's importance remained limited to the enforcement of the no-fly zone over Northern Iraq. As a US State Department official put it: 'Turkey was not considered a country of the Middle East. It was a NATO member. We viewed it as part of Western Europe.'[29]

To a role in the Middle East

At the very beginning of the 1990s, as relations between Turkey and Israel were growing fast, pro-Israeli groups in Washington became involved in an organized effort by the Israeli government to explain to the Jewish-American community the importance to Israel of its relations with Turkey.[30] Gradually, they also began to get more and more mobilized within Congress and the administration, some of them often in co-operation with Turkey's supporters in Washington, with the aim of underlining Turkey's importance for the security of Israel as well as for the wider US strategic interests in the Middle East.[31] Before long the Israeli embassy, AIPAC (with its huge network of contacts throughout the US political system) and a number of major Jewish-American organizations were energized in order to bolster interest in Turkey in Congress and within foreign policy circles. Pro-Israel think tanks, of which the most prominent was the Washington Institute for Near East Policy (WINEP), also became active to the same effect. The general objective was to help fulfil the Turks' expectations for dividends in Washington in return for their relations with Israel. In the phrase of an analyst for AIPAC, 'we believe, and have been told by Israeli officials, that whatever we can do for Turkey helps the Turkey-Israel relationship.'[32] It is a measure of the perceived strategic importance to Israel of its relations with Turkey that pro-Israeli groups and individuals, regardless of their important political differences, including opposite positions concerning Rabin's peace policy, were keen to put in more than a good word for Turkey. The intensity of the effort directly reflected progress made in bilateral ties. So this became noticeably much more systematic and persistent as from 1993, a landmark year in the growth of the relationship, for it marked the first official visit of a Turkish minister of foreign affairs to Israel (13–15 November).

It was also the same year that Rabin's government appointed Professor Itamar Rabinovich as Israel's new ambassador to the US (1993–96). Rabinovich, a renowned historian of Arab-Israeli relations who had Rabin's ear, recalls that soon after he took his position he set to work in order to familiarize US officials with the idea that Turkey could play a constructive role in the Middle East.[33] To this end he worked closely with those pro-Israeli groups who favoured the Israeli government's peace policies. Rabinovich remembers that he discussed Turkey's strategic importance with Deputy Secretary of State Strobe Talbott (1994–2001) already in one of their first meetings.[34] Besides being deputy secretary of state, Talbott was Clinton's close friend and much more influential on foreign policy issues than Anthony Lake, the national security advisor.[35] Rabinovich used three main arguments. First, Turkey was a moderate force in the Middle East, a barrier against any kind of fundamentalism. Second, it was an important contributor to the peace process, as its growing relations with Israel challenged the dominant paradigm of prejudice and confrontation between Muslims and Israelis. Third, Turkey was a considerable player for the economic development of the Middle East within the context of Shimon Peres's vision for a New Middle East,[36] where forces of regional co-operation and mutual development were expected to prevail.[37] This was the conceptual basis which would support the Israeli government's effort to stir US interest in the Turkey-Israel engagement and hence in Turkey. In short, Turkey was a positive force whose rapprochement with Israel could help strengthen US strategy in the Middle East. According to Rabinovich, these arguments made an impression on Talbott.[38] Besides working the administration channels, the Israeli embassy also *openly* lobbied Congress on the side of Turkey, something unprecedented according to those familiar with the pressure game in Washington.[39]

The same line of argumentation was used by Jewish-American organizations which supported (or at least did not have a reason to oppose) Yitzhak Rabin's peace policy. So, basically, they echoed the Israeli embassy. It should be noted that the clash about the peace policy conducted by Rabin's government between the left-wing and the right-wing pro-Israeli groups[40] could also be seen in the way the latter lobbied in favour of Turkey. Right-wing groups who wished to undermine Rabin's peace policy (which also meant that they had less access to the Cinton administration) essentially argued that the Turks' co-operation with Israel strengthened the Israelis against their major enemies, Iran, Saddam Hussein and terrorism, all three of which also happened to be enemies of the US.[41]

An important underpinning of the combined effort of the Israeli embassy and the Jewish-American groups was the argument that Turkey was a potential security partner of Israel, and further that Turkey, Israel and the US could perhaps develop a latent trilateral security co-operation. The idea that such co-operation could even develop to become tantamount to an alliance consolidating US influence from the Caspian Sea to the Middle East was also aired by the Rabin government.[42] Within the context of this ambitious design, the US was expected to provide mainly diplomatic and economic support, while military backing could be offered only if needed. Right-wingers and neoconservatives were also very keen on trilateral military co-operation. It is interesting to note that in the early 1990s the Jewish Institute for National Security Affairs (JINSA), one of Washington's less prominent pro-Israel think-tanks, whose mandate was to strengthen US-Israel security co-operation (with an emphasis on military co-operation), declared in its mission statement that it also wished to play a key role in strengthening security co-operation between the three countries.[43] Richard Perle sat on the advisory board of JINSA, which was closely linked with US neoconservative and right-wing Israeli circles.

The Israeli embassy and pro-Israeli groups also joined forces with the Turkish lobby for the promotion of a number of major items on Ankara's policy agenda, which were also of interest to Israel and in line with US policies.[44] These included Turkey's accession to the European Union (EU) and the construction of the Baku-Ceyhan pipeline to transport Azerbaijan's significant oil reserves to the Mediterranean via Turkey (a project the Turks were most keen on and for which they were lobbying very intensely). In the view of the Israeli Ministry of Foreign Affairs, Turkey's accession to the EU would be beneficial for Israel because it would transform the geopolitical map of the area and move Israel closer to Europe. The Israelis also had very good reasons to vigorously support the materialization of the Baku-Ceyhan pipeline. The success of this project would serve Israel's energy security through the construction of pipelines connecting Ceyhan with the Israeli port of Ashkelon. In fact, this was quite an old project for the Israelis, which they had already begun lobbying Washington for in the very early 1990s.[45] Also, the Israelis were eager to support the construction of a westbound (via Turkey) energy route from Azerbaijan, as the second alternative and much cheaper southbound route (via Iran) would increase Tehran's cash flow (because of transit rights) and consequently enhance the regional influence of Iran, which the Israeli security establishment considered as Israel's main enemy after Saddam Hussein's defeat in the Gulf War. Apparently, pro-Israel groups did not actively lobby for issues that interested Turkey but did not also concern Israel or were controversial, at least for some within the Jewish-American community,[46] for instance the question of blocking passage of a congressional Armenian

Genocide Resolution.[47] Actually, this particular issue generated a debate within the community – that spilled over into Congress – over the dilemma between realism and the sacrifice of values the Jews ought to stand for.[48] But the heart of the matter was that the community had thrown its support behind Turkey with a zeal that was never done before for any other country besides Israel.[49] Therefore, at the end of the day active involvement was not always essential for 'Jewish-American organizations had made it clear to their congressional allies that whatever is good for Turkey is also good for Israel and that they should support Ankara.'[50]

The continuing transformation of the US foreign policy–making system in the post-Cold War period, its becoming 'more similar to its domestic counterpart, with multiple interest groups using channels to try to influence policy choices'[51] and the slow, uncertain formulation of Clinton's foreign policy favoured efforts by organized interests to affect US foreign policy decisions. Jewish-American groups and organizations in particular were perhaps better positioned than ever before to influence the foreign policy debate. Most of them had unlimited access to the Clinton administration. This was due to the president's wish (Clinton was by general acknowledgement the most pro-Jewish, pro-Israeli Democratic president in US history[52]) to repair ties with the Jewish-American community, 'which felt that had been kicked around' by the Bush administration.[53]

But much more importantly the Clinton administration allowed a strong pro-Israel/pro-Rabin sentiment to prevail when it came to policy in the Middle East.[54] Further, a significant number of alumni from WINEP, the leading pro-Israel think tank in Washington, served in key foreign policy positions. As Zachary Lockman observes, most of them while at WINEP 'worked hard to strengthen Israel's standing in Washington as the key U.S. ally in the Middle East and to ensure that U.S. policy in the region coincided with the policies and strategies of the Israeli government.'[55]

The most prominent example was Martin Indyk, founding executive director of WINEP in the second half of the 1980s, whose public 'emergence' in 1993 'exemplified the Clinton administration's desire to ease relations with Israel and the American-Jewish community.'[56] Previously, Indyk, who was Jewish, had worked as deputy research director for AIPAC. During Clinton's first term he served as special assistant to the president on issues relating to the Middle East and was senior director for Near East and South Asia in the National Security Council. Also, he was a senior member of Warren Christopher's Middle East peace team and during Clinton's second term he became assistant secretary of state for Near East affairs (1997–99).[57] Indyk 'helped shape and reinforce a trend that was already clear' within the administration. This was to regain the confidence of the Israelis so that the peace process would have a chance.[58] According to Aaron David Miller, the result was that 'a clear pro-Israel orientation' was given to the peace-process planning.[59] Influenced by this overall political purpose, Indyk, Thomas Dine says, was receptive to the views of the Israeli government concerning

Turkey as he was looking for building blocks in order to support the peace process.[60]

By early 1994 the credibility of the idea that Turkey might be able to contribute to the success of the peace process grew within the administration. Indyk had a big role to play in this. On 17 May 1994 Anthony Lake in his address to the Washington Institute's Soref symposium, a very high-profile annual event, outlined the political goals of the Clinton administration for the Middle East. The US National Security Advisor spoke about how the peace process was changing the 'political paradigm' of hatred against Israel and mentioned Turkey on top of the list of 'moderate Islamic states [*sic*]' (the other states were Saudi Arabia, Morocco and Pakistan) that would 'constrain the capacity of rogue states and organizations to extend their influence and their message of hate and violence'. And 'with Syria and all other states in this camp of peace with Israel the balance of power in the Middle East' would 'shift decisively in favor of moderation'.[61] It was still a rather general and vague perspective on Turkey's role, but it was a new perspective. Indyk was the main framer of Lake's speech.[62] The Israeli embassy and all those who had worked diligently to promote the idea that Turkey had a role to play in building a new security environment in the Middle East must have been very pleased. Certainly the Turks were.[63]

As the Clinton administration was in the midst of drawing up a clearer road map for the Middle East, the message that Turkey was potentially a Middle East security actor was repeated many times to different influential audiences by different influentials. In early June, two weeks after Lake's address at WINEP, the United States Institute of Peace (USIP),[64] organized a two-day conference under the title 'A Reluctant Neighbour: Analysing Turkey's Role in the Middle East'. According to the organizers, the major goal of the conference was to 'initiate discussion on Turkey's relations with the countries of the Middle East and its role in the regional peace process'. The organizers justified the need for such a discussion by stressing that

> despite their recognition of Turkey's strategic location among regions in flux, scholars and policymakers have tended to disregard the fact that Turkey is part of the Middle East, long an unstable region. Although any Middle East specialist will acknowledge that Turkey has both a significant history in the region and distinctive relationships with Israel and the Arab states, Turkey is not often spoken of as a factor in the Middle East peace process.[65]

Paul Wolfowitz was the conference keynote speaker. Wolfowitz had worked in the Nixon, Ford and Carter administrations before he served in important posts both at the State and Defense Departments in the Reagan and the George H. W. Bush administrations. One of the things he was known for in Washington (but also in Ankara) was that he was a staunch supporter of Israel.[66] (Some years later as an assistant secretary of defense during the presidency of George W. Bush he would gain notoriety for being the architect of the administration's policy towards Iraq.) His appearance as a keynote speaker at the USIP conference was a manifestation of the interlinking networks of pro-Israel groups and Turkey's traditional supporters and their mutually beneficial agendas. Neoconservative Wolfowitz was a close friend of Richard Perle. He was also a disciple of Albert Wohlstetter and, like Perle, had been much influenced by the latter's strategic thinking.[67] As a young graduate student he was recruited by Wohlstetter, along with Perle, to work in the Washington office created by Dean Acheson and Paul Nitze and was also exposed to, and influenced by, their hawkish foreign policy views.[68] Later on, together with Perle, he worked at Senator Jackson's office. In the Carter administration he had taken the Pentagon job of deputy assistant secretary of defense for regional programs. In this capacity during the early days of the administration he directed a project that was the first extensive effort by the Pentagon to study the US need to defend the Persian Gulf. One of the major conclusions of the report produced under his guidance was that the US needed new bases in the region and that it had to develop the general infrastructure that would allow it to quickly bring its military forces to the defence of the Gulf.[69] The impact of these conclusions, though initially negligeable, would eventually shape US military thinking toward the Middle East[70] and, by extension, Turkey in the closing days of the 1970s.[71] He too had very close ties with the Turkish military establishment and was always connected with Turkey, even when this connection was indirect through Perle.[72] He was interested in Turkey's potential role in the security of the Middle East in general and of Israel in particular.

In his keynote address at the USIP conference, Wolfowitz stressed the strategic relevance of Turkey by saying that 'there is no other country in the world to which the word "strategic" applies more'. He stated that in the post-Cold War era Turkey was still strategically important, arguing along the lines underscored by the Turks themselves and those US strategic analysts[73] whose thinking had been seasoned by the Cold War. So, he mentioned the conflicts in the Balkans, Turkey's 'crucial' proximity to the Black Sea, its role as a 'critical' bridge to the Caucasus and Central Asia. But he also noted Turkey's 'least analyzed role' in that it occupied 'a strategic and possibly growing position in the Middle East.' His conclusion echoed very closely the Turks' perspective: Turkey, he noted, was reluctant 'though not unwilling' to become involved in the affairs of the Middle East.[74] Throughout the 1990s Wolfowitz was often invited to be a keynote speaker at conferences on Turkey in Washington as well as in Turkey. He would invariably stress Turkey's strategic role mainly in the Middle East, within the context of the peace process, and underscore how natural it was for the Turks to develop relations with the Israelis.[75] According to some well-informed observers, his interest and public support for Turkey was primarily fuelled by his wish to strengthen Israel.[76]

Professor Alvin Rubinstein, a well-known expert on Russian foreign policy and US security issues, who was also participating at the conference, emphasized

Wolfowitz's points even more. Exactly what stimulated his interest in Turkey is hard to say, but a number of factors worked together. Rubinstein was also known for his strong interest in the affairs of the state of Israel.[77] But it seems that his thinking regarding Turkey was also grounded on his concept for a new security system in the Middle East. Since the Gulf War he had been advocating the need for the US to develop a security vision that would help transform the Middle East and establish a stable regional order in the region.[78] In his view, Turkey would also have a big part to play in a new regional security arrangement. At the USIP conference Rubinstein certainly did not understate his case. He declared that Turkey 'was simply the most important country in the Middle East'. But, he commented, 'no major country in the Middle East has been less studied by American scholars or more ignored by the American media.' In his mind 'what Turkey' did or did not do would 'critically affect the course of events, including stability, not only in the Middle East but also in the Caucasus, Central Asia, the Balkans, and the West'. Finally, he cautioned those who took Turkey's allegiance to the West for granted by stating that 'the growing ambivalence in the West toward Turkey is reflected in Turkey's growing ambivalence toward the West.'[79]

Two important players

It can be said that the year 1994 was indeed critical in the increase of American attention on Turkey. By the end of that year the rise of interest in Turkey would start becoming palpable within the administration. This was mainly the result of the actions of two US officials, who with considerable zeal championed Turkey's strategic importance and in co-ordination with each other sought to renew US–Turkey strategic ties.[80] They were Richard Holbrooke, the influential assistant secretary of state for European and Canadian sffairs (September 1994–February 1996), and Marc Grossman, the US ambassador to Ankara (September 1994–June 1997), who in 1997 was appointed to the assistant secretary position (August 1997–May 2000) previously held by Holbrooke.[81]

In the early 1990s Marc Grossman was already known in Washington as an 'ardent supporter' of US–Turkey strategic relations.[82] He had served in Ankara for over three years as deputy head of mission (1989–92) under Morton Abramowitz. When Abramowitz left (July 1991), Grossman assumed the duties of the head of mission until Richard Barkley took up his position as the new US ambassador (November 1991). Even before Grossman was confirmed as the US ambassador to Turkey (September 1994)[83] he was thought to be 'Mr Turkey' in Washington. Grossman recalls that during his first stint in Ankara he witnessed Turkey's strategic value decline fast as a result of the end of the Cold War.[84] He lamented it. He thought that Turkey should not lose its strategic value simply because the Cold War was over. Grossman, who had a strong interest in geopolitics, believed that Turkey's strategic value to the US was long term, due to its location at the crossroads of Europe, the independent states of the former USSR, the Balkan states and also the Middle East. In his mind its key value lay in its potential role in the creation of an East-West energy corridor from the Caspian Sea. But his perspective was also influenced by other strategic considerations. Turkey was a barrier to the revival of Russian power. Because of its democratic style of politics it stood as a model among Muslim countries. It was an ally against Islamic terrorism that was feeding on anti-Western fervour. It was on the right side in the global confrontation between the forces supporting political reform and open society and their opponents, which also included Islamic fundamentalists. Thus, he was convinced that the US 'should get the relationship back on track'. Grossman shared the view of those experts on Turkey who argued that unless the country sorted out its extremely serious internal problems, namely its faltering economy and the Kurdish issue, it could never become an effective US ally.[85] But to him the crux of the matter was not Turkey's weaknesses but rather that the country was too important to the US for the Americans to afford to let it go astray and finally have it collapse under the weight of its own shortcomings. In short, this was the message that Grossman wished to inject into the perspective of the administration.

From his vantage point as an old Turkey hand, Grossman thought that to anchor Turkey in the West and for the relationship to have a future the US, for its part, should provide greater predictability and consistency in its dealings with Ankara. In other words, the US administration should have a clear policy of commitment to Turkey, which would help serve mutual interests. Grossman's assessment was that the Turks could not, and essentially would not, come to accept US goals (including the necessity to contain Saddam Hussein) unless they received US support on issues of major interest to them, namely the Kurdish issue, Turkey's accession to the EU (something that incidentally President Bush had promised Özal in the wake of the Gulf War[86]) and Turkey's economic restructuring. By choosing to support Ankara on these matters, thought Grossman, the US would demonstrate its serious interest in Turkey, while at the same time it would assist the Turks by increasing their confidence about the future prospects of their country. When gauging the future Grossman knew that there was another harder task that had to be accomplished. The bilateral relationship was too narrow and thus essentially the responsibility of the American and Turkish military, who basically shaped the Turkish approach to the US. For Grossman, the long-term viability of the relationship demanded that it was taken away from the hands of the military and that it was broadened. Actually, Ambassador Morton Abramowitz had urged this point when he was head of the mission in Ankara and Grossman was his deputy. Abramowitz watched the growing liberalization of Turkey as the 1980s were coming to a close and foresaw that soon there would be a strong public opinion and a strong parliament to reckon with. So, he argued, the relationship should be shifted from the military-to-military track into the hands of the State Department and the Turkish government, otherwise it would have no future.[87] This would be only a beginning. Abramowitz thought it essential that the heavily lopsided relationship, which was

90 per cent based on military ties, should be rebalanced to include more civilian aspects of interaction, with an emphasis on the growth of business ties.[88] These viewpoints, first developed by Abramowitz in the very early 1990s, also guided Grossman and grew in his mind as he was thinking of the long-term viability of the relationship. One of his main ideas was that the US needed to increase the private sector investment in Turkey, to stimulate the kind of co-operation that was linking private American interests with private Turkish interests.[89]

No sooner was Grossman confirmed ambassador than he set to work in order to transform the unequal relationship with the Turks into an effective partnership and to open up opportunities for the building of business-to-business ties. As he recalls he had to work hard to convince the administration. The major thrust of his argument was that Central Asia and the Balkans were going to be important and Turkey could be an effective ally in both these areas in a variety of ways. While traditional military ties had been the core of US–Turkey co-operation until then, Grossman pointed out that the US presently had an opportunity to develop a different relationship with the Turks because Turkey *was changing*; it was catching up with modernity at a fast pace. Grossman recalls that it was not easy to attract the attention and gain the co-operation of administration officials behind the idea that the US should strengthen and expand its ties with Turkey.[90] But in the end he succeeded. Morton Abramowitz underscores that 'Turkey is one of the handful of countries where the U.S. ambassador can exert real and continued influence in Washington.'

> In great part this arises from the complexity and unfamiliarity of Turkish problems coupled with the lack of general knowledge about the country at high policy levels and the absence of high-level personal relationships; language also can sometimes be a problem inhibiting high-level Washington-Ankara direct discussion. Much obviously depends on the character and drive of the ambassador and the issues in play.[91]

Clearly Marc Grossman had what it took. A native of California and an international relations graduate, he was 43 years old at the time. A lean man, of medium-height with an easy-going, smooth manner and an attentive gaze, he had taken an interesting path within the State Department which helped him accumulate a lot of knowledge and experience on how to integrate political, economic and security issues into policy. Before his first appointment to Ankara (1989–92) Grossman had served for seven years (1976–83) at the US embassy in Pakistan during the period of military rule (1977–88) before he became deputy director (1984–86) of the private office of the secretary general of NATO, Lord Carrington, in Brussels. His other appointments included that of principal deputy assistant secretary of state for the Bureau of Political Military Affairs – the main bridge of the State Department with the Department of Defense – whose mission was to integrate diplomacy with defence – and executive secretary of the Department of State (January 1993–September 1994).

A very driven, intelligent, hard-working man with a lot of fire underneath his understated, low-key manner he was an extremely serious official who wanted to get things done. He proved that he had both the capacity and the temperament to deal with the challenge of engineering alliances of interests that could help drive policies. Grossman's effectiveness was strengthened by the fact that his boss at the State Department, Assistant Secretary of State Richard Holbrooke, was sympathetic to Turkey and immediately endorsed both Grossman's perspective and his proposed frame of action in order to strengthen US–Turkey ties.[92] In Holbrooke's own words in an interview he gave to the daily Turkish *Milliyet* a short while after he left his post:

> Soon after we started our new jobs, Grossman in Ankara and I in Washington, we sat down to discuss what Turkey meant for us in the post-Cold War era. We developed a new concept which was fully backed by the White House and Pentagon, that Turkey was the new front state for the West, and in that sense, she had taken up the role of Germany during the Cold War.[93]

Not only did Holbrooke approve Grossman's viewpoint but he actively promoted it within the administration and in Congress. This added extra weight to Grossman's effort. Over the next two years Holbrooke emerged as a staunch advocate of Turkey's strategic value and a strong US–Turkey relationship. He would consistently refer to Turkey as a 'front-line state'[94] and in concert with Grossman would underline the importance of building closer ties with the Turks. According to the astute analyst of US–Turkey relations, Alan Makovsky, 'only Richard Perle … had previously exerted such strong influence in favour of strong U.S. strategic bonds with Turkey.'[95] Holbrooke's title, assistant secretary of state, belied his influence. Although only a middle-level official (like Perle) he was extremely influential within the administration because, according to savvy political observers, it is not the rank that mostly determines influence (although it does play a role) but the force of the personality. All in all, prospects for effectively promoting Grossman's proposed frame of action were good. Grossman's and Holbrooke's presentation of Turkey as a 'front-line state' had all the aspects that, according to Ryan Beasley's analysis,[96] would make it very likely to be adopted by the administration: it was simple; it was backed by an expert, Grossman, who had established beyond doubt his expertise on Turkey due to his prior service in Ankara in the late 1980s/early 1990s; it had the backing of a strong official, Richard Holbrooke. Furthermore, the proposed frame of action could be seen as an incremental outgrowth of what had been done in the past, another important element that made it easy to be adopted.[97] Grossman successfully registered also the backing of Deputy Secretary of State Talbott. As an expert on the Soviet Union, Strobe Talbott belonged to those who viewed Turkey as a strategic asset in relation to the USSR, which in his mind was replaced by Russia after the end of the Cold War. Samuel (Sandy) Berger, Clinton's deputy national security advisor under Anthony Lake (1993–97) and a close friend of the president, also endorsed Grossman's viewpoint.[98] Talbott and Berger, recalls Grossman, became big supporters of his initiatives.[99]

Grossman and Holbrooke, who co-ordinated their actions, initiated and implemented important policy measures that would shape the Clinton administration's policy toward Turkey from the end of 1994 onwards.[100] Grossman's first initiative that was meant to open the way for the strengthening of US–Turkey ties developed as soon as he was appointed ambassador to Ankara. In the autumn of 1994 before taking up his position Grossman effectivelly 'encouraged' the under-secretary of commerce for international trade, Jeffrey Garten, to include Turkey in the list of the ten so-called big emerging markets.[101] What this meant in practice was that the secretary of commerce gave priority to improving market access, providing financing and otherwise supporting US companies that were interested in developing trade relations with or investing in Turkey. It was a grand public gesture of US confidence in the Turks and their continuing efforts to fully liberalize their economy. Predictably, it was highly appreciated in Ankara for the Turks until that point had felt that the US had done very little to constructively assist their efforts for economic development.[102] At the same time, Grossman was working at another much more exciting policy initiative, from Ankara's standpoint. As mentioned earlier, in the early 1990s one of the major goals of the Turks was to secure a share in the development of a Caspian oil pipeline. The Turks were after a piece of the main export pipeline from Baku, which was still to be built. As the route of the pipeline was under discussion they lobbied hard in Washington for it to pass via Georgia and Turkey and end up in the Turkish Mediterranean port of Ceyhan, instead of going through Russia or Iran. Designed to carry almost a thousand barrels of oil a day, it was going to be a lucrative source of income for Turkey because of transport fees. It was also expected to turn Turkey into an energy hub, thus enhancing its strategic importance. Prime Minister Çiller met with President Clinton in 1993 and laid out the Turkish government's strategy plan for Ceyhan. Clinton was sympathetic but non-committal.[103] In fact, until Grossman came into the picture in late 1994 the Clinton administration had given the Turks little reason to be seriously optimistic concerning US support. Grossman was very supportive of the Turkish proposal. In his mind, the development of the Baku-Ceyhan route was a very important strategic issue for both political and economic reasons. It would serve as an important underpinning of Turkey, help tie it more firmly to the West and help boost the confidence of the Turks, which was necessary if they were to successfully engage in a more active foreign policy course in the Caucasus and Central Asia that would be helpful to American interests.[104] Essentially it would boost the confidence of the Turks in the US as an ally and a friend. It really helped that around the time Grossman was appointed to the ambassadorial position the energy task force of Rosemarie

Forsythe, the director for Russian, Ukrainian and Eurasian affairs at the National Security Council, reached the conclusion that US interests demanded that the pipeline did not go via Russia. The decision benefited Grossman, who sought to build a consensus around the Baku-Ceyhan route. His basic strategy was to engage the full attention of the State Department on the pipeline issue and then get the approval of a number of other departments, including those of defense, energy and commerce. As he recalls, he was at first amazed when he realized that an issue of such strategic significance was essentially dealt with by the 'pipelines and the economy people'.[105] Grossman worked incessantly in Washington to push through the administration the idea that the US ought to support the Baku-Ceyhan option in order to enhance Turkey's regional importance and thus strengthen it as a westward channel of influence for the newly independent states in the Caucasus and Central Asia.[106] His hand was very much strengthened by the backing of Rosemarie Forsythe, who was looking for a way to convince Strobe Talbott that a pipeline independent of Moscow should not be seen as incompatible with Washington's policy of seeking not to antagonize Russia.[107] Finally approval did come through as he was getting ready to leave for Turkey and he worked around the clock in order to get clearance to mention in his first press conference in Ankara that the US supported the Baku-Ceyhan route. So, soon after the presentation of his credentials (3 January 1995) he delivered in his first press conference the statement that the US government had already informed several governments in the region that they would endorse construction of a pipeline via Turkey. He recalls with a smile the big sensation his statement aroused in Turkey: 'The Turks could hardly believe it'.[108] According to LeVine, Grossman became instantly 'a local hero'.[109]

Clearly, Washington's new approach concerning the pipeline encouraged Turkish officials to think that with US support the chances of achieving their objectives had multiplied.[110] In reality, the Clinton administration could not have made, and had not, any promises that the Baku-Ceyhan pipeline plan would finally materialize. The general diplomatic support Washington was talking about was expected to help the Turks' own efforts. Thus, it successfully delivered the message that Washington was a true ally and friend of Turkey, at no cost to the US. All the same, Grossman's hard work in Washington and his ability to produce policy resulted in striking in Ankara a new optimistic note about its relationship with the US. It also greatly enhanced Grossman's own standing in official Turkish circles, who correctly understood that his initiatives had a lot to do with this bonanza of good-will gestures coming from Washington.[111]

Inside the administration Grossman was not alone in thinking that Turkey retained its strategic importance in the post-Cold War era and in believing that there was need of a more engaged US policy towards the Turks. For one, Morton Abramowitz had already been arguing that the US had 'a major stake' in the success of the 'unique' Turkey 'experiment': 'a secular democracy in a Muslim country in an area of turbulence, poverty and religious radicalism'. Abramowitz's viewpoint was that preserving that stake would 'demand more concentrated and sympathetic attention than senior US officials had usually been willing to devote'.[112] Certain Pentagon circles also lamented the lack of a clear-cut US policy towards Turkey. Since the collapse of the Soviet Union they had been arguing that Turkey due to its strategic location could emerge as an important US strategic partner in the post-Cold War era.[113] A December 1993 report written by three security experts at the Strategic Studies Institute of the US Army War College entitled *Turkey's Strategic Position at the Crossroads of World Affairs* captured this perspective. The authors argued that Turkey because of its strategic location 'at the intersection of Europe and Asia' played 'a pivotal role in the post-Cold War system of states.'[114] Therefore the report – which clearly intended to influence the thinking of the new Clinton administration – called 'for a clear U.S. strategy and concept of U.S. and Turkish interests in the regions of mutual engagement so that the United States can help Ankara overcome its problems.'[115]

Actually, Holbrooke's statement to *Milliyet* that it was himself and Grossman who at the end of 1994 came up with the idea that Turkey was 'a front-line state' raises questions about its accuracy. At no time, Grossman says, did he come up with this idea nor does he know who did.[116] In fact, the idea that Turkey was 'a front-line state' for the West was already established in Ankara before the two US officials assumed their positions, although it is difficult to trace its origins.[117] There is evidence showing that since the very early 1990s the Turkish general staff often referred to Turkey as a 'front-line state'. For instance, in February 1992 Lieutenant-General Çevik Bir, the Turkish general staff director of operations, in his speech in Washington at the American Turkish Friendship Association underscored that Turkey was a 'front-line state'.[118] This event took place two and a half years before Holbrooke and Grossman assumed their positions in September 1994. The topic of Bir's presentation was the new NATO strategy and Turkey's security in the post-Cold War international environment. Bir stated that the new threats originating in the Middle East as well as instability in the Caucasus meant that within the context of Western security Turkey was transformed from a flank country of the North Atlantic Treaty alliance to a 'front-line state'. Hence, Turkey had to adopt a forward defence position, which, he argued, created a pressing need for the military modernization of the country.[119] In April 1993 (one and a half years before Holbrooke's and Grossman's appointments) Chief of the Turkish General Staff General Doğan Güreş, summing up the general staff view of Turkey's strategic position in the post-Cold War security environment, also stated that Turkey was a 'front-line state' and not a flank country.[120]

There was an underlying assumption behind the Turks' 'front-line state' idea, and this was spelled out by Ambassador Morton Abramowitz in a piece for *Foreign Policy* that appeared in the summer of 1993, long before the idea of Turkey as a 'front-line state' was promoted in the US administration by Holbrooke and Grossman. Abramowitz identified that

> the Turks proudly sense a new international prominence for themselves; they enjoy their position as a major regional power in the Caucasus, Central Asia, and the Persian Gulf. They believe their country has recovered its strategic importance to the West, which seemed lost with the end of the Cold War and the decline of NATO.[121]

But there was a significant gap between the Turks' perception and reality. Although in the very early 1990s Turkey's foreign policy objectives and its expectations about its international role had been expanded with US encouragement,[122] Turkey lacked the capacities to achieve most of them without US support,[123] while the US did not seem interested, or focused, enough to help the Turks upgrade their international position. As it happened, Marc Grossman's and Richard Holbrooke's appointments greatly worked to Turkey's advantage for they significantly contributed to redefining and focusing US policy toward Turkey on the basis of the idea that the US should support the Turks' objectives.

Making Turkey relevant to a broader constituency

By the end of President Clinton's second year in office his foreign policy team started giving more emphasis to the security aspects of foreign policy and began to pursue more traditional US foreign policy goals. If this hadn't happened, Grossman and Holbrooke might not have been able to formulate and sustain a US policy aiming at strengthening ties with Turkey. But the success of this policy also depended upon the Turks' ability and willingness to work with the Americans in order to identify how to achieve increased co-operation on the basis of Turkey's capabilities and mutual interests.[124] In short, the Turks were called upon to make their own policy adjustments and so they eventually did.[125] By 1994 Turkish leaders came to accept that their resistance to US efforts to contain Saddam Hussein was counter-productive. They also came to realize that they had to cut down to size their ambitions to create a zone of Turkish influence in the Caucasus and Central Asia. This objective, which initially was encouraged by the US, was not only proved unrealistic but, more importantly from a US point of view, was causing rivalry with Russia, threatening to complicate relations between Washington and Moscow.[126] But the more spectacular policy change was the decision to expand relations with Israel into the military field.

In February 1996 Turkey and Israel announced that they had signed a military co-operation agreement which included joint air-force training, mutual naval visits, as well as exchanges of military information, experience and personnel. The agreement expanded the military training co-operation that was initiated in September 1995 with the signing of a Memorandum of Understanding for the training of pilots of both countries in each other's airspace. Bilateral military co-operation was further strengthened with the signing of a defence industries co-operation agreement in August 1996.[127] Throughout the rest of the decade Turkey-Israel military ties would flourish while the US selectively joined in the co-operation.

The 1996 military co-operation agreement, which took a year of negotiations, was a landmark in the history of the bilateral relationship that had been developing relatively slowly since the late 1980s and in a quite rapid fashion since the early 1990s. In essence, it reflected the political and strategic changes in the Middle East sub-system after the Gulf War which created new risks but also new strategic options for Turkey. Some analysts argue that the agreement signified the end of Turkey's long-standing policy of non-involvement in Middle Eastern affairs.[128] Others take the view that change should not be seen as the full reversal of the traditional policy of non-involvement, but rather the adoption of a more flexible policy.[129] In any case, it was a sea change in Ankara's carefully woven policy vis-à-vis the Arab-Israeli conflict, for in this context Turkish governments had tended to favour the Arabs. The Turks' decision to develop military ties with Israel served a number of key Turkish priorities.[130] The strong desire of the Turkish military establishment to develop joint industrial defence projects with the Israelis, in addition to Turkey's already established interest in diversifying its supply market for modern weapons, provided a strong impetus. Also, military co-operation with Israel was expected to strengthen Ankara's hand in the escalating confrontation with Damascus over the latter's support for the Kurdish PKK guerillas. In the words of Mehmet Ali Birand, it offered a kind of security guarantee regarding Turkey's eastern border that the Turks intensely desired.[131] Most importantly, it was another necessary step within the context of the effort to boost support for Turkey in Washington.[132] Şükrü Elekdağ, Turkey's influential ambassador to Washington in the 1980s (1979–89), who had understood – and made sure that Ankara did too – the importance of enlisting the support of the Jewish-American lobby groups on Turkey's behalf, wrote in a much quoted article in November 1994:

> The Israeli lobby in the United States is far superior to all other ethnic lobbies put together. Whenever this lobby has worked for us, Turkey's interests have been perfectly protected against the fools in the United States. The development of relations between Turkey and Israel and the formalisation of their *de facto* alliance will place this lobby permanently on our side.[133]

Elekdağ's statement was noteworthy not only because of his former position and his continuing influence among Turkey's foreign policy–making circles, but also because his views echoed the thinking of the majority of the Turkish foreign policy–making establishment. His opinion piece revealed that the Turks realized that 'enhanced efforts' were necessary in order to gain the full-hearted support of the pro-Israeli lobby.[134] Although, since the very early 1990s Turkey's relations with Israel were steadily advancing, the Israelis drove a hard bargain with the Turks over Israel's intervention on Turkey's behalf in Washington,[135] while persistently promoting in Ankara the value of bilateral military co-operation. As a matter of fact, since the very early 1990s there had been a 'careful cultivation' by the Israelis of top officers in the Turkish defence establishment,[136] who eventually became the main architects of the military co-operation on the Turkish side.[137] Actually, according to Özdem Sanberk, the Israelis' efforts to this effect can be dated even earlier, since the late 1980s.[138] Around the mid-1990s it was not only the Israelis who were working hard to persuade the Turks but the Americans too as by late 1994 the Clinton administration was actively pressing the Turks to enter into security co-operation with the Israelis.

Most students of the development of Turkey-Israel relations in the 1990s do not link Turkey's decision to develop bilateral military ties to an active US diplomatic effort.[139] The US has been by and large presented as an endorsing observer watching from the sidelines while leaving the initiative to the Turks and the Israelis. Along this general line, Henri Barkey does state that Washington provided 'some initiatives' but he does not elaborate on this point, except for saying that the Americans essentially left the two countries to decide the limits of their co-operation.[140] Offra Bengio points out that the US was 'ready to play a part, albeit minor, in the new alignment'. She also states that according to the Israeli military attaché in Ankara during the 1990s Rabin had gotten the Clinton administration interested in the Israel-Turkey strategic co-operation rapprochement, but then she does not discuss whether the Clinton administration had any influence on the Turks' decision to develop military ties with Israel.[141] Yet the US administration played an active and it seems decisive role.[142]

Evidently the Israelis and Jewish-American groups sought to enlist Washington's support in the effort to convince the Turks to expand relations also into the military field.[143] But it is impossible to assess the impact that this persistent lobbying had on the Clinton administration's growing interest in the Turkey-Israel alignment. In any case, the development of military co-operation between the two US allies was clearly attractive to many Clinton administration officials because it served a number of US regional interests and objectives.[144] Those US officials who were involved in the peace process had come to accept the argument that Israel's military co-operation with Turkey would strengthen the peace camp for it helped increase pressure on Syria. Therefore, it was expected that the Turkish-Israeli alignment would be another factor that would make Assad reconsider his 'hard' policy towards Israel[145] as US officials believed that the Syrian leader 'calculated the balance of power like a computer', to use Martin Indyk's words.[146] There was also the supporting argument that military ties with Turkey offered Israel a strategic advantage that would make it feel less isolated and more secure.[147] For a long time the prevailing view among the Americans was that the more secure the Israelis felt, the more willing they would be to make the necessary concessions for the peace process to move forward. There was moreover the belief that whatever supported the peace process indirectly backed the Clinton administration's dual containment policy for the peace process and dual containment were seen in Washington as 'symbiotic'.[148] In other words, military co-operation between Turkey and Israel would help isolate those who were against the US, such as Iraq and Iran by affecting the fragile military and political balances in the Middle East in favour of the regional forces friendly to the US.[149] Also, US officials saw an opportunity for putting in place a kind of loose trilateral military co-operation between Israel, Turkey and the US that could be useful at times of regional crises.[150] Essentially, the Turkey-Israel military co-operation was from an American perspective perfectly in line with the post-Cold War US security strategy that has been described as relying on the 'rise of new security geometries or alliances in critical regions', involving co-operation with states that were friendly to the US, which allowed Washington to serve its interests in their wider area.[151] Those US officials who advocated stronger US–Turkey ties were also keen on Turkey's military co-operation with Israel. For one thing, this development would help consolidate US–Turkey relations as the Turks' co-operation with Israel would be supporting a number of US regional objectives. Furthermore, Israel could become a conduit for providing Turkey with US military technology and thus assist the US executive to bypass congressional opposition.[152] Also, military co-operation with Israel was expected to help dull congressional opposition to Ankara on account of its handling of the Kurdish issue.[153] At the same time, US officials knew that Washington had to be careful lest Turkey-Israel military ties undermined other US interests. Military sales to Turkey were one of them. The other was not to undermine and alienate the Arab forces who were friendly to the US by offering open support to the new alignment.[154] However, these concerns did not hold a prominent place in the minds of State Department officials.[155]

It was at some point in 1994 that the Clinton administration began to show more than an approving interest in the Turkey-Israel relationship and actually began to encourage the Turks to consider adding a military dimension to it.[156] Apparently it was a slow moving act, but when Marc Grossman was appointed US ambassador to Ankara the matter was pushed further. Grossman placed the question of the Israel-Turkey relationship high on his agenda and made a big effort to persuade the Turks that they should strengthen and deepen relations with Israel.[157] Grossman acted because the relationship was 'very important to the US',[158] but he was also motivated by his interest in injecting new life into US–Turkey relations. For Grossman regarded the strengthening of the Turkey-Israel relationship – which, had begun as a result of Özal's policies – as fundamental to the strengthening of US–Turkey relations.[159] As it became more obvious that Turkey could not play the influential role it aspired to in the area of the former Soviet Union, the clearer it was for Grossman – and for all those who advocated Turkey's strategic value – that Turkey needed to identify new reasons in order to justify again its importance to the US. Thomas Dine, staff director of the AIPAC in the early 1990s, coming from a different perspective succintly makes the point that US support for Turkey really depended upon the Turks: 'The lobby could influence

Congress and the administration on Turkey's behalf only to an extent. The rest depended on the Turks themselves. Turkey needed to do something to prove in Washington that it was worthy of support.'[160]

Grossman believed that deeper co-operation with Israel would first of all help change Turkey's image in the US.[161] Improving Turkey's image was an issue of major importance to those in Washington who, like Grossman, wished to boost the US–Turkey relationship. Richard Perle noted that whilst there were many reasons that accounted for the congressional reaction to the Reagan administrations' requests for significant military assistance to Turkey, in his view the biggest impediment to building Turkey as a major ally with American money was its image in the popular media. This was influenced by Alan Parker's film *Midnight Express* (1978), which portrayed the Turks as barbarous, cruel and anti-American.[162] Grossman recalls that the issue of Turkey's image was immensely frustrating.[163] Not only was his generation, at least, influenced by *Midnight Express*, but in the early 1990s Turkey's negative image was compounded due to US media reports about the harsh way the Turkish state was responding to the Kurdish insurgency and also as a result of the actions of those who were interested in the Cyprus issue and Turkey's relations with Greece. He remembers how 'it was impossible to frame Turkey in any other light.'[164] Besides, stresses Grossman, Turkey was considered important and worthy of attention only by a handful of officials, most of them to be found at the Pentagon. 'When you wanted to talk to someone about Turkey he would exclaim, "Turkey!" and he would not listen. He would glaze over.'[165] As all students of politics know, successful policy-making depends on building coalitions. In Grossman's mind 'Turkey badly needed to find public allies in the US.'[166] He was aware that to this effect the Turks had to broaden the context in which their country was viewed. The way to go about it was to identify an angle that served various agendas and interests. This would make Turkey relevant to many in Washington. The trial and error of experience hard taught him that such an angle would tend to unify many officials both in the administration and in Congress. 'It would have them work together on policy issues that mattered to Turkey even if normally, perhaps, they would not even talk to each other.'[167] In his judgement, a strong, expanded Turkey-Israel relationship would be just the issue that would get different people interested in Turkey, for all the reasons outlined earlier.[168]

So as soon as he arrived in Ankara he began to work systematically and persistently in order to convey the value of deepening relations with Israel to the Foreign Ministry and the military. The timing was extremely good. There existed a large number of issues in Turkish foreign policy, whether these concerned relations with the US or the Arabs, that had ripened to a point that called for some variety of approach. An interest in pushing relations with Israel further into the hard security field was, in fact, already present in the minds of many senior foreign policy-makers in Ankara and particularly in the military establishment.[169] Therefore Turkish rulers were receptive to the US ambassador's arguments. According to Grossman, 'the Turkey-Israel relationship fit well the needs of both countries. All I did was to structure the arguments for the Turks'.[170] So he told them to consider that the US was very much interested in the Turkey-Israel relationship. He underscored that Turkey needed public allies in the US and said that strengthening relations with Israel would both contribute to this and improve its public image there. Further, it would help register the support of Israel behind Turkey's effort to join the EU.[171] The Turks listened. In the words of Mehmet Ali Birand, the bottom line of the US message at the time was 'a security relationship with Israel – latent trilateral – will give you a golden opportunity in Washington'.[172] But according to Birand there were no promises of specific US rewards. Nor did Grossman make the US some kind of guarantor of the Turkey-Israel security co-operation. It would have to develop on a bilateral basis to the degree that fit the needs of the Turks and the Israelis.[173]

Any other US ambassador might have been less effective. But Grossman was a man of immense ability. Also, his recent policy initiatives gave him impeccable credentials as a friend of Turkey. There was still another reason contributing to his success. During his previous service as deputy head of mission in Ankara he built excellent channels of communication with Turkey's military establishment, which dominated foreign policy, as well as with a number of senior officials in the Foreign Ministry bureaucracy, some of whom now had Prime Minister Çiller's ear. Actually, his close acquaintance with many senior Turkish military officers, including Deputy Chief of Staff General Çevik Bir (1995–98), the architect of the military alignment with Israel on the Turkish side (who apparently also happened to have strong ties with the US Pentagon),[174] dated back to the mid 1980s when Grossman was the deputy director (1984–86) of the private office of the secretary general of NATO, Lord Carrington.[175]

According to Mehmet Ali Birand and another Turkish source, Grossman played an important role in the decision of the Turkish military leadership and the Foreign Ministry to co-operate with Israel also in the military field. In their minds he was instrumental in igniting the interest that was there already.[176] For Mehmet Ali Birand, by and large the spectacular development of the military aspect of the Turkey-Israel relationship should be considered Grossman's personal achievement. According to the Turkish journalist and commentator, without the US ambassador's influence security ties might still have materialized but they would have developed in a very slow, much more cautious way.[177] Of course, the deepening of the Turkey-Israel relationship, a major regional development, featured many players in prominent roles, but it can be safely said that Grossman played the leading part on the US side. Grossman himself prefers to underplay his personal contribution. Instead he underscores that many people in Washington and Ankara worked for the strengthening of relations between Turkey and Israel.[178]

Students of Turkish-Israeli relations tend to discuss the importance of Turkey's decision to militarily side with Israel within the context of Turkey's Middle

East policy and the development of a post-Cold War Turkish foreign policy activism.[179] They tend to overlook the significance of the decision within the context of Turkey's policy toward the US. Yet military co-operation with Israel signified Turkish support, albeit through the back door, for a number of major US policy goals in the Middle East, including the peace process and the containment of Iran and Iraq. It also reflected the Turks' changed perspective concerning military co-operation with the US in the area. As Turkish Foreign Minister Hikmet Çetin put it during his 1994 visit to Israel, a new order was emerging in the Middle East and Turkey was determined to co-operate in its creation.[180] After 1998 Turkey, Israel and the US began to participate in annual joint naval exercises. Their stated purpose was that they constituted an effort for the Israeli, Turkish and United States navies to learn each other's capabilities and get accustomed to each other's procedures so as to achieve co-ordination and inter-operability for a rapid response to a humanitarian emergency.[181] Yet, clearly, such experience could be useful not only in a humaritanian, but also in a military context in the event of a crisis in the region. Actually, during the second exercise a small task force also performed surface manoeuvering of a military nature, which made it obvious that the framework for even wider future manoeuvers was being prepared.[182] There were also joint air-manoeuvers, and apparently trilateral theatre missile defence talks were also held.[183] In other words, from the perspective of the Turkey-US relationship, the Turkish-Israeli alignment revealed that Turkish leaders and primarily the military, who dominated the foreign policy–making process, came to realize that in order to promote their major security/political/economic goals,[184] they had to back a number of US strategic objectives in the Middle East. In effect, Turkey's alignment with Israel was another major step in the gradual shift, selectively, away from the former policy of keeping a safe distance from US objectives in the area. This shift was first seen with the 1982 COB agreement and then with Turkey's participation in the Gulf War.

The decision to enter into military co-operation with Israel – and thus to inevitably identify its policy in the Middle East more with that of the US – did not remain unchallenged within the Turkish foreign policy–making apparatus. Even though the military pushed hard for it and it had the approval of Prime Minister Tansu Çiller, while it was endorsed by some of his close advisers, it was resisted by a significant number of Foreign Ministry bureaucrats who thought that a reversal of Turkey's traditional policy in the area would not prove to be prudent in the longer run.[185] Eventually, the argument that a change in the course of Turkish foreign policy was necessary won the day. Actually, it would have been difficult not to as the military was still at the helm of Turkish foreign policy in the 1990s, even though the Foreign Ministry maintained a significant degree of influence. As Alan Makovsky pointedly puts it, at the time a policy strongly advocated by the military would almost certainly have been implemented; a policy strongly opposed by the military almost certainly would not.[186] It was the Turkish Islamists who during their short period in power (June 1996–June 1997) as members of a coalition government under their leader, Necmettin Erbakan, resisted ties with Israel. Erbakan employed an anti-Western, anti-Israel rhetoric and seemed determined to stop the military co-operation with Israel. But his efforts were in vain against the resolution and strong reaction of the military with the support of the Kemalist political establishment.

It has been argued that as the Gulf War undermined the foundations of Arab solidarity Turkey had the opportunity to act more freely in the area. This freedom of action, it is said, was clearly reflected in its growing relationship with Israel.[187] Yet the exact opposite argument can be made. The reversal of Turkey's policy of non-involvement in the conflicts in the Middle East and in conflicts between the states of the area and external powers can be seen as a sign of Ankara's lack of freedom of choice, at least without a significant cost. Turkey's alignment with Israel and consequently its indirect support for a number of US strategic goals in the Middle East undoubtedly reflected the ambitions of Turkish leaders at the time as much as the challenges that concerned them. But had there been an alternative way for the Turks to advance their objectives, most probably they would have preferred to advance relations with Israel cautiously and to continue with their policy of keeping a safe distance from US policies in the Middle East. Essentially there had been no radical change in the Turkish leaders' conviction that the US was an unreliable interlocutor and ally.[188] And the general staff did not really wish for Turkey to get militarily involved in the Middle East.[189] By and large, Ankara's new policy in the Middle East betrayed Turkey's weakness and lack of necessary tools to deal with challenges and promote its political and economic objectives without the support of the US and Israel. Turkish Prime Minister Mesut Yilmaz in a laconic manner acknowledged as much when he stated to the Arab weakly *Al-Wasat* (a few months after the signing of Turkey's military co-operation agreement with Israel was announced) that Israel was an important power influencing the global balance of power and Turkey took this into consideration.[190]

A 'pivotal state' is born

The turning point in post-Cold War US–Turkey relations occurred around the autumn of 1994 and winter of 1995, which saw the beginnings of the 'partnership for the twenty-first century', as Turkey's supporters within the Clinton administration decided to brand the relationship. It was when Grossman was appointed US ambassador to Ankara and Turkey-Israel discussions concerning military co-operation turned into meaningful negotiations.[191] Not surprisingly, the same period witnessed the emergence of the Turks' euphoria concerning their relations with the Americans, while the thought that the US was 'Turkey's best friend' internationally began to emerge in Ankara.[192] A strong telling sign that Washington's policy towards Turkey was becoming more focused was the important but little publicized agreement (3 October 1994) to transfer $1.5 billion from the Turkish Defense Fund (in a special account at the Federal Reserve)[193] to the Central Bank of Turkey. The actual transfer took place in January 1995. It constituted perhaps the largest single transfer of funds from the US to Turkey in the history of the bilateral relationship.[194] The objective was not to cover Turkey's defence needs but to boost Turkey's foreign currency reserves[195] in order to restore its international creditworthiness. This had collapsed due to a dramatic currency crisis that developed against the backdrop of growing fiscal imbalances. In the first quarter of 1994 Turkey's Central Bank lost 50 per cent of its currency reserves, the Turkish lira more than 50 per cent of its value against the US dollar and inflation reached three digit numbers.[196]

In late February 1995 Richard Holbrooke on an official visit to Turkey stated to the press that Turkey's importance had increased after the end of the Cold War.[197] Around the same time the expression 'front-line state' became inseparable from any mention of Turkey by the State Department. In March 1995 Holbrooke in his statement outlining the policy of the Clinton administration before the House International Relations Committee underscored Turkey's importance as a 'front-line state' because it stood 'at the crossroads of almost every issue of importance to the U.S. on the Eurasian continent.'[198] The phrase that Turkey stood 'at the crossroads' would soon become the 'battle cry' for those favouring strong ties with Turkey, as Makovsky aptly puts it.[199] According to the administration's public rhetoric the list of the areas of US concern that Turkey could affect could not be more impressive: NATO, the Balkans, the Aegean, sanctions on Iraq, Russia's relations with the former Soviet republics, peace in the Middle East, energy routes.[200]

In April 1995 Deputy Secretary of State Strobe Talbott in his Ankara speech in Hobrooke's presence fully supported the Turks' aspirations to regional importance and influence and underlined Turkey's value for US security objectives.[201]

> Looking beyond Europe, the United States and Turkey have vital roles to play in the Middle East and Central Asia. Turkey is the European nation most closely linked to those regions by geography, history, culture, and, of course, by religion. … Your country's accomplishments in the twentieth century give you the potential to be a leader in the twenty-first. This is just one reason among many why the United States is proud to stand with you as we work to build a safer and more prosperous future.[202]

He boldly declared that Turkey was

> yet again on the front line of the world's most important struggles just as it was during the Cold War from the late 1940s to the late 1980s and just as it was during the first major post-Cold War crisis – the repulse of Iraqi aggression and the liberation of Kuwait in 1990–91.[203]

Talbott also sent a message of optimism concerning how much the two countries could achieve together for mutual benefit. The deputy secretary spoke in the self-assured US traditions of manifest destiny and liberal internationalism. 'If we continue *to act together*, we can seize a historic opportunity not just to combat new threats but also to shape a world that reflects our shared ideals and promotes our common interests.'[204] This was of course the language of public rhetoric. But it was crystal clear that the Clinton administration had departed from its lukewarm approach to Turkey. Bilateral security co-operation, Talbott noted, was 'especially vital' when it came to dealing with Iraq, Iran and terrorist organizations like the PKK and Hamas.[205] As a reward to the Turks for having adjusted their policy and 'acting together' with the Americans, the Clinton administration had become convinced that it had to show much more understanding of Ankara's policy concerning the Kurdish issue. It was Holbrooke's statement during his visit to Turkey earlier that year that first revealed the big change of perspective that was underway within the administration. Holbrooke stressed at the press conference he held in Ankara that although human rights were important they would not be allowed to rupture bilateral relations.[206] It was as if the Cold War had never ended. His statement, which reflected the new focus of US foreign policy on more traditional security concerns, dismayed human rights activists[207] and also many liberals in Turkey, all the more so because it took place in the midst of reports about an escalation in human rights violations by the Turkish state, which even refused to accept that they were happening.[208] The administration's new stance was fully confirmed during Prime Minister Çiller's visit in Washington in late April 1995 when Clinton did not raise (at least publicly) concerns over the human rights problem. In June of the same year, when the State Department in response to a congressional request submitted to Congress a report acknowledging violations of human rights by the Turkish military in which US-origin equipment was 'highly likely' to have been used, Chairman of the Joint Chiefs of Staff General John Shalikashvili in a letter urged Congress not to cut aid to Turkey because of human rights abuses, for Turkey occupied 'the new front line in the post-Cold War era.'[209] In September 1995 House Representative Christopher H. Smith, Chairman of Commission on Security and Cooperation in Europe in his opening statement at the Commission hearing entitled "Turkey-United States Relations: Potential and Peril" underlined that since 1992 'Turkish security forces 'evacuated or destroyed more than 2,000 Kurdish villages in southeast Turkey and displaced more than 2 million in a campaign frighteningly similar to ethnic cleansing'.[210] But that did not matter much for the unarguable fact was, as Marshall Adair Hobrooke's deputy put it at the hearing: Turkey was 'uniquely important to the United States. We now have a strong and positive relationship with Turkey which seeks to promote our interests there and in the region. There is both tremendous potential and peril for U.S. interests, and by our actions, we can promote our interests or we can endanger them. The issue of human rights is an important part of this equation'.[211] In short, as from 1995 the

Clinton administration was calling for a policy that essentially resembled Reagan's policy concerning Turkey's democratization process. Although the administration fully recognized that 'significant human rights abuses' were taking place in Turkey, it concluded as summarized by the words of John Shattuck, assistant secretary of the Bureau of Democracy, Human Rights and Labor at the State Department, that the US should encourage 'above all the strengthening of good relations between Turkey and the United States', while also encouraging changes in the interests of human rights and democracy.[212]

Talbott's April visit to Ankara coincided with a large-scale cross-border Turkish military operation involving 30,000 troops against the Kurdish guerillas in Northern Iraq. This had been launched by the Turkish armed forces on 20 March and would continue until early May. The previous large-scale operation had taken place in 1992. The US administration gave the Turks its full support even though it was not entirely happy and had certain reservations in relation to the scope and duration of the operation. The Americans wanted to make sure that care would be taken to avoid civilian casualties, and a main concern was that the operations should not give the Arabs the impression that the Turks were after oil-rich Mosul.[213]

By the end of 1995 the administration's policy of support for the Turks over a good number of issues that greatly mattered to them was well established. Congress with a few exceptions rode along. At the end of 1995 Turkey became the first foreign country to be sold the surface-to-surface long-range Army Tactical Missiles Systems (ATACMS). The Human Rights Watch Arms Project protested the sale on account of its potential consequences for the Kurdish civilian population. The Pentagon, however, argued that the Turkish state needed the missiles to defend itself against its rogue neighbours, namely Iraq and Iran. Congress authorized the sale.[214] At that point there was a remarkable degree of unity in Congress over efforts to find ways to support Turkey. This was because Congress had bought the idea that Turkey was a crucial state, due to its emerging security relationship with Israel and its potential role in the attainment of many US objectives in the Middle East.[215] In the words of Abramowitz 'the emergence of an Israel-Turkey axis added grist to a continually revised official view of Turkey's place in the world and helped generate political support for Turkey in the United States,'[216] as Grossman had foreseen.

The Clinton administration also fervently supported the construction of the Baku-Ceyhan pipeline, although it limited its efforts to diplomatic means and did not offer the economic support that the Turks were so much after.[217] According to Morton Abramowitz, while the construction of the pipeline served a number of US goals (to prevent Iran from becoming an energy outlet for the Caspian Sea, to increase the independence from Russia of the former Soviet republics in Central Asia and the Caucasus) the primary motive behind the US decision to favour the pipeline was to demonstrate support for Turkey.[218]

The new policy endorsed by the administration was soon reflected in the print media's coverage of Turkey and in the approach taken by Washington's think tanks. During the earlier part of Clinton's first term, Turkey's public image was coloured by press items focusing on the forced evacuation of Kurds from their villages and the attacks by the Turkish military on Kurdish civilians. This visibly began to change. Within the context of public debate attention now shifted to Turkey's significance to the US as a 'front-line state'.[219] To this effect, academics also played a major role. The much publicized article 'Pivotal States and U.S. Strategy' (which would later appear in book form) by Professor Paul Kennedy, the well-known historian at Yale, was a prominent case in point.[220] The article, co-authored by Kennedy and two PhD students, appeared in *Foreign Affairs*' winter 1996 issue, the Council of Foreign Affairs' publication that bridged the world of politics and academia. Due to Kennedy's acclaim the article attracted a lot of attention among political analysts and experts on Turkish foreign policy around the world and was instantly given a prominent place in the relevant bibliography. In the article the three authors included Turkey among the states they regarded as pivotal.[221] The term was used in reference to 'a hot spot that could not only determine the fate of its region but also affect international stability'.[222] Essentially, the authors echoed the basic arguments employed by the champions of a strong US–Turkey relationship within the administration and suggested a US policy that in reality was already there. Specifically, the paper pointed out that,

> at a multifold crossroads between East and West, North and South, Christendom and Islam, Turkey has the potential to influence countries thousands of miles from the Bosporus. … A Turkey engulfed by civil wars and racial and religious hatreds, or nursing ambitions to interfere abroad, would hurt American interests in innumerable ways and concern everyone from pro-NATO strategists to *friends of Israel*.[223]

As the stated objective of the article was to feed into the unfolding debate concerning the shape that US policy should take in the new world order, its authors underscored that the new pivotal states, including Turkey, 'no longer need assistance against an external threat from a hostile political system; rather, the danger is that they will fall prey to internal disorder. … Chaos and instability may prove a greater and more insidious threat to American interests than communism ever was.'[224] Therefore, they concluded that it was 'vital' for the US to focus its efforts on these states and help them succeed through a multitude of diplomatic, security and economic efforts, including providing them with aid 'despite congressional pressure to reduce or eliminate overseas assistance'.[225] 'In short the United States must use all the resources at its disposal to buttress' their stability.'[226]

There lay the conceptual framework of the administration's new more focused and energetic policy toward Turkey. The idea of Turkey as a 'pivotal state' was an effective addition. In contrast to the idea of 'front-line state', which was like a throwback to the Cold War mentality, that of a 'pivotal state' was much more in tune with the new international environment and the new security posture of the US. Certainly, it was a more scholarly term and had much more gravitas, for as the authors did not fail to point out it had 'a distinguished pedigree reaching back to the British geographer Sir Halford Mackinder in the 1900s and earlier.'[227]

The Kennedy article was much appreciated in Ankara. Many Turkish officials viewed it not only as a weighty affirmation of Turkey's importance as a regional actor,[228] a role to which Turkish leaders aspired, but apparently also as assisting the effort to find public allies of their country among US political circles.[229]

In the second half of the 1990s Washington also extended its full backing to the Turkish military in their confrontation with the rise of political Islam in the guise of the Islamist Prime Minister Necmettin Erbakan, although the Clinton administration was careful in its public rhetoric not to appear to be taking sides.[230] That confrontation ended with Erbakan's ousting from power in 1997 by what has been called a postmodern coup, the fourth military coup in Turkey since 1960. On the economic front, Washington's support was displayed by making sure that the IMF would underpin Turkey's stabilization efforts.[231] Moreover, the US played a major part in the attempts in the late 1990s to resolve the question of Turkey's future accession to the EU. A few voices were raised in Congress arguing that the US ought to see improvements and progress in Turkey concerning democratization, the issue of human rights and over Cyprus before the US supported Turkish EU candidacy. But not much attention was given to them. According to Richard Holbooke, the administration's policy was to support Turkey's entry to the EU and it 'would hope that changes would occur afterwards because of this support.'[232]

Actually, the Americans became diplomatically very active in major European capitals in order to have reversed the 1997 Luxembourg EU decision,[233] which had shut the accession door on Turkey due to its poor human rights record and its dispute with Greece. President Clinton himself had telephone conversations with European political leaders in anticipation of the European Council Helsinki meeting in December 1999, which would readress the issue of Turkey's prospects of achieving EU membership. Clinton's personal involvement was rather unusual. Normally, presidential involvement in support of foreign policy actions occurs when there is a major US interest at stake, or the president has a personal interest in the issue. Whatever Clinton's inner motives it was meant to serve as a gesture of American good will toward the Turks,[234] who greatly appreciated it.[235]

According to Marc Grossman, 'Clinton got interested in Turkey. He immediately realised its strategic significance', recalls the ambassador.[236] To a few well-informed observers of the US–Turkey relationship Clinton's interest in Turkey had to be fully credited to Grossman. In the quest for support for a more committed US policy toward Turkey the US ambassador succeeded in bringing the issue of its strategic importance to the attention of the president himself, mainly thanks to Sandy Berger (Clinton's National Security

Advisor 1997–2000).[237] Turkey's growing relationship with Israel, in Grossman's view, helped a lot to attract the president's attention.[238] If it was not the only reason one can assume that it must have played a major role as the peace process was a top foreign policy priority for Clinton.

'Turkey', wrote President Clinton in his autobiography,

> was one of a handful of countries whose future course would have a large impact on the twenty-first-century world. If it could resolve the Cyprus problem with Greece, reach an accommodation with its restive and sometimes repressed Kurdish minority, and maintain its identity as a secular Muslim democracy, Turkey could be the West's gateway to a New Middle East. If peace in the Middle East fell victim to a rising tide of Islamic extremism, a stable democratic Turkey could be a bulkwark against its spread into Europe.[239]

It is remarkable, but not surprising, that Clinton's few lines about Turkey's international role focused mainly on its potential contribution within the context of the Middle East and the wider drama of its conflicts.

For the Turks and those in Washington who followed closely the US-Turkey relationship, Mark Grossman and Richard Holbrooke were undoubtedly the main architects of the new US policy toward Turkey. As Holbrooke remarked, with a touch of self-importance, this policy was not formulated in response to events but was the product of a careful design and effective co-ordination between Grossman and himself.[240]

In May 1996 Holbrooke was awarded the Atatürk Peace and Democracy Award by the newly founded Atatürk Society of America, based in Washington. It was the second Peace and Democracy Award given by the society. The recipient of the first one the previous year was Democratic Senator Robert C. Byrd, who according to the society was one of the Senate's biggest supporter of Turkey.[241] Grossman for his part received a lot of high praise among official circles but also public acknowledgement in Turkey. According to a Turkish journalist and close observer of US–Turkey relations, the first half of Grossman's term was a period of 'unprecedented achievements' within the context of the bilateral relationship.[242] As Grossman's term in Ankara drew to a close, Ilnur Çevic, the editor-in-chief of the English-language newspaper *Turkish Daily News*, remarked in a farewell article to the US ambassador (the central piece of the newspaper that day) that he had acted beyond the call of duty in order to strengthen relations between the US and Turkey.[243]

Grossman's and Holbrooke's impact on US policy was too visible to be missed. But the Israelis and pro-Israeli interest groups also performed a crucial role in the process that focused US interest on Turkey, even though they did not openly receive credit in Ankara in this respect. Nonetheless, in private, many Turkish officials acknowledged the importance of Israel's role. The Israelis' contribution lay in that that they effectively linked the success of a number of US strategic objectives in the Middle East with Turkey's alignment with Israel. It was they who introduced the idea of a broadly defined, flexible strategic co-operation framework that would involve Turkey, Israel and the US in the security of the area. In the words of Mark Parris, who succeeded Grossman as head of mission in Ankara (1997–2000), 'Turkey and Israel discovered one another in the mid-1990s. And the blossoming of that relationship underscored the commonality of the US-Turkish strategic vision, and very importantly, it changed the dynamics in Washington.'[244]

Notes

1 D. McDowall, *Palestine and Israel: The Uprising and Beyond*, Berkeley, CA: University of California Press, 1989, p. 2.
2 Author's interviews with Barlas Özener, Turkey's ambassador to Israel (1995–99) (a) and Yalım Eralp (a).
3 For an excellent concise discussion of Turkey's objectives in seeking to develop ties with Israel in the early 1990s, see A. Makovsky, 'Israeli-Turkish Relations. "A Turkish Periphery Strategy"?', in H. J. Barkey (ed.), *Reluctant Neighbor: Turkey's Role in the Middle East*, Washington DC: United States Institute of Peace Press, 1996, pp. 155–9; G. E. Gruen, 'Dynamic Progress in Turkish-Israeli Relations', *Israel Affairs,* vol. 1, 1995, pp. 40–70.
4 Author's interview with Barlas Özener (a) and Yalım Eralp (a). Also author's interview with Mehmet Ali Birand (a).
5 For a comprehensive account of the clash between the old and the new trends in Turkish foreign policy at the time, see M. Mufti, 'Daring and Caution in Turkish Foreign Policy', *Middle East Journal*, vol. 52, 1998.
6 On Turkey's foreign policy–making centres during this period, see M. Mufti, *Daring and Caution in Turkish Strategic Culture: Republic at Sea*, Houndmills, Basingstoke: Palgrave, Macmillan, 2009, pp. 96, 89–109 and passim; specifically on the role of the military, see also G. Özcan, 'The Military and the Making of Foreign Policy in Turkey', in B. Rubin and K. Kirişci (eds), *Turkey in World Politics: An Emerging Multiregional Power*, Boulder, CO: Lynne Rienner, 2001.
7 Author's interviews with Barlas Özener and Özdem Sanberk; Mufti, *Daring and Caution*, pp. 95–109 and passim.
8 M. Aydin, *Turkish Foreign Policy during the Gulf War of 1990–1991*, Cairo: Cairo Papers in Social Science, 1998, p. 71.
9 Author's interviews with Yalım Eralp and Ambassador Süha Umar, who in the early 1990s was deputy director of the Directorate of Arms Control and Disarmament Bureau at the Turkish Ministry of Foreign Affairs before he was appointed ambassador to Jordan (1995–98).
10 E. Athanassopoulou, 'Ankara's Foreign Policy Objectives after the End of the Cold War', *ORIENT*, vol. 36, 1995, p. 272. Author's interviews with Yalım Eralp (a) and Özdem Sanberk.
11 The conference heralded the beginning of the peace process under the aegis of the US.
12 *Türkiye*, 25 October 1991, quoted in *Turkish Press Review*, Directorate General of Press and Information, Ankara.
13 Author's interview with David Granit, Israel's ambassador to Turkey (1993–95) (a).
14 However, Turkey was included in the multilaterals as an extra-regional state along with Canada, China, the EU, Japan, Russia and the US.
15 Author's interviews with Süha Umar and with Mr L., an official of the Israeli Ministry of Defense who spoke on condition of anonymity due to active service, Tel Aviv, December 1998; G. F. Gruen, 'Turkey and the Middle East after Oslo

I', in R. O. Freedman (ed.), *The Middle East and the Peace Process: The Impact of the Oslo Accords*, Gainesville: University Press of Florida, 1998, pp. 182–5.

16 Author's interviews with Henri Barkey (a), with Sonar Cagaptay, director of the Turkish Research Program at the Washington Institute for Near East Policy and with Mehmet Ali Birand (a).

17 K. Kirişci and G. M. Winrow, *The Kurdish Question and Turkey: An Example of a Trans-state Ethnic Conflict*, London: Routledge-Curzon, 2004, p. 138; H. J. Barkey and G. E. Fuller, *Turkey's Kurdish Question*, Lanham: Rowman and Littlefield Publishers, 1998, pp. 133–51.

18 According to one source it appears that the Turks were also relying on reconnaissance information provided by the US forces stationed in Turkey, authors' interview with Mehmet Ali Birand (a).

19 H. J. Barkey, 'The Push and Pull of Strategic Cooperation: The US Relationship with Turkey in the Middle East', in David W. Lesch (ed.), *The Middle East and the United States: A Historical and Political Reassessment,* Boulder, CO: Westview, 2007, p. 451.

20 Quoted in A. Tovias and E. Inbar, 'Potential Effects of Turkey's Membership in the EC on Israel's Economy', in A. I. Bağış (ed.), *Actual Situation and Prospects of Turkey's Bilateral Relations with Israel: Potential and Opportunities,* Ankara: TES-AR Yayınları, 1992, no. 4, p. 108.

21 M. B. Aykan, 'Turkish Perspectives on Turkish-US Relations Concerning Persian Gulf Security in the Post-Cold War Era', *Middle East Journal*, vol. 50, 1996, pp. 346–9.

22 M. B. Aykan, 'The Palestinian Question in Turkish Foreign Policy from the 1950s to the 1980s', *International Journal of Middle East Studies*, vol. 25, 1993, p. 103.

23 Author's interviews with Yalım Eralp and with Mr K., a senior Turkish Foreign Ministry official who spoke on condition of anonymity due to active service, December 2006, Istanbul.

24 Author's interview with Thomas Dine.

25 Author's interviews with Alan Makovsky (a) and Mr P., a State Department official who spoke on condition of anonymity due to active service, July 2007, Washington.

26 Author's interview with Daniel Kurtzer, deputy assistant secretary of state for Near Eastern Affairs (1989–94) and US ambassador to Israel (2001–05). Also author's interview with Mr A. and Mr S. two Israeli Foreign Ministry officials who spoke on condition of anonymity due to active service, December 1998, Jerusalem.

27 Ibid. Also O. Bengio, *The Turkish-Israeli Relationship: Changing Ties of Middle Eastern Outsiders*, New York: Palgrave Macmillan, 2004, p. 101.

28 Author's interviews with Mr P., July 2007, Washington, Henri Barkey (a) and Sonar Cagaptay.

29 Author's interview with July 1997, Washington.

30 E. Inbar, *The Israeli-Turkish Entente*, London: King's College Mediterranean Studies, 2001, p. 41.

31 Author's interviews with Andrew Manatos and Thomas Dine. See also T. Ambrosio, 'Entangling Alliances: The Turkish-Israeli Lobbying Partnership and Its Unintended Consequences', in T. Ambrosio (ed.), *Ethnic Identity Groups and U.S. Foreign Policy*, Westport, CT: Praeger, 2002.

32 Quoted in Ambrosio, 'Entangling Alliances', p. 147.

33 Author's interview with Itamar Rabinovich.

34 Author's interview with Itamar Rabinovich.

35 W. G. Hyland, *Clinton's World: Remaking American Foreign Policy*, Westport, CT: Praeger, 1999, p. 23; D. Halberstam, *War in a Time of Peace: Bush, Clinton, and the Generals*, New York: Simon and Schuster, 2001, p. 243.

36 S. Peres and A. Naor, *The New Middle East*, New York: Henry Holt, 1993.
37 Author's interview with Itamar Rabinovich.
38 Author's interview with Itamar Rabinovich.
39 Author's interviews with Andrew Manatos and with Peter Marudas.
40 Both sets were not coherent blocks but rather weak coalitions. This clash was present within AIPAC where a powerful leading group was against Rabin's approach: J. J. Goldberg, *Jewish Power: Inside the American Jewish Establishment*, Reading, MA: Addison-Wesley, 1996, pp. 225–6; also author's interview with Thomas Dine.
41 The above are based on the author's interviews in Washington and in Israel. Among these the interview with Thomas Dine was particularly illuminating.
42 For the airing of this idea in Turkey by Shimon Peres, see D. Jung and W. Piccoli, *Turkey at the Crossroads: Ottoman Legacies and a Greater Middle East*, London: Zed Books, 2001, p. 165.
43 JINSA's mandate, [n.d.], available online at www.jinsa.org/about/agenda/agenda.html (accessed 20 February 1998).
44 The following are based on the author's interviews with Thomas Dine, David Granit and Mr A. and Mr S, December 1998, Jerusalem. For a discussion of the alliance between American-Jewish groups and the Turkish lobby concerning the promotion of a number of issues, see Ambrosio, 'Entangling Alliances', pp. 150–54.
45 And not after the Baku-Ceyhan pipeline was a reality, as some publications claim. For such claims, see for instance R. Ibrahimov, 'Israeli Pipeline. Ashelon-Eilat-The Second Breath', *Journal of Turkish Weekly*, 9 April 2007, available online at http://www.turkishweekly.net (accessed 20 September 2007).
46 Author's interviews with Thomas Dine (a), Alan Makovsky (a) and Andrew Manatos.
47 On the attitude of the American-Jewish groups concerning the Armenian Genocide Resolution, see Ambrosio, 'Entangling Alliances', pp. 156–9.
48 Author's interview with Thomas Dine.
49 The closest example would be that of Iran. Back in the 1960s Israel did lobby in Washington on behalf of Iran – Israel's regional ally – for greater US military support and modern military equipment. I want to thank Roland Popp at the Center for Security Studies (CSS) / ETH Zurich for bringing this fact to my attention. His forthcoming book, *Nach Mossadeg: Die USA und Iran, 1957–67*, throws more light on this particular aspect of Israel's lobbying effort in Washington.
50 Ambrosio, 'Entangling Alliances', p. 149.
51 J. W. Dietrich, 'Interest Groups and Foreign Policy: Clinton and the China MFN Debates', *Presidential Studies Quarterly*, vol. 29, 1999, p. 280; T. Ambrosio, 'Ethnic Identity Groups and U.S. Foreign Policy', in Ambrosio (ed.), *Ethnic Identity Groups*, pp. 7–9.
52 Goldberg, *Jewish Power*, p. 364; A. D. Miller, *The Much Too Promised Land: America's Elusive Search for Arab-Israeli Peace*, New York: Bantam Books, 2008, p. 79.
53 Miller, *Much Too Promised Land*, p. 242 and passim.
54 Miller, *Much Too Promised Land*, pp. 242–4 and passim.
55 Z. Lockman, *Contending Visions of the Middle East: The History and Politics of Orientalism*, Cambridge: Cambridge University Press, 2004, p. 247; author's interview with Andrew Manatos.
56 Miller, *Much Too Promised Land*, p. 243.
57 During Clinton's second term Indyk served twice as US ambassador to Israel (1995–97; 2000–01).
58 Miller, *Much too Promised Land*, p. 243; author's interview with Daniel Kurtzer.

59 Miller, *Much too Promised Land*, p. 243. Indyk was not the only one in the peace team thinking along these lines, Miller, *Much too Promised Land*, p. 243 and passim.
60 Author's interview with Thomas Dine.
61 A. Lake, 'Conceptualizing U.S. Strategy in the Middle East', 17 May 1994, keynote address, Soref Symposium, The Washington Institute for Near East Policy, Washington, DC.
62 Author's interview with Thomas Dine.
63 Author's interview with Yalım Eralp (b).
64 USIP is a non-partisan federal institution created and financed by Congress. Its mandate is to help the US government deal with international conflicts without the use of violence and to enhance national security.
65 P. Carley, *Turkey's Role in the Middle East*, conference report, Washington DC: United States Institute of Peace, 2005, p. viii.
66 According to J. Mann, *Rise of the Vulcans: The History of Bush's War Cabinet*, New York: Viking, 2004, p. 113, as head of the State Department's policy planning staff during the Reagan years, Wolfowitz 'demonstrated himself to be one of Israel's strongest supporters' in the administration. He challenged the wisdom of selling AWACS aircraft to the Saudis and sought to slow down the growing momentum within the US government to engage with the Palestinian Liberation Organization.
67 E. Drew, 'The Neocons in Power', *The New York Review of Books*, 12 June 2003, available online at www.nybooks.com/articles/16378 (accessed 7 October 2008); Mann, *Rise of the Vulcans*, pp. 29–31.
68 Mann, *Rise of the Vulcans*, pp. 31–2.
69 Mann, *Rise of the Vulcans*, pp. 79–82.
70 Mann, *Rise of the Vulcans*, pp. 87–90.
71 Author's interviews with Mehmet Ali Birand (a) and Yalım Eralp (a).
72 Author's interview with Mehmet Ali Birand (a).
73 S. J. Blank, S. C. Pelletiere and W. T. Johnsen, *Turkey's Strategic Position at the Crossroads of World Affairs*, Carlisle Barracks, PA: Strategic Studies Institute, US Army War College, 3 December 1993.
74 Carley, *Turkey's Role*, p. 2.
75 Author's interviews with Mehmet Ali Birand (a) and Cengiz Çandar (b).
76 Author's interviews with Mehmet Ali Birand (a) and Thomas Dine.
77 D. Ackerman, 'Memorial Honors Life of Penn Prof', 22 January 2002, *The Daily Pennsylvanian*, available online at http://media.dailypennsylvanian.com (accessed 3 March 2009).
78 A. Z. Rubinstein, 'New World Order of Hollow Victory?', *Foreign Affairs,* vol. 70, 1991.
79 Carley, *Turkey's Role*, p. viii.
80 A. Makovsky, 'U.S. Policy toward Turkey: Progress and Problems', in M. Abramowitz (ed.), *Turkey's Transformation and American Policy,* New York: The Century Foundation Press, 2000, p. 224; M. Abramowitz, 'The Complexities of American Policymaking on Turkey', in M. Abramowitz (ed.), *Turkey's Transformation and American Policy,* New York: The Century Foundation Press, 2000, p. 176.
81 In 2001 Grossman was appointed under-secretary of state for political affairs, which was the third most important position at the State Department.
82 Author's interview with Andrew Manatos; Makovsky, 'U.S. Policy toward Turkey', p. 224
83 Grossman's confirmation took place two and a half months before Barkley's tour of duty was over. Grossman presented his credentials to President Demirel on the 3 January 1995.
84 Grossman's thinking as described below is based on the author's interviews with Ambassador Marc Grossman.

85 Author's interview with Ian Lesser (a). Also see Blank *et al.*, *Turkey's Strategic Position.*
86 George Bush Public Papers, Remarks Following Discussions with President Turgut Ozal of Turkey, South Portico, White House, 25 September 1990, available online at www.bushlibrary.tamu.edu/ research/public_papers.php (accessed 10 January 2006); Remarks at a Dinner Hosted by President Turgut Ozal in Istanbul, Turkey, Dining Room, Dolmabahce Palace, 21 July 1991, George Bush Presidential Library and Museum, available online at www.bushlibrary.tamu.edu/ research/public_papers.php (accessed 14 April 2006).
87 Author's interviews with Morton Abramowitz (b), Marc Grossman and Mehmet Ali Birand (b).
88 Author's interviews with Morton Abramowitz and Marc Grossman.
89 Author's interviews with Marc Grossman.
90 Author's interview with Marc Grossman (b).
91 Abramowitz, 'American Policymaking on Turkey', pp. 176–7.
92 Author's interviews with Marc Grossman.
93 *Milliyet*, 17 March 1996, quoted in Y. Çongar, 'The State of Turkish-American Dialogue: Do You Understand What I Am Saying?', *Private View* 3, no. 7, Spring 1999, available online at www.tusiad.org.tr/yayin/private/spring99/html/ sec9.html (accessed 20 June 2007).
94 Author's interview with Andrew Manatos. Also, Makovsky, 'U.S. Policy toward Turkey', p. 224.
95 Makovsky, 'U.S. Policy toward Turkey', p. 224
96 R. Beasley, 'Collective Interpretations: How Problem Representations Aggregate in Foreign Policy Groups', in D. A. Sylvan and K. F. Voss (eds), *Problem Representation in Foreign Policy Decision Making*, Cambridge: Cambridge University Presss, 1998, pp. 90–94.
97 V. M. Hudson, *Foreign Policy Analysis: Classic and Contemporary Theory*, Lanham, MD: Rowman and Littlefield, 2007, p. 92.
98 During Clinton's second term Berger succeeded Lake as US national security advisor (1997–2000).
99 Author's interviews with Marc Grossman.
100 Abramowitz, 'American Policymaking on Turkey', p. 176; Makovsky, 'U.S. Policy toward Turkey', p. 224.
101 Author's interview with Marc Grossman (a).
102 Author's interview with Yalım Eralp (b).
103 Author's interview with Yalım Eralp (b).
104 Author's interviews with Marc Grossman.
105 Author's interviews with Marc Grossman.
106 Author's interviews with Marc Grossman.
107 S. LeVine, *The Oil and the Glory: The Pursuit of Empire and Fortune on the Caspian Sea*, New York: Random House, 2007, pp. 223–4.
108 Author's interviews with Marc Grossman.
109 LeVine, *The Oil and the Glory*, p. 225.
110 Author's interviews with Marc Grossman; LeVine, *The Oil and the Glory*, p. 225.
111 Author's interview with Mehmet Ali Birand (b).
112 Abramowitz, 'Dateline Ankara: Turkey after Özal', *Foreign Policy*, no. 91, 1993, p. 181.
113 Author's interview with Ian Lesser (b).
114 Blank *et al.*, *Turkey's Strategic Position*, foreword.
115 Blank *et al.*, *Turkey's Strategic Position*, p. iv.
116 Author's interview with Marc Grossman (b).
117 Author's interview with Lale Sarıimbahimoğlu.

118 For the text of the speech, see Çevik Bir, 'Nato'nun Yeni Stratejisi ve Türkiye', *Savunma ve Havacılık*, vol. 6, 1992, pp.16–22.
119 Bir, 'Nato'nun Yeni Stratejisi', p. 17.
120 Özcan, 'The Military and the Making of Foreign Policy', p. 25.
121 Abramowitz, 'Dateline Ankara', p. 164.
122 Author's interview with Morton Abramowitz (a); Blank et al., *Turkey's Strategic Position*, introduction, conclusions; S. Hunter, 'Bridge or Frontier? Turkey's Post-Cold War Geopolitical Posture', *The International Spectator*, vol. XXXIV, 1999, p. 71.
123 Author's interview with Morton Abramowitz (a); Blank *et al.*, *Turkey's Strategic Position*, conclusions.
124 Author's interview with Warren Christopher.
125 Author's interviews with Alan Makovsky (a), Marc Grossman, Thomas Dine; also Makovsky, 'U.S. Policy toward Turkey', p. 223.
126 Author's interview with Alan Makovsky (a); S. J. Blank, 'Turkey's Strategic Engagement in the Former USSR and U.S. Interests', in Blank *et al.*, *Turkey's Strategic Position*.
127 For an excellent, very detailed account of developments in bilateral relations in this period, see A. Nachmani, 'Bridge across the Middle East: Turkey and Israel in the 1990s', unpublished manuscript. I am grateful to Professor Nachmani for providing me with a copy. For a concise version of Nachmani's paper, see A. Nachmani, *Turkey: Facing a New Millennium; Coping with Intertwined Conflicts*, Manchester: Manchester University Press, 2003, ch. 7 and passim; also A. Nachmani, 'The Remarkable Turkish-Israeli Tie', *Middle East Quarterly*, vol. 5, 1998; Makovsky, 'Israeli-Turkish Relations', pp. 160–69 covers developments up to 1995.
128 Jung and Piccoli, *Turkey at Crossroads*, pp. 154–5; Mufti, *Daring and Caution*, p. 107; see also Bengio, *Turkish-Israeli Relationship*, p. 104.
129 W. Hale, *Turkish Foreign Policy, 1774–2000*, London: Frank Cass, 2000, pp. 296, 301; G. Özcan, 'Apologismos 50 Hronon ton Sheseon Tourkias-Israil', in F. Sönmezoğlu (ed.), *Mythos ke Pragmatikotita: Analysi tis Tourkikis Exoterikis Politikis*, Athens: Infognomon, 2001, tomos A, pp. 239, 249, 251.
130 On the Turks' motives in seeking military co-operation with Israel, see A. Gresh, 'Turkish-Israeli-Syrian-Relations and Their Impact on the Middle East', *Middle East Journal*, vol. 52, 1998, passim; Nachmani, 'Remarkable Turkish-Israeli Tie', passim; Lesser, 'Turkey's Strategic Options', pp. 84–5; Jung and Piccoli, *Turkey at Crossroads*, pp. 166–71; Özcan, 'Apologismos 50 Hronon', p. 238; Bengio, *Turkish-Israeli Relationship*, pp. 78–80, 86–8; Mufti, *Daring and Caution*, pp. 107–9; Barkey, 'Push and Pull', p. 453.
131 Author's interview with Mehmet Ali Birand (b).
132 Author's interviews with Mehmet Ali Birand and Yalım Eralp.
133 *Milliyet*, 7 November 1994.
134 Jung and Piccoli, *Turkey at Crossroads*, p. 169. However, usually Elekdağ's statement is quoted merely to show that the Turks thought their relations with Israel will be useful in Washington.
135 Author's interview with David Granit, (a). Also, author's interviews with Mr A. and Mr S., December 1998, Jerusalem.
136 P. Robins, *Suits and Uniforms: Turkish Foreign Policy since the End of the Cold War*, London: Hurst and Co, 2003, p. 257, n. 43; Bengio, *Turkish-Israeli Relationship*, p. 107,
137 Özcan, 'Apologismos 50 Hronon', p. 249; Bengio, *Turkish-Israeli Relationship*, pp. 80–89; Mufti, *Daring and Caution*, p. 109.
138 Author's interview with Özdem Sanberk.
139 For the relevant literature see n. 130 in this chapter.

140 Barkey, 'Push and Pull', p. 454.
141 Bengio, *Turkish-Israeli Relationship*, pp. 98–9. Bengio quotes a Turkish source which maintains that President Clinton played a leading role concerning the Turkey-Israel military agreement, but she points out that the source is unreliable, p. 99
142 Author's interviews with Marc Grossman, and with Mr P., July 2007, Washington.
143 Author's interview with David Granit (b); also Bengio, *Turkish-Israeli Relationship*, p. 99.
144 Makovsky, 'U.S. Policy toward Turkey', p. 236; Bengio, *Turkish-Israeli Relationship*, p. 100; Barkey 'Push and Pull', p. 454.
145 Author's interview with Daniel Kurtzer. Dr Kurtzer was one of the four people who composed the core Middle East team at the State Department (1991–94); the others were Dennis Ross, Bill Burns and Aaron David Miller. See also A. Makovsky, 'Israeli-Turkish Co-operation; Full Steam Ahead', *Policywatch*, no. 292 (Jan 1998).
146 M. Indyk, *Innocent Abroad: An Intimate Account of American Peace Diplomacy in the Middle East*, New York: Simon and Schuster, 2009, p. 22.
147 Author's interviews with Alan Makovsky (b) and Henri Barkey (b).
148 Indyk, *Innocent Abroad*, p. 43.
149 Author's interviews with Henri Barkey (b) and Alan Makovsky (b).
150 Makovsky, 'U.S. Policy toward Turkey', p. 236; author's interviews with Sonar Cagaptay and Mehmet Ali Birand (b).
151 I. O. Lesser, 'Western Interests in a Changing Turkey', in Z. Khalilzad, I. O. Lesser and F. S. Larrabee (eds), *The Future of Turkish-Western Relations,* Santa Monica, CA: RAND, 2000, pp. 56–7; Barkey, 'Push and Pull', in D. Lesch (ed.), *The Middle East and the United States*, p. 454.
152 Makovsky, 'U.S. Policy toward Turkey', p. 236. In the 1970s the Americans used this technique to bypass congressional opposition to selling arms to China.
153 Author's interviews with Marc Grossman.
154 Author's interview with Mr P; July 2007, Washington; Makovsky, 'U.S. Policy toward Turkey', pp. 236–7; Bengio, *Turkish-Israeli Relationship*, p. 101.
155 Author's interviews with Marc Grossman; author's telephone interview with Aaron David Miller, Middle East analyst, State Department advisor to secretaries of state on Arab-Israeli negotiations (1978–2003), October 2010, Washington. Also author's interview with Daniel Kurtzer, and with Mr P., July 2007, Washington.
156 Author's interviews with Mehmet Ali Birand.
157 Author's interviews with Marc Grossman, Mehmet Ali Birand and Yalım Eralp.
158 Author's interviews with Marc Grossman.
159 Author's interviews with Marc Grossman, Mehmet Ali Birand and Yalım Eralp.
160 Author's interview with Thomas Dine.
161 Author's interviews with Marc Grossman.
162 A. Weisman, *Prince of Darkness: Richard Perle. The Kingdom, the Power and the End of Empire in America*, New York: Union Square Press, 2007, p. 117.
163 Author's interviews with Marc Grossman.
164 Author's interviews with Marc Grossman.
165 Author's interviews with Marc Grossman.
166 Author's interviews with Marc Grossman.
167 Author's interviews with Marc Grossman.
168 Author's interviews with Marc Grossman.
169 Author's interviews with Mehmet Ali Birand, Yalım Eralp and Süha Umar.
170 Author's interviews with Marc Grossman.
171 Author's interviews with Marc Grossman and with Mehmet Ali Birand.
172 Author's interview with Mehmet Ali Birand (a).
173 Author's interview with Mehmet Ali Birand (a).

174 Author's interviews with Mehmet Ali Birand (a) and Cengiz Çandar (a).
175 Bir between 1973 and 1985 served at the central command of NATO military forces (Supreme Headquarters Allied Powers Europe (SHAPE)) in Belgium.
176 Author's interviews with Mehmet Ali Birand and Mr K., December 1996, Istanbul. Ambassador Yalım Eralp in his interview with the author (b) said that it was 'likely that Grossman played a role' in Ankara's decision to expand the relationship into the security field.
177 Author's interview with Mehmet Ali Birand (b).
178 Author's interview with Marc Grossman. According to Yalım Eralp, the Pentagon promoted the idea of Turkey-Israel military co-operation: author's interview with Yalım Eralp (b). The author was told the same by Mr L., Tel Aviv, December 1998.
179 For the relevant literature see n. 130 in this chapter. A comprehensive discussion of the Turkey-Israel relationship of the 1990s is beyond the scope of this book, which is concerned with it only to the extent that it is relevant to Turkey's relations with the US.
180 Statement by the Turkish foreign minister during his 1994 visit to Israel, quoted in G. E. Gruen, 'Dynamic Progress in Turkish-Israeli Relations', *Israel Affairs*, vol. 1, 1995, p. 58.
181 *Jerusalem Post*, 16 December 1999.
182 *Jerusalem Post*, 16 December 1999; author's interview with Mehmet Ali Birand (a) and with Amnon Barzilai, defence correspondent, *Ha'aretz* (a).
183 Bengio, *Turkish-Israeli Relationship*, pp. 100, 114.
184 For a discussion of these goals see earlier on in this chapter.
185 On the different views concerning military ties with Israel within the circles of the Turkish foreign policy–making elite see, Mufti, *Daring and Caution*, pp. 107–9.
186 A. Makovsky, 'The New Activism in Turkish Foreign Policy', *Insight Turkey*, vol. 1, 1999, p.18.
187 Özcan, 'Apologismos 50 Hronon', p. 239.
188 C. Çandar, 'Some Turkish Perspectives on the United States and American Policy toward Turkey', in M. Abramowitz (ed.), *Turkey's Transformation and American Policy*, New York: The Century Foundation Press, 2000, pp. 135–46; Mufti, *Daring and Caution*, pp. 92–3.
189 Author's' interviews with Henri Barkey and Mehmet Ali Birand; M. B. Aykan, 'The Turkey-US-Israel Triangle: Continuity, Change and Implications for Turkey's Post Cold War Middle East Policy', *Journal of South Asian and Middle Eastern Studies*, vol. XXII, 1999, pp.12–13.
190 Quoted in the *Jerusalem Post*, 8 May 1996.
191 Bengio, *Turkish-Israeli Relationship*, p.107. This is also confirmed by the author's own research.
192 Makovsky, 'U.S. Policy toward Turkey', p. 224.
193 The fund was created after the Gulf War, see Chapter 4 in this book.
194 *MEED*, 3 February 1995, p. 22; *The Turkish Yearbook of International Relations*, Ankara: Ankara Üniversitesi Basımevi, vol. XXXI, 2000, p. 257.
195 P. L. Thomson, 'United States-Turkey Military Relations: Treaties and Implication', *The International Journal of Kurdish* Studies, vol. 9, 1996, p. 109.
196 On the 1994 crisis in Turkey, see among others, O. Celasun, *The 1994 Currency Crisis in Turkey*, Washington DC: World Bank Policy Research Working Paper no. 1319, April 1998.
197 Anadolu Agency, 20 February 1995.
198 Assistant Secretary of State for European Affairs Richard C. Holbrooke, statement before the International Relations Committee, US House of Representatives, 9 March 1995, quoted in Makovsky, 'The New Activism of Turkish Foreign Policy', pp. 108–9.

199 Makovsky, 'U.S. Policy toward Turkey', p. 224.
200 Author's interviews with Marc Grossman and with Alan Makovsky (a).
201 On the Turk's aspirations, see among others, Blank, 'Turkey's Strategic Engagement', passim; Hunter, 'Turkey's Geopolitical Posture', pp. 69, 71–3; I. O. Lesser, 'Turkey and the West after the Gulf War', *International Spectator*, vol. 72, 1992, pp. 87–8.
202 S. Talbott, 'U.S. Turkish Leadership in the Post-Cold War World', address at Bilkent University, Ankara, Turkey, 11 April 1995.
203 Talbott, 'U.S. Turkish Leadership'.
204 Talbott, 'U.S. Turkish Leadership', my emphasis.
205 Talbott, 'U.S. Turkish Leadership'.
206 Transcript of press conference by US Assistant Secretary of State Richard Holbrooke, 21 February 1995, Ankara.
207 Author's interviews with two Turkish human rights activists who spoke on condition of anonymity, March 1995, Ankara.
208 Amnesty International, *Turkey: A Policy of Denial*, 8 February 1995, available online at http://amnesty.org/en/library/asset/EUR44/001/1995/en/3a88f8ee-f8bf-11dd-b40d-7b25bb27e189/eur440011995en.pdf (accessed 20 Feb. 2005).
209 Human Rights Watch, *Weapons Transfers and Violations of the Laws of War in Turkey*, New York: 1995, p. 146.
210 United States Congress, Commission on Security and Cooperation in Europe, *Turkey-United States Relations: Potential and Peril*, hearing before the Commission on Security and Cooperation in Europe, 104th Congress, first session, 19 September 1995, Washington DC: US Government Printing Office, 1996, p. 2.
211 US Congress, Commission of Security and Cooperation in Europe, *Turkey-United States Relations*, p. 13.
212 US Congress, Commission of Security and Cooperation in Europe, *Turkey-United States Relations*, p. 10.
213 Author's interview with Mr P., July 2007, Washington; Mufti, *Daring and Caution*, pp. 99–102; F. Keskin, 'Turkey's Trans-Border Operations in Northern Iraq: Before and After the Invasion of Iraq', *Research Journal of International Studies*, issue 8, 2008, p. 63. This is an interesting article that looks at the Turkish military operation in Northern Iraq from an international law perspective.
214 C. Migdalovitz, *Greece and Turkey: Current Foreign Aid Issues* (CRS, Issue Brief, 1996), available online at www.fas.org/man/crs/86–065.htm#summ (accessed 16 June 2006).
215 Author's interviews with Alan Makovsky (a), with Morton Abramowitz (a) and with Thomas Dine.
216 M. Abramowitz, 'American Policymaking on Turkey', p. 158.
217 J. Joseph, 'Pipeline Diplomacy: The Clinton Administration's Fight for Baku-Ceyhan', WWS Case Study 1/99, Woodrow Wilson School for Public Affairs, Princeton University, available online at wws.princeton.edu/research/cases/pipeline.pdf (accessed 2 February 2001). The US government made it clear that once the pipeline consortium had secured financing which proved that the pipeline was commercially viable then Trade and Development funds would be provided: Makovsky, 'U.S. Policy toward Turkey', p. 241.
218 Author's interview with Morton Abramowitz (b); also Abramowitz, 'American Policymaking on Turkey', p. 180.
219 A good example is the opinion piece by Thomas Friedman, 'Foreign Affairs: The Turkish Nightmare', *New York Times*, 17 May 1995.
220 Paul Kennedy became an academic 'celebrity' to a wider audience of policy makers globally in the end of the 1980s following the publication of his book, *The Rise and Fall of the Great Powers* (1987), which became a bestseller. In his book he argued from a historical perspective that expanding military commitments undermined a country's economy, leading to decline in the long run. He

predicted that the outlook for the USSR was bleak due to the lack of a strong productive base, but he also suggested, causing a stir, that problems of 'military overstretch' were well under way in the case of the US.

221 According to the authors, the other 'pivotal' states were Indonesia, India, Pakistan, Egypt, South Africa, Brazil, Algeria and Mexico.

222 R. S. Chase, E. B. Hill and P. Kennedy, 'Pivotal States and U.S. Strategy', *Foreign Affairs*, Jan/Feb 1996, p. 33.

223 Chase, Hill and Kennedy, 'Pivotal States', pp. 47–8, my emphasis.

224 Chase, Hill and Kennedy, 'Pivotal States', p.34.

225 Chase, Hill and Kennedy, 'Pivotal States', pp. 33, 49.

226 Chase, Hill and Kennedy, 'Pivotal States', p. 49.

227 Chase, Hill and Kennedy, 'Pivotal States', pp. 33–4.

228 Author's interview with Yalım Eralp (a).

229 Author's interview with Mehmet Ali Birand (a).

230 See the US Department of State daily press briefing transcripts of the period.

231 Çongar, 'State of Turkish-American Dialogue'.

232 United States Congress, Commission on Security and Cooperation in Europe, *Turkey-United States Relations*, p. 24.

233 Author's interview with Marc Grossman (a).

234 Author's interviews with Morton Abramowitz (a) and Mark Grossman (b).

235 Author's interviews with Mehmet Ali Birand (a) and Morton Abramowitz (a).

236 Author's interviews with Mehmet Ali Birand (a) and Morton Abramowitz (a).

237 Author's interviews with Marc Grossman.

238 Author's interviews with Marc Grossman.

239 B. Clinton, *My Life*, New York: Alfred A. Knopf, 2004, pp. 876–7.

240 Çongar, 'State of Turkish-American Dialogue'.

241 On the society's website Byrd is described as 'a great American and a great friend of Turkey', Atatürk Society of America, Atatürk Awards, available online at http://ataturksociety.org/content.asp?id=1&sID=2 (accessed 2 February 2007). Byrd was particularly known in Turkey for supporting Turkey over the issue of the Armenian genocide resolution: see for instance 'Turkey's "Best Friend" in Senate Died at Age 92', *Hurriyet Daily News*, 28 June 2010, available online at http://www.hurriyetdailynews.com/default.aspx?pageid=438&n=turkey8217s-8216 best-friend8217-in-us-senate-dead-at-92-2010-06-28 (accessed, 30 June 2010). It is worth mentioning that the third – and so far the last – recipient of the award was Admiral William J. Crowe, Jr. (1998), chairman of the joint chiefs of staff (1985–89). The award was given to him 'for his much publicized appreciation and admiration of Atatürk'.

242 Çongar, 'State of Turkish-American Dialogue'.

243 I. Çevic, 'A Top Class Diplomat, a Gentleman and a Friend' (editorial), *Turkish Daily News*, 16 May 1997.

244 M. Parris, 'The U.S. and Turkey', in B. Maddy-Weitzman and A. Susser (eds), *Turkish-Israeli Relations in a Trans-Atlantic Context: Wider Europe and the Greater Middle East*, conference proceedings, Tel Aviv: The Moshe Dayan Center for Middle Eastern and African Studies, 2005, p. 28.

7 More questions than answers

The renewal of US–Turkey ties that Özal eagerly sought, but without much success, first became apparent half way through Clinton's first term. This period was also marked by high-level officials' interest in Turkey, at least momentarily, as the number of their visits increased when compared to the 1980s. Turkish affairs attracted attention even at the highest level, that of the office of the president, mainly thanks to Grossman's efforts. This delighted the Turks, who for a very long time felt indignant because Turkish issues were not given the attention which they considered appropriate.[1] But high-level attention was not present on a steady basis for Turkey had not been upgraded on to the list of foreign countries that demanded constant high-level attention within the US foreign policy–making apparatus. Ankara's hope for Turkey to become a partner of the US did not materialize. Relations with Turkey continued to be handled and managed at the middle level of under-secretary of state and most of the time at the lower level of the director of the office for southeast Europe and his subordinates within the Bureau of European Affairs. The Turks could only console themselves because Assistant Secretaries Hobrooke and Grossman had a strong presence within the foreign policy–making apparatus, like Richard Perle did in the 1980s.

Having said all that, it has to be noted that there was a qualitative change of sorts concerning US interest in Turkey. In the past, high-level interest in Turkey was either the result of a major crisis (Cyprus in 1974) or a pressing need to secure Turkey's support (the Gulf War). In the second part of the 1990s, the sporadic high-level interest in Turkey was expressed specifically to show US support for Turkey. But these are rather fine details. The most significant qualitative change in the bilateral relationship, which would have great implications for its future course, was shifting the security dialogue, which had been entirely in the hands of the Turkish military and the Pentagon, to the State Department and the Turkish government. Turgut Özal initiated this change on the Turkish side. On the US side it was Marc Grossman who deserved the credit for moving the relationship back to the State Department.[2] There was another – not less important – promising change in the bilateral relationship, which also worked in favour of the previous one mentioned. This was the emergence of a broader strategic dialogue, something that again Turgut Özal had been pursuing since the 1980s. The beginnings of a US–Turkey dialogue in the field of energy augured well for developing relations beyond their traditional narrow security paradigm, which was defined by hard security considerations born out of the exigencies of the Cold War.[3] Indeed, this change of paradigm was what President Clinton underlined in his November 1999 speech to the Turkish parliament.[4] It was also what Grossman sought to impress upon the Turks. He recalls that he urged them to do more business with the US, to seek for ways to engage with the broader American society.[5] In Grossman's assessment, by the end of the 1990s the bilateral relationship that had been until then so heavily lopsided in favour of military issues was rebalanced at least to some extent reflecting the growth of non-military mutual interests.[6] Yet this new kind of dialogue was still at an embryonic stage until the end of the 1990s. Furthermore, the Turks continued to shy away from the effort to seriously engage with the Americans outside the state-to state framework.

Actually, it was hard not to see that in spite of the rhetoric on both sides about a 'partnership for the twenty-first century' the nature and objectives of this partnership were not properly defined. Strobe Talbott in his 1995 Ankara speech mentioned earlier spoke about the US and Turkey 'acting together'.[7] But how much and what kind of future acting together did the Clinton administration have in mind? To properly answer this question would necessitate devising a mechanism of mutual consultation on military, economic and political issues, as a next step, that could help advance co-operation and strengthen the relationship. But this was apparently of no real interest to Washington at the time. In fact, already when Grossman succeeded Holbrooke at the State Department the energy that these two officials had injected into US policy toward Turkey had dissipated. Far more importantly, US policy toward Turkey seemed somewhat to drift. Decisions affecting the bilateral relationship tended to be taken in a piecemeal fashion. As late as December 1997 both sides were still talking about the need to focus their bilateral co-operation and develop a clear agenda in areas of mutual interest such as energy, trade, security and regional matters. And although the two sides agreed then to work toward this end,[8] concrete achievements were hard to come by in the remaining years of the Clinton administration. For some this lack of coherence and consistency was related to Holbrooke's departure from the State Department in February 1996.[9] There was also the complementary fact that many US officials were still primarily interested in traditional security co-operation when dealing with Turkey. Actually, a strong preference for working through the more 'reliable' military-to-military channel was still lingering in Washington, something that became evident when Erbakan was in power.[10] But another major reason was that there was a wide range of issues that separated the two countries. During most of the Cold War, US–Turkey co-operation was born out of a specific security need, to deal with the Soviet threat, and was in tune with the simple pattern of the Cold War international order. This simple pattern was there no more. For one, it was impossible to predict the US side of the story. More importantly, however, it was difficult for the Americans and the Turks to square between them the complexities of the new international environment and harmonize their interests in a way that would allow them to tighten their relationship, let alone broaden it. Although the two allies shared a number of broad security objectives (fighting terrorism, containing Iraq, checking upon Iran's weapons of mass destruction capabilities, facilitating the peace process) Ankara did not see eye to eye with Washington concerning a number of significant details and priorities when it came to policy towards Iraq, Iran and Syria.[11] Also, there were still substantial differences regarding Turkey's relations with Greece and Cyprus[12] and human rights, even though the Clinton administration chose to put the strategic relationship above them.[13] Until Marc Grossman assumed his post in Ankara very little action had been taken to help minimize the impact of all these differences. Grossman regarded it as essential to get around them. 'That's why we sought ways to support Turkey. This was the job. That was what we were working for, to help overcome these differences; to help pave the way for better mutual understanding of each other's political realities and domestic political constrains.'[14] By the end of his term it was obvious that progress had been made. Nevertheless, differences still had to be dealt with, and this most of the time was an uphill struggle.

In fact, it soon became evident that the scope of Turkey's security co-operation with the US in the Middle East could not be stretched to the point that the US desired. To comprehend the difficulties in cementing a strong US–Turkey partnership it is worth elaborating on this point. Turkey's alignment with Israel had encouraged ideas and ambitious calculations about the role that Turkey could further play in support of US interests the Middle East. For some State Department and Pentagon officials dealing with Middle East security, Turkey's military co-operation with Israel was a first step toward the creation under US backing of a new security arrangement in the Middle East, a kind of a regional pact with the participation of the Arab regimes that were friendly to the US.[15] Initially, it could be based on the co-operation of Jordan with Turkey and Israel. It was an idea that Israeli Prime Minister Shimon Peres aired to the Americans in late 1995 and had been gestating in certain circles in Washington, even though the Clinton administration was rather cool towards it out of fear that it might jeopardize the peace process.[16] Even so, the Turkish-Israeli alignment was considered by a few US officials as a first step toward Turkey becoming much more actively supportive of US strategic objectives in the area.[17] This optimism was partly based on the conviction that the US would manage to shape security in the area in its own image. It was also supported by the observation that Turkey's alignment with Israel was not an isolated decision. A number of Ankara's actions were seen as sending the message that the Turks entertained an interest in becoming more engaged in Middle East security in a variety of forms: for example, Turkey's participation in the Temporary International Presence in Hebron[18] – at least, this was what some officials thought. Ankara's decision to host some of the meetings of the Arms Control and Regional Security working group of the peace process multilateral track was seen in the same light.[19]

State Department officials who worked on Turkey and Turkey experts injected a note of skepticism into these calculations and deliberations. Although they did not question the Turks' interest in becoming more active in Middle Eastern affairs, they doubted their willingness to enter into closer co-operation with the US. In their assessment this might happen only selectively, on a case-by-case basis, if the Turks thought that supporting the US would serve their own narrow interests. The overriding belief of those arguing along these lines was that Turkey's foreign policy doctrine of non-involvement in the Middle East as an ally or a close partner of the US had not been rejected outright. In their view Turkish leaders sought to balance a course of action that was largely independent of the US in the area with selective, mostly indirect support of a number of US goals.[20] The hard reality on top of all this was that Ankara's political priorities in relation to Iran, Iraq and Syria significantly differed from those of the US.

It was an accurate reading of the Turkish perspective. The Turks turned a new page concerning their co-operation with the US in the Middle East when they aligned with Israel. But this by no means meant that they were ready to become the subcontractors of the US in the area, in the phrase of a senior official of the Turkish Ministry of Foreign Affairs.[21] On top of this, as mentioned earlier, there was no reversal of the perception – deeply rooted in the Turkish psyche – of the US as an unreliable interlocutor and a hegemonic partner. General Kemal Yavuz, a former army commander and head of the Turkish War Academies, described well Ankara's pulse when he said that Turkey's co-operation with the US was only a temporary expedient born out of the necessities created by changes in the international environment; in the long run, Turkey could not trust the US.[22] US policy in Northern Iraq, which contributed to the development of an autonomous Kurdish entity with all the consequences that this had for Turkish security and even territorial integrity, was a good case in point, as far as the Turks were concerned. In short, Özal's 'blind, at least in the eyes of the Turkish military',[23] pro-American attitude was but an interlude.

Had the Americans and the Turks shared an overriding security concern in the Gulf, Ankara might have felt the need to further adjust its position and enter into much closer security co-operation with the Americans and the Israelis in the Middle East, with or without the co-operation of an Arab regime. But such a concern did not exist. So the Turks apparently rejected the idea presented to them by Israeli Prime Minister Benjamin Netanyahu of a military agreement which would be the main 'axis' of a regional security system.[24] Essentially, Ankara offered its co-operation à la carte and refused to support security initiatives that were determined by the hegemonic imperatives of the US.[25] Turkey's relationship with Iran was an emblematic case in point, for Turkish leaders refused to accommodate the US policy of isolating Tehran and insisted on maintaining good economic relations with the Iranian regime.

It is most revealing that Ankara did not seriously seek to develop a formal strategic dialogue with Washington, despite the evolution of the bilateral relationship. Apparently the two sides came close to developing such a dialogue only during a very short period, between the years 1997 and 1999.[26] This effort on the part of the Turks seemed to be at least partly a reaction to the December 1997 EU decision to reject Turkey's candidacy, which caused anger and frustration in Ankara. In the final analysis whatever thoughts might have been entertained for a closer US–Turkey co-operation in the Middle East they were short lived. By the end of the 1990s it was crystal clear to Washington that the Turks should not be expected to support US military operations in the Gulf unless these served Turkey's narrow national interests.[27]

Irrespective of differences in security interests and policy perspectives, building a more mature relationship was difficult for other reasons too. Turkey was changing and changing fast under the impact of both external and internal political developments. In December 1999 the EU decision to grant Turkey candidate-member status raised for the Turks a new foreign policy challenge. From now on when deciding on a foreign policy issue they needed to also factor in the reaction of the major European players, whose perspectives by no means always coincided with Washington's. There was one other factor of greater importance. The Turks felt vulnerable on many fronts when the Clinton administration came to power. This began to change by the latter part of the decade, in no small way also as a result of the new US policy toward Turkey. Turkey's internal stability increased after the Turkish Armed Forces broke the back of the Kurdish insurgency. Also, after a major showdown in 1998 between Turkey and Syria, Ankara's strained relations with Damascus came to end. Assad stopped harbouring the Kurdish leader Abdullah Öcalan – who was eventually captured in 1999 – and the two countries entered a new period of improved political as well as economic relations. Thus, a major security thorn was removed from Turkey's side. By the end of 1998 the crucial Baku-Ceyhan pipeline project was gaining momentum, as finally this option seemed to prevail among all others, a development that fuelled Ankara's hopes for Turkey becoming an energy hub. Moreover, the Turkish leaders' European aspirations received a tremendous boost after the 1999 EU decision to move into an accession partnership with Turkey. Around the same time relations with Greece began to improve dramatically as Ankara and Athens agreed to implement a policy of rapprochement. Admittedly, the Turks still found it difficult to turn their economy around, but the involvement from 1998 of the IMF in a supervisory role over the Turkish economy had generated some optimism. Therefore the Turks' expectations for their country to become an influential regional actor were better grounded. In short, by the end of the 1990s the Turks were regaining their confidence. This was clearly visible, as was the rise of nationalist trends, which grew partly as a result of Turkey's increased self-assurance. Furthermore, although Turkey's military modernization programme continued to largely depend on US weaponry and technology, the weight of this dependence was lessened, partly due to the fact that the Turks had successfully diversified their sources of military goods and services,[28] but mainly because all US subsidized military assistance to Turkey ended after fiscal year 1977.[29]

Before long, political developments in Turkey would add another element to the picture. The rise of the pro-Islamist Justice and Development Party to power in 2002 would raise new questions regarding the future course of Turkish foreign policy and hence affect perceptions of co-operation with the US.

Contradictions

Turkish leaders sought to reconcile two contradictory goals. They wished to promote Ankara's interests and increase its regional influence through co-operation with Israel and the US while at the same time they wanted to preserve Turkey's independent policy in the Middle East as much as possible. Turkish leaders were under no illusions that this act would be easy or would not have unpleasant consequences for Turkey's position in the Middle East. But the chiefs of staff, the government and a good number of officials at the Ministry of Foreign Affairs reached the conclusion that it was worth it on the basis of a cost-benefit analysis.[30] The Turks were resolved to face up to Arab and Iranian criticism and indignation. Their defensive line was to insist that Turkish policy had not changed. It simply reflected changes in the region, they argued. When confronted on this issue in regional capitals, they usually retorted, why should Turkey have to be more royal than the king, while so many Arab states are developing relations with Israel?[31] It was a delicate act but it was possible to carry it off just as long as the peace process continued – or at least while there was hope for peace between the Israelis and the Arabs – and US influence in the area remained strong. Of course the Turks had to continue to believe that the gains outweighed the costs.

It has been argued that the contradictions in Turkish foreign policy during the 1990s reflected the interaction, tension and competition of two opposite strategic culture paradigms, the 'Imperial' and the 'Republican'.[32] The former is characterized by militarism, a more aggressive posture abroad and an interest in exclusive alliances; while the latter is characterized by suspicion of the West, a strong aversion to foreign entanglements and an outlook that is strongly anti-Imperial and minimalist.[33] This is an interesting perspective that deserves to be explored further. However, Ankara's choices concerning its relationship with the US within the Middle East strategic context can also be explained in an alternative way, if looked at through the prism of relations between a great power and a weak state. In the final analysis the Turks sought to respond under the circumstances as effectively as possible to what constitutes, as Michael Handel points out, a major question for most weak states in the international system: how to commit a powerful state to supporting their interests while at the same time maintaining their integrity and independence.[34] 'To conduct politics with big states is like sharing the same bed with a tiger', said Ismet Inönü when he was once asked to comment on Turkey's relations with the US.[35] The relationship between the US and Turkey was an unequal one. And as is usually the case when a weaker state enters into an unequal partnership, the Turks had to accept some dangers and even some liabilities in order to reap benefits.[36] But they also had to keep their guard up.

Notes

1 Author's interview with Mehmet Ali Birand (b). H. Laipson, 'US Policy towards Greece and Turkey Since 1974', in D. Constas (ed.), *The Greek-Turkish Conflict in the 1990s: Domestic and External Influences*, Houndmills, Basingstoke: Macmillan, 1991, p. 175.
2 Author's interviews with Mehmet Ali Birand and Marc Grossman.
3 Author's interviews with Morton Abramowitz (b), Mark Grossman (a, b) and Alan Makovsky (b).
4 'Remarks by the President in Address to the Turkish Grand National Assembly', General Assembly Hall, Ankara, Turkey, the White House, Office of the Press Secretary (Ankara, Turkey), 15 November 1999.
5 Author's interviews with Marc Grossman.
6 Author's interviews with Marc Grossman.
7 S. Talbott, 'U.S. Turkish Leadership in the Post-Cold War World', address at Bilkent University, Ankara, Turkey, 11 April 1995.
8 Speech by the US ambassador to Ankara, Mark Parris, to the 19th convention of the Assembly of Turkish American Associations, 8 October 1998, published in [*Turkey*] *Briefing*, 12 October 1998, p. 18.
9 Author's interview with Alan Makovsky (b).
10 [*Turkey*] *Briefing*, 20 April 1998. Author's interview with Mehmet Ali Birand (b).
11 For a detailed discussion of these differences, see A. Makovsky, 'U.S. Policy toward Turkey: Progress and Problems', in M. Abramowitz (ed.), *Turkey's Transformation and American Policy,* New York: The Century Foundation Press, 2000, pp. 230–35, 238–40; H. J. Barkey, 'The Push and Pull of Strategic Cooperation: The US Relationship with Turkey in the Middle East', in D. W. Lesch (ed.), *The Middle East and the United States: A Historical and Political Reassessment*, Boulder, CO: Westview, 2007, pp. 451, 454–55.
12 When the two countries came close to a war in 1996 Congress delayed the planned transfer of two frigates to Turkey for about two years.
13 J. Tirman, 'Improving Turkey's "Bad Neighborhood": Pressing Ankara for Rights and Democracy', *World Policy Journal*, vol. 15, 1998, pp. 60–67. It is worth noticing that in his address to the Turkish parliament in November 1999 President Clinton elaborated on Turkey's strategic world importance, even as he nudged the Turks on the human rights issue. Specifically, he noticed that despite progress concerning this issue Turkey had still 'far more to do', and he made the poignant point that progress on that front would be 'the most meaningful measure' of Turkey's progress. 'Remarks by the President in Address to the Turkish Grand National Assembly', General Assembly Hall, Ankara, Turkey, the White House, Office of the Press Secretary, 15 November 1999. It should be mentioned that two months earlier a Turkish journalist, Abdurraham Dilipak, had published an 'Open Letter to Mr Bulent Ecevit [the Turkish prime minister], c/o President Clinton', which criticized the government particularly on human rights issues. Copies of the newspaper were confiscated and legal proceedings against him were inititiated although his article did not contain incitement to hatred or violence. This had been publicized by human rights organizations in the US.
14 Author's interview with Marc Grossman (b).
15 Makovsky, 'U.S. Policy toward Turkey', p. 236; Bengio, *Turkish-Israeli Relationship*, p. 99. Jordan was gradually developing strategic ties with both Israel and Turkey in the second half of the 1990s. These were kept as much as possible out of the public eye.

16 Author's interviews with Itamar Rabinovitz, Amnon Barzilai (a) and Mr P., July 2007, Washington DC. See also, I. Rabinovich, *The Brink of Peace; The Israeli-Syrian Negotiations*, Princeton, NJ: Princenton University Press, 1998, p. 206; *Ha'aretz*, 15 December 1995.
17 Author's intevriews with Henri Barkey (a) and Sonar Cagaptay.
18 Hebron is demographically a Palestinian city located in the West Bank. The Temporary International Presence in Hebron (TIPH) was a civilian observer mission that was established in the city in 1994 in order to monitor efforts to maintain normal life in the city following an attack by an Israeli which left 29 Palestinians dead and over 100 wounded. Turkey joined TIPH in 1997.
19 Author's interviews with Henri Barkey (a), Alan Makovsky (b) and Sonar Cagaptay.
20 Author's interviews with Henri Barkey, Sonar Cagaptay, Ian Lesser, Alan Makovsky.
21 Quoted in Mufti, *Daring and Caution in Turkish Strategic Culture: Republic at Sea*, Houndmills, Basingstoke: Palgrave, Macmillan, 2009, p. 105; M. B. Aykan, 'The Turkey-US-Israel Triangle: Continuity, Change and Implications for Turkey's Post Cold War Middle East Policy', *Journal of South Asian and Middle Eastern Studies*, vol. XXII, 1999, pp. 12–13.
22 Quoted in Mufti, *Daring and Caution*, p. 93.
23 Author's interview with Cengiz Çandar (b).
24 Author's interviews with Mr A. and Mr S., December 1998, Jerusalem. Also Aykan, 'Turkey-US-Israel Triangle', pp. 10–11.
25 For some insight into the thinking of the Turkish leadership on the issue, see Aykan, 'Turkish Perspectives', pp. 348–49; Mufti, *Daring and Caution*, pp. 92–109.
26 Author's interviews with Alan Makovsky (a) and Ian Lesser (b).
27 A. H. Cordesman, *After Desert Fox: Our Policy for the Gulf and Iraq*, Washington DC: CSIS, 1999, p. 3.
28 Israel, Russia and Germany were the other main beneficiaries of Turkey's defence contracts.
29 T. Gabelnick, W. D. Hartung, and J. Washburn, with research assistance by M. Ciarrocca, *Arming Repression: U.S. Arms Sales to Turkey During the Clinton Administration*, a joint report of the World Policy Institute and the Federation of American Scientists, October 1999, available online at www.fas.org/asmp/library/reports/turkeyrep.htm (accessed 4 March 2000), table II.
30 Author's interview with Barlas Özener. Of course as it has been discussed not everybody within the Foreign Ministry bureaucracy agreed with this conclusion.
31 Author's interview with Barlas Özener. Also author's interview with a Jordanian (January 1999, Amman) and an Egyptian diplomat (June 1999, Ankara) who spoke to the author on condition of anonymity due to active service.
32 Mufti, *Daring and Caution*, pp. 87, 92–3.
33 Mufti, *Daring and Caution*, pp. 1–6.
34 M. I. Handel, *Weak States in the International System*, London: Frank Cass, 1981, pp. 121–2.
35 Quoted in Muammer Kaylan, *The Kemalists: Islamic Revival and the Fate of Secular Turkey*, Amherst, NY: Prometheus Books, p. 96.
36 Handel, *Weak* States, p. 131.

Epilogue

The Washington-Ankara strategic relationship from the end of the 1970s till the end of the 1990s can be examined through a variety of alternative interpretative frameworks and hence understood in different ways. This book has tried to map, in a broad outline, the parameters that, to my mind, determined the evolution of the bilateral relationship – with a focus on the Middle East strategic context – which have not been adequately examined in the mainstream literature.

The most important of these was Turkey's relative weakness. In this time period the majority of Turkish political and military leaders would have preferred, if they could have afforded it, to have maintained their security co-operation with the Americans strictly confined within the NATO framework while avoiding becoming too closely connected with the US. Had they chosen this path they would also have had the support of the vast majority of the Turkish people. Turgut Özal was the exception, although perhaps not to the extent that his critics and political opponents claimed in the impression of him they disseminated.

In the scholarly literature the Turks' wish to re-engage with the Americans at the dawn of the 1980s is mainly attributed to security concerns due to political developments in the greater Middle East. The close US–Turkey security relationship in the 1950s, after all, was built on a common perception of the Soviet security threat shared between American and Turkish leaders. With this in mind, wasn't it entirely reasonable that Ankara chose once more to tighten its strategic ties with Washington against the new security challenges that rose as a result of Moscow's policies following the Soviet invasion in Afghanistan? Yet this story could be told in a different way. This book suggests that for Turkish leaders it became imperative to move again closer to the US primarily because of the collapse of the economic statism model which produced dire economic consequences that, in combination with other domestic factors, shook the Turkish social and political system. Since the mid 1960s the various political currents in the country had found more or less common ground around the idea of resistance to US hegemonic leadership. It was the loss of optimism about the prospects of the Turkish republic without external help and lack of alternatives that created the urgent need for the coalition governments under Demirel, the leader of the centre right, and under the social democrat Ecevit, who succeeded each other in the premiership from 1975 to 1980, to re-establish a close connection with the US. This by no means suggests that developments around Turkey's borders in the closing days of the 1970s played no part in determining policy. Rather, this book argues that at the time security concerns related to domestic rather than external pressures and risks were primarily driving the Turks closer to the US.

The ambitious plans of the Turkish leaders, the military in particular, for military modernization and the development of a defence industry attuned to contemporary technological advances was the other major parameter that determined the evolution of the bilateral relationship. These plans were initially born partly out of frustration with the US arms embargo. But later they expanded rapidly as a result of ample US military co-operation with Turkey. In fact, they were fully endorsed and even promoted by US officials who wished to turn Turkey into a strong US military ally not only within NATO but also within the context of US strategic planning in the Middle East. Thanks to US assistance the Turks' military modernization designs were successful to a large extent. But inevitably there were consequences for the bilateral relations.[1] For one thing, security assistance levels became the measuring rod of the value of maintaining a close strategic co-operation with the US. Equally important, from a Turkish perspective, military modernization plans resulted in Turkey's becoming dependent on the US for military aid, credit, advanced weapons systems and technological support. Essentially, Turkey was faced with the paradox that confronts many a weak state in the international system. As they seek to enhance their military power in order to become stronger they end up losing part of their independence, for most weak states lack the necessary resources they need in order to increase their power but instead have to rely on foreign assistance.

It is within this context that Turkey's co-operation concerning the use of the bases during the Gulf War should be primarily viewed. Mainstream studies argue that Turkish participation in the Gulf War was the result of the decisions and actions of the 'visionary' or 'pro-American' Turgut Özal in response to post-Cold War realities. But this explanation overlooks Turkey's growing dependence on the US for its military modernization, which developed during the Reagan administrations. It also overlooks that the bases were the focal point of US interest in Turkey and therefore it would have taken more luck than skill for the Turks to have maintained their aloofness, if the question of their use ever acquired urgency for the Americans. Of course, had Turkish rulers no longer been interested in sustaining a close security relationship with the US, then the story might have been different. But this was not the case. Post-Cold War changes in the international environment urged the Turks to avoid jeopardizing their ties with the Americans. Furthermore, the Turks did not give up their military modernization plans after the end of the Cold War. In fact, their designs grew even more ambitious, and even though levels of US-appropriated military funds were declining, Turkey's military modernization was still primarily dependent on US security assistance, broadly defined. In short, Turkey could not avoid its military involvement in the Gulf War for, as has been pointed out, 'there is little doubt that the selling of weapons to weak states is one of the most important, and perhaps one of the most efficient means available to the powers in their struggle for hegemony.'[2]

Students of Turkey's foreign policy underline that one of the central elements of Turkey's dominant (at least until the end of the Cold War) strategic culture, which is rooted in the history of the republic, is a strong commitment to independence. Hence there is the imperative to resist foreign influences. Yet the ambitious military modernization designs, which could not be achieved based on Turkish resources alone, constituted a big compromise as far as Turkey's independence was concerned. As Turkey's long-term military modernization programme became heavily dependent on US resources the Americans were placed in a better position to extract concessions. This issue has not been a subject of discussion in the mainstream literature on Turkish foreign policy. However, it is a particularly interesting one for those studying the interaction between Turkish culture, identity and foreign policy. It is worth asking why Turkish military leaders did not follow, for instance, India's example? India, a poor, weak state during the Cold War, was very sensitive when it came to matters of foreign influence and pressure. Even though its leaders, like Turkey's, were very much interested in building up its military power and creating its own regional sphere of influence, throughout the Cold War years they kept at arms' length US military and financial 'gifts'. In fact, they consistently held the line that India had 'no intention of surrendering or bartering her freedom for any purpose or under any compulsion whatever.'[3] Rhetoric aside, in practice this meant that Indian leaders tended to prefer US loans at low rates than outright presents,[4] in direct contrast to the Turks, who strongly preferred aid versus credit. Only further empirical study will help explain the Turks' approach and hopefully offer enough material which could be used for fruitful cross-national comparative analysis in the field of identity and foreign policy behaviour.

Geopolitical factors were the deeper reasons accounting for the renewal of Washington's strategic interest in Turkey in the latter half of the 1990s. But this interest did not emerge automatically. It grew out of specific ideas, actions and the synergy of many actors. In other words, geopolitical factors alone are not adequate to explain 'how' and 'why' US interest in Turkey was conceptualized with a new vocabulary, or why a policy that aimed to broaden the basis of co-operation was developed. To answer these questions I tried in this book to draw attention to those actors who greatly contributed to the development of a more focused US policy toward Turkey.

As the latter part of the 1990s ran its course, many hands at different levels within the US bureaucracy helped give shape to a new policy toward Turkey, which in its important details emerged as a result of the beliefs, ideas and actions of Marc Grossman, which were fully supported and promoted by

Richard Holbrooke. Both proved to be strong players within the foreign policy decision-making apparatus during the 1990s, as Richard Perle was during the 1980s. And while one has to be careful not to exaggerate the role of officials in explaining foreign policy, it is difficult not to note that in the decades before and after the end of the Cold War these personages commanded the direction and implementation of US policy toward Turkey. Grossman's most important contribution was that he energetically acted upon the realization that as the ability of the US to provide assistance at the levels required by the Turks was diminishing, a security relationship could not be maintained unless the US broadened the definition of the strategic relationship so that it would no longer be dependent on assistance funds. He and Holbrooke worked to communicate this perspective to the administration, and together they gave a sense of direction and conviction to US policy, which had lost its enthusiasm for Turkey. As a result, a lot of the tension between Turkey and the US was resolved as the usefulness of the US as an ally grew in the eyes of the Turks, who for their part responded by making their own policy adjustments in order to stimulate US interest. Thus, Grossman and Holbrooke became the authors of a major new chapter in the history of the bilateral relationship during the crucial fluid period of the post-Cold War decade. Of course, having illuminated their role and underlined their importance, the question of the role played by Turkish actors within the context of the bilateral relationship rises. Hopefully, further research will provide us with answers which will help us better understand the Turkish foreign policy outcomes.

Here it should be mentioned that this study has no intention of offering insightful observations within the context of the agency/structure debate. Furthermore, by no means does it suggest, let me repeat, that geopolitical factors did not play an important role in determining US policy towards Turkey in the 1990s. Had Turkey not been at the crossroads of three areas important to the US it would have not been possible for the US interest to have been stimulated and maintained the way it was. Yet the definition of this interest and the form that US policy took were determined by various actors' perceptions and indeed agendas. In other words, the macro-approach that the mainstream literature mainly employs is not enough to help us fully understand the evolution of US policy toward Turkey in the 1990s. In short, there is too much focus on structure and hardly at all on agency. One of the objectives of this book has been to help redress this imbalance. It is to be hoped that it will be of some value in this regard.

Turkey's decision, with US prodding, to move closer to Israel resulted in an unprecedented alignment of domestic and non-domestic actors favourably disposed toward Turkey in Washington. As a result, US officials who advocated the need for a strong US–Turkey relationship were able to achieve objectives that otherwise might have been hard to realize. In essence, the story of how the new US policy toward Turkey came into place in the second half of the 1990s partly demonstrates what Robert Putnam calls the entanglement between domestic and international politics.[5] In other words, the Turkey-Israel military co-operation opened up 'the possibility of synergistic issue linkage, in which strategic moves at one game-table [that of international politics in this case] facilitate unexpected coalitions at the second table [of domestic politics]'.[6]

Within this story there was an interesting chapter, the support given to Turkey by Jewish-American groups. Their activities were a notable example of the energy spent by groups in the pro-Israeli lobby in order. 'to ensure', as John Mearsheimer and Stephen Walt note, 'that American power is used to shape the Middle East environment in ways they believe would advance Israel's interests, especially in security.'[7] Within this context the two analysts focus on how Jewish-American groups have been using their influence to make the US contain the various regional threats to Israel's security, in addition to maintaining generous amounts of aid to Israel.[8] Their lobbying on behalf of Turkey in the 1990s shows that Israel's strategic imperatives also translated into directing US support *in favour of* a state which the Israelis wished to entice into closer political and military co-operation.

The Turks' decision to support through their military co-operation with Israel the order that the US sought to establish in the Middle East was a further erosion of their long-standing resistance to becoming too closely associated with US policies in the area. The first signs of this erosion date back to the early 1980s, when the Turkish military chiefs agreed to sign the COB agreement that essentially paved the way for Turkey's military involvement in the Gulf War. Initially, this erosion partly reflected state and regime changes that were taking place in Turkey, which removed many of the bureaucratic and political constraints that might have prevented it. In the 1990s the erosion became more dramatic, although the norms with deep historical roots which constrained the Turks' co-operation with the US were still in existence. This was the result of a combination of macro-level factors. The changes that were taking place around Turkey's borders were one of them. In addition, Turkish and US interests in the Middle East converged much more in the 1990s than had been the case in the past three decades. The new order that the US was eager to establish in the area was attractive to the Turks both for economic and security reasons. Turkey's collaboration also reflected the heavy dependence of its military modernization plans on the US, which could not be easily broken even though the Americans were changing many of the basic rules of the game against the backdrop of the post-Cold War security environment. Finally it was a manifestation of Turkey's relative weakness, which prevented Ankara from fulfilling its regional goals without external backing for most of the post-Cold War decade; Turkey, like most weak states, had to derive its strength from external sources.[9] It has been argued that dramatic foreign policy change, in itself something rare, is more likely the result of 'perceived losses … than perceived opportunities for gain.'[10] The case of the Turkish change of policy in the Middle East in the second half of the 1990s does not support this theory. Actually, all available evidence shows that

Turkish leaders decided to abandon their traditional policy in quest for multiple gains, not out of fear of perceived losses.

While a key motivation behind the change of Turkish policy in the Middle East was the desire to boost Turkey in Washington, it would be wrong to assume that Turkish foreign policy makers resolved that they had to fully identify with US interests or that allowed their decisions to be dominated by a US agenda. The Turks were prepared to stand up to the US when they thought it was necessary in order to protect certain major interests, while the Americans allowed them room to pursue their own objectives. The Turks were hardly unique in this respect. As Nick Cullather has shown in his excellent study of US-Philippines relations in the 1950s, or Fred Halliday in his work on the Shah's Iran, ties of dependency do not automatically translate into either a full surrender of national interests or an end to opposition to US demands.[11]

'There's no such thing as gratitude in politics.'[12] On 1 May 2003 during the run-up to the invasion of Iraq, after months of intensive negotiations between Washington and Ankara and despite strong US pressure, the Turkish parliament in a close vote refused to allow the US Fourth Infantry Division to deploy in Turkey in order to open up a second front against Saddam Hussein. Soon it became clear that the parliament's decision was not an isolated act but was supported by the majority of Turkish foreign policy decision-makers, including the military. The refusal stunned Washington. No one in the US capital expected the Turks to decline to support the US as for nearly a decade the Americans had backed Ankara concerning a number of issues that greatly mattered to Turkish leaders. In fact, it was only a couple of years earlier that the George W. Bush administration had propped up Turkey's economy through a gigantic IMF rescue package. And yet, if there is something to ponder in this story it is not the Turks' refusal but Washington's surprise.

In the latter part of the 1990s, the new kind of 'mutual understanding' that emerged between the Americans and the Turks[13] fuelled US officials' optimistic expectations concerning the future of the relationship, but undoubtedly there were also serious challenges ahead, as many observers noted at the time. The Turks needed US diplomatic, political and military support, but they also wished to preserve as much freedom of action as possible. In addition, they continued to distrust the US and doubt its reliability. While they saw benefits in supporting certain US strategic objectives in the Middle East, they refused to discuss further regional co-ordination of action. At the end of the day there were a considerable number of differences between the two countries concerning important issues and Iraq was number one.

Grossman and a number of other US officials believed that the Turks would be more prepared to co-operate with the Americans if the US gave more attention to Turkey and backed its major goals. The early results were promising. In the second half of the 1990s the Turks were driven closer to the US under the influence of a complex set of parameters, some of which this book has sought to illustrate. However, sustaining the policy that Grossman and

Holbrooke advocated, leaving all else aside, demanded a focused effort on the part of the bureaucracy that would have been difficult to maintain even in the best of circumstances for a country which in the final analysis did not occupy a central place within the context of US foreign policy. By the end of the decade a new partnership designed for the post-Cold War era was still far from having taken shape. The framework of US–Turkey strategic co-operation for 'the twenty-first century' and its main objectives were not properly discussed and agreed upon. Actually, both sides found it hard to bring into the relationship a new purpose and enthusiasm and even more difficult to maintain it in spite of some effort. To a large extent the relationship continued to be coloured by historical experience while, however, US security assistance to Turkey was coming to an end. This state of affairs both reflected and strengthened the Turks' ambivalence towards the US. Also Turkey was changing. A new powerful political force in the form of the pro-Islamist Justice and Development Party was re-shaping the domestic political dynamics and affected foreign policy behaviour. In parallel, as the relationship shifted from an exclusive military-to-military track to a State Department-to-civilian government track Washington's channels of communication with Ankara could no longer be what they used to be, although the US still had strong bridges in the country. Much more importantly, Turkey was becoming stronger, and as Turkey's confidence was advancing it was inevitable that the balance of the relationship was going to change. Turkey's moving closer to the US during the 1980s and to the US and Israel in the 1990s essentially reflected its relative weakness. This thesis has been presented in different ways throughout the book. But at the dawn of the new century its internal stability had increased. Its potential to become a regional actor in the Middle East was better perceived in the region, while the Turks could see that the influence of the US in the Middle East had fallen from the high point it occupied in the early part of the 1990s. In these circumstances, and as US security assistance to Turkey had come to an end while a new broader relationship was too slow to develop, the Turks' tendency not to allow their interests in the Middle East to be dictated by the wishes of the US was bound again to strengthen.

Notes

1 These plans also had significant negative consequences for the economic and political development of Turkey, but this discussion is beyond the scope of the present study.
2 M. I. Handel, *Weak States in the International System*, London: Frank Cass, 1981, p. 86.
3 Statement by Jawaharlal Nehru to India's parliament in 1953 following the news of US military aid to Pakistan, quoted in A. J. Rotter, *Comrades at Odds: The United States and India, 1947–1964*, Ithaca, NY: Cornell University Press, 2000, p. 67. For an analysis of India's approach toward the US, see also Rotter, *Comrades at Odds*, passim.
4 K. Knorr, *Power and Wealth: The Political Economy of International Power*, New York: Basic Books, 1973, p. 172.

5 R. D. Putnam, 'Diplomacy and Domestic Policy: The Logic of Two Level Games', *International Organization*, vol. 42, 1988.
6 Putnam, 'Diplomacy and Domestic Policy', p. 460.
7 J. J. Mearsheimer and S. M. Walt, *The Israel Lobby and U.S. Foreign Policy*, New York: Farrar, Straus and Giroux, 2007, p. 200.
8 Mearsheimer and Walt, *Israel Lobby*.
9 Handel, *Weak States*, p. 257.
10 D. A. Welch, *Painful Choices: A Theory of Foreign Policy Change*, Princeton, NJ: Princeton University Press, 2005, p. 229.
11 N. Cullather, *Illusions of Influence: The Political Economy of United States – Philippines Relations, 1942–1960*, Stanford, CA: Stanford University Press, 1994. F. Halliday, *Iran. Dictatorship and Development*, Harmondsworth: Penguin Books, 1979. Of course, the US–Turkey relationship does not compare with the US–Philippines one, which constituted a classic client relationship.
12 G. Greene, *The Quiet American*, London: Vintage Books, 2004, p. 168.
13 Author's interviews with Marc Grossman.

Bibliography

Unpublished archival material

NATO archives (Brussels, Belgium)

Document Series:

North Atlantic Council, Records of Meetings (C-R), 1977–80.
Private Office of the Secretary General (PO), 1977–79.
Military Committee Records (MC), 1979–80.
International Military Staff Working Memoranda (IMSWM), 1979–80.
Chairman of the Military Committee Memoranda (CHAMILCOM), 1979–80.

Ronald Reagan Presidential Library (Simi Valley, California)

Collections:

White House Staff and Office Files, 1981–1989:
European and Soviet Affairs Directorate, NSC: Records, 1983–89:
Series III. Trip File: RAC Box 14: Under-secretary Armacost's Trip to Turkey, 10/31/1985–11/01/1985 (Binder) (1)–(6).
Series IV. Visit File: RAC Box 15: Ozal Visit 04/02/1985, (1)–(5).

Executive Secretariat, NSC: Country File: Records 1981–85: Box 20: [The majority of documents in these files were still classified].
Turkey (01/21/1981–07/06/1981)
Turkey (07/07/1981–11/10/1981)
Turkey (11/24/1981–01/25/1982)
Turkey (01/29/1982–05/10/1982)
Turkey (05/13/1982–05/27/1982)
Turkey (05/28/1982–06/24/1982)
Turkey (06/28/1982–09/10/1982)
Turkey (10/05/1982–01/30/1983)
Turkey (02/16/1983–10/05/1983)
Turkey (10/11/1983–12/23/1983)
Turkey (01/04/1984–02/22/1984)

Published archival material

George Bush Presidential Library (College Station, Texas)

Collections:

Memoranda of Meetings and Telephone Conversations (Memcons/Telcons):
Turkey, 1989/02/24-1992/04/28. Online. Available, HTTP: <http://bushlibrary.tamu.edu/research/memcons_telcons.php> (accessed 20 Feb. 2010).

Public papers:
'Remarks Following Discussions with President Turgut Ozal of Turkey', South Portico, White House, 25 Sept. 1990. Online. Available, HTTP: <http://www.bushlibrary.tamu.edu/ research/public_papers.php> (accessed, 10 January 2006).
'Remarks at a Dinner Hosted By President Turgut Ozal in Istanbul', Turkey, Dining Room, Dolmabahce Palace, 21 July 1991. Online. Available, HTTP: <http://www.bushlibrary.tamu.edu/research/public_papers.php> (accessed, 14 April 2006).
'Remarks at the Departure Ceremony for Prime Minister Suleyman Demirel of Turkey', South Lawn, White House,11 Feb.1992. Online. Available, HTTP: <http://www.bushlibrary.tamu.edu/research/public_papers.php> (accessed, 10 Jan. 2008).

Foreign Relations of the United States, Washington, D.C: U.S. Government Printing Office.

Volumes used:
1955–1957, vol.XII, *Near East Region; Iran; Turkey* (1991).
1958–1960, vol.X, part 2 (1993).
1961–1963, vol. XVI, *Eastern Europe; Cyprus; Greece; Turkey* (1994).
1964–1968, vol. XIII, *Western Europe Region* (1995).

NATO archives

NATO, *Final Communiqué*, 05 Dec. 1978–06 Dec. 1978, 15 May 1979–16 May 1979, 11 Dec. 1979–12 Dec. 1979. Online. Available, HTTP: <http://www.nato.int/cps/en/natolive/official_texts.htm> (accessed, 15 Jan. 2010).

US Department of State

The American Embassy, Ankara to the Secretary of State, Washington, 2 March 1975, Telegram 2621, Electronic Telegrams 1/1/1975–12/31/1975, no. 18, available online at http://aad.archives.gov/aad/createpdf?dt=2476&rid=70336&dl=1345 (accessed 20 December 2007).
The American Embassy, Ankara to Secretary of State, Washington, Telegram 2584, 1 April 1975, 'Demirel Government's Coalition Protocol: Foreign Policy and National Security Section: Implications for USG-GOT Security Relationship', Electronic Telegrams 1/1/1975–12/31/1975, no. 14, available online at http://aad.archives.gov/aad/createpdf?dt=2476&rid=70336&dl=1345 (accessed, 20 December 2007).
The American Embassy, Ankara to the Secretary of State, Washington, Telegram 7985, 20 October 1976, Electronic Telegrams 1/1/1976–12/31/1976, no. 19, available online at http://aad.archives.gov/aad/createpdf?dt=2476&rid=70336&dl=1345 (accessed, 20 December 2007).

'U.S.-Turkey Defence and Economic Cooperation Agreement', 29 March 1980, available online at http://photos.state.gov/libraries/turkey/461177/pdf/32t3323.pdf (accessed, 29 October 2007).

'Agreement between the United States and Turkey Supplementing and Extending the Agreement of March 29, 1980 for Cooperation on Defense and Economy. Effected by Exchange of Letters at Washington', 16 March 1987, 'Entered into Force March 16, 1987', available online at http://photos.state.gov/libraries/turkey/461177/pdf/ctia5977_001.pdf (accessed, 22 May 2010).

Other published official documents

Binnendijk, H., and Friendly, A., Jr., *Turkey, Greece, and NATO: The Strained Alliance*, staff report to the Committee on Foreign Relations, United States Senate, Washington DC: US Government Printing Office, March 1980.

Commission on Integrated Long-Term Strategy (US), *Discriminate Deterrence*, report of the Commission on Integrated Long-Term Strategy, Washington DC: US Government Printing Office, January 1988.

Congressional Research Service, Foreign Affairs and National Defense Division, *Turkey's Problems and Prospects: Implications for U.S. Interests*, report prepared for the Subcommittee on Europe and the Middle East of the Committee on Foreign Affairs, US House of Representatives by the Foreign Affairs and National Defense Division Congressional Research Service, Library of Congress, Washington DC: US Government Printing Office, 1980.

Congressional Research Service, *The Persian Gulf: Are We committed? At What cost?: A dialogue with the Reagan Administration on U.S. Policy*, prepared for the use of the Joint Economic Committee, Congress of the United States with the assistance of the Congressional Research Service, Library of Congress, Washington DC: US Government Printing Office, 1981.

'Fiscal Year 1992 Security Assistance Budget Request by the Honorable Reginald Bartholomew, Under Secretary of State for International Security Affairs', *The DISAM Journal*, Spring 1991.

Migdalovitz, C., *Greece and Turkey: Current Foreign Aid Issues*, CRS, Issue Brief, 1996, available online at www.fas.org/man/crs/86–065.htm#summ (accessed 16 June 2006).

Sanford, J. E., *Debt Owed to the United States by Foreign Countries: Recent Rescheduling and Forgiveness*, CRS report for Congress, Washington DC: Congressional Research Service, The Library of Congress, US Government Printing Office, 19 November 1993.

United States Congress, Commission on Security and Cooperation in Europe, *Turkey-United States Relations: Potential and Peril*, hearing before the Commission on Security and Cooperation in Europe, one hundred and fourth Congress, first session, 19 September 1995, Washington DC: US Government Printing Office, 1996.

United States Congress, House Committee on Armed Services, Subcommittee on Military Installations and Facilities, *Hearings, on H.R. 1816 (H.R. 2972) to Authorize Certain Construction at Military Installations for Fiscal Year 1984, and for Other Purposes*, ninety-eighth Congress, first session, 1983, Washington DC: US Government Printing Office, 1983.

United States Congress, House Committee on Foreign Affairs, Subcommittee on Europe and the Middle East, *Supplemental Aid Requests for Fiscal Years 1979 and*

1980 for Turkey and Oman. Hearings, 15 and 31 May 1979, ninety-sixth Congress, first session, Washington DC: US Government Printing Office, 1979.

United States Congress, House Committee on Foreign Affairs, Subcommittee on Europe and the Middle East, *United States-Turkey Defense and Economic Cooperation Agreement, Hearing before the Subcommittee on Europe and the Middle East of the Committee on Foreign Affairs*, House of Representatives, ninety-sixth Congress, second session, 7 May 1980, Washington DC: US Government Printing Office, 1980.

United States Congress, House Committee on Foreign Affairs, *United States Political-Military Relations with Allies in Southern Europe: Report of a Staff Study Mission to Portugal, Spain, Greece and Turkey, October 15–30, 1986, to the Committee on Foreign Affairs, U.S. House of Representatives*, Washington DC: US Government Printing Office, 1987.

United States Congress, Senate Committee on Armed Services, *The Military Aspects of Banning Arms Aid to Turkey. Hearing before the Committee on Armed Services*, United States Senate, ninety-fifth Congress, second session, 28 June 1978, Washington DC: US Government Printing Office, 1978.

United States Congress, Senate Committee on Foreign Relations, *United States-Turkish Defense Cooperation Agreement: Hearing before the Committee on Foreign Relations*, United States Senate, ninety-fourth Congress, second session, on S. J. Res. 204, 15 September 1976, Washington DC: US Government Printing Office, 1976.

United States Congress, Senate Committee on Foreign Relations, *Fiscal Year 1980 International Security Assistance Authorization. Hearings, February 28 – April 30, 1979*, ninety-sixth Congress, first session on S. 584, To Amend the Foreign Assistance Act of 1961 and the Arms Export Control Act, and for Other Purposes, Washington DC: US Government Printing Office, 1979.

United States Congress, Senate Committee on Foreign Relations, *Perspectives on NATO's Southern Flank: Senate Delegation Report, April 3–13, 1980: A Report to the Committee on Foreign Relations*, Washington DC: US Government Printing Office, 1980.

United States Department of Defense, *Conduct of the Persian Gulf War: Final Report to Congress, 1991*, Responsibility Sharing, appendix P, Washington DC: US Government Printing Office, 1992.

United States Department of the Treasury, *Historical Debt Outstanding-Annual, 1950–1999*, available online at http://www.treasurydirect.gov/govt/reports/pd/histdebt/histdebt.htm (accessed 20 March 2006).

United States General Accounting Office, *The Defense and Economic Cooperation Agreement – U.S. Interests and Turkish Needs: Report by the Comptroller General of the United States*, Washington DC and Gaithersburg, MD: US General Accounting Office, 1982.

Public speeches

Lake, A., 'Conceptualizing U.S. Strategy in the Middle East', 17 May 1994, keynote address, Soref symposium, The Washington Institute for Near East Policy.

Talbott, S., 'U.S. Turkish Leadership in the Post-Cold War World', address at Bilkent University, Ankara, Turkey, 11 April 1995.

The White House, Office of the Press Secretary, 'Remarks by the President [Clinton] in Address to the Turkish Grand National Assembly', General Assembly Hall, Ankara, Turkey, 15 November 1999.

Interviews

Americans

Morton Abramowitz, US ambassador to Turkey (1989–91), assistant secretary of state for intelligence and research (1985–89): a) July 2007; b) October 2010, Washington DC.

Henri Barkey, professor of international relations, member of the Department of State Policy Planning Staff (1998–2000): a) July 1999, b) July 2007, c) October 2010, Washington DC.

Warren Christopher, US secretary of state (1993–97): August 2003, Los Angeles, CA.

Thomas Dine, executive director of the American Israel Public Affairs Committee (AIPAC) (1980–93): June 2013, Washington DC.

Marc Grossman, under-secretary of state for political affairs (2001–5), assistant secretary of state for European affairs (1997–2001), US ambassador to Turkey (1994–97): a) July 2007; b) October 2010 (discussion); c) June 2013, Washington DC.

Daniel Kurtzer, US ambassador to Israel (2001–5), US ambassador to Egypt (1997–2001), deputy assistant secretary of state for Near Eastern affairs, (1989–94): July 2008, Athens.

Michael Ledeen, foreign policy analyst, consultant to the US National Security Council and the State Department during the Ronald Reagan administration: December 1997, Washington DC.

Ian O. Lesser, foreign and security policy analyst, specialist on U.S.-Turkey relations: a) July 2007, Washington DC; b) June 2008, Athens.

Alan Makovsky, senior professional staff member with responsibility for the Middle East and Turkey, Committee on Foreign Affairs, US House of Representatives (2001–13): a) July 2007; b) October 2010, Washington, DC; c) February 2011 (electronic conversation).

Aaron David Miller, Middle East analyst, State Department adviser to secretaries of state on Arab-Israeli negotiations (1978–2003): October 2010, Washington DC (telephone interview).

Andrew Manatos, lobbyist: July 2007, Washington DC.

Peter Marudas, chief of staff, Senator Paul S. Sarbanes office: July 1999, Washington DC.

Israelis

Amnon Barzilai, defence correspondent, *Ha'aretz*: a) December 1998; b) January 1999, Tel-Aviv.

David Granit, Israel's ambassador to Turkey (1993–95): a) December 1998; b) February 1999, Jerusalem.

Itamar Rabinovitz, professor of history, expert on the politics and policies of the Middle East, Israel's ambassador to the US (1993–96) and Israel's chief negotiator with Syria (1992–95): July 2008, Athens.

Turks

Mehmet Ali Birand, journalist, political commentaror and writer: a) February 2007, Athens; b) November 2008, Istanbul.

Sonar Cagaptay, director of the Turkish Research Program at the Washington Institute for Near East Policy: July 2007, Washington DC.

Sami Cohen, foreign affairs journalist and columnist, *Milliyet*: June 2008, Istanbul.

Cengiz Çandar, political columnist and writer, special adviser to President Turgut Özal (1991–93): a) December 2006, Istanbul; b) November 2008, Athens; c) October 2010, Washington DC.
Selim Egeli, member of the board of directors of Turkey's Foreign Economic Relations Board (DEIK), adviser to President Turgut Özal (1990–93): November 2008, Istanbul.
Yalım Eralp, ambassador, adviser (1991–96) to Prime Ministers Mesut Yilmaz and Tansu Çiller while director general of NATO affairs, Turkish Ministry of Foreign Affairs: a) December 2006; b) November 2008, Istanbul.
Ali Karaosmanoğlu, professor of international relations, expert on security and civil-military issues: June 1999, Ankara (discussion).
Hasan Köni, professor of international relations: June 1999, Ankara.
Özdem Sanberk, ambassador, permanent under-secretary at the Turkish Ministry of Foreign Affairs (1991–95), foreign policy chief adviser (1985–87) to Prime Minister Turgut Özal: December 2006, Istanbul.
Barlas Özener, Turkey's ambassador to Israel (1995–99): a) December 1998; b) February 1999, Tel-Aviv.
Lale Sarıibrahimoğlu, defense affairs columnist: September 1995, Ankara.
Süha Umar, ambassador to Jordan (1995–98), deputy director for disarmament affairs, Turkish Ministry of Foreign Affairs (1991–94): July 2008, Athens.

Press conferences material

Under-secretary of State Richard Holbrooke, press conference, 21 February 1995, Ankara.

Memoirs

Brzezinski, Z., *Power and Principle: Memoirs of the National Security Adviser, 1977–1981*, New York: Farrar, Strauss, Giroux, 1983.
Clinton, B. *My Life*, New York: Alfred A. Knopf, 2004.
Evren, K., *Kenan Evren'in Hatıraları*, Istanbul: Milliyet Yayınları, 1991, vol. 3.
Ford, G. R., *A Time to Heal*, New York: Harper and Row, 1979.
Indyk, M., *Innocent Abroad: An Intimate Account of American Peace Diplomacy in the Middle East*, New York: Simon and Schuster, 2009.
Spain, J. W., *American Diplomacy in Turkey: Memoirs of an Ambassador Extraordinary and Plenipotentiary*, New York: Praeger Publishers, 1984.
Torumtay, N., *Orgeneral Torumtay'ın Anıları*, Istanbul: Milliyet Yayınları, 1994.
Yirmibeşoğlu, S., *Askeri ve Siyasi Anıları*, Istanbul: Nisan, 1999.

Books, articles and other cited sources

Abramowitz, M.I., 'Dateline Ankara: Turkey after Özal', *Foreign Policy*, no. 91, 1993, pp. 164–81.
——'The Complexities of American Policymaking on Turkey', in M. Abramowitz (ed.), *Turkey's Transformation and American Policy*, New York: The Century Foundation Press, 2000, pp. 153–84.
Ackerman, D., 'Memorial Honors Life of Penn Prof', 22 January 2002, *The Daily Pennsylvanian*, available online at http://media.dailypennsylvanian.com (accessed 3 March 2009).

Ahmad, F., *The Making of Modern Turkey*, London: Routledge, 1993.

Akçam, T., *Türk Ulusal Kimliği ve Ermeni Sorunu*, Istanbul: Iletişim Yayınları, 1992.

Akder, H., 'Turkey's Export Expansion In the Middle East 1980–85', *Middle East Journal*, vol. 41, 1987, pp. 553–67.

Allison, G. T., and Zelikow, P., *Essence of Decision: Explaining the Cuban Missile Crisis*, New York: Longman, 1999.

Ambrosio, T, 'Ethnic Groups and U.S. Foreign Policy', in T. Ambrosio (ed.), *Ethnic Identity Groups and U.S. Foreign Policy*, Westport, CT: Praeger, 2002, pp. 1–19.

——'Entangling Alliances: The Turkish-Israeli Lobbying Partnership and Its Unintended Consequences', in T. Ambrosio (ed.), *Ethnic Identity Groups and U.S. Foreign Policy*, Westport, CT: Praeger, 2002, pp. 143–67.

American Hellenic Institute, Policy Statements, 'Critical Review of U.S. Policy toward Turkey Needed' [n.d.], available online at www.ahiworld.com/policy_statement.html#6a (accessed 20 September 2008).

American Presidency Project, 'An American Vision: For Our Children and Our Future', in J. T. Woolley and G. Peters, The American Presidency Project, Santa Barbara, CA, [n.d], available online at www.presidency.ucsb.edu (accessed, 20 February 2010).

Amnesty International, *Turkey: Testimony on Torture*, London: Amnesty International Publications, 1985.

——*Turkey: A Policy of Denial*, 8 February 1995, available online at http://amnesty.org/en/library/asset/EUR44/001/1995/en/3a88f8ee-f8bf-11dd-b40d-7b25bb27e189/eur440011995en.pdf (accessed 20 February 2005).

Atalay, S., 'ABD Güvenlık Yardımı ABD Türkiye Ilişkileri', *Avrasya Dosyası*, vol. 1, 1994, pp. 236–56.

Athanassopoulou, E., 'Turkey and the Black Sea Initiative', in R. Gillespie (ed.), *Mediterranean Politics*, London: Pinter Publishers, vol. 1, 1994, pp. 130–47.

——'Ankara's Foreign Policy Objectives after the End of the Cold War', *ORIENT*, vol. 36, 1995, pp. 269–85.

——*Turkey: Anglo-American Security Interests, 1945–52: The First Enlargement of NATO*, London: Frank Cass, 1999.

——'American-Turkish Relations since the End of the Cold War', *Middle East Policy*, vol. VIII, 2001, pp. 144–64.

Aydin, M., *Turkish Foreign Policy during the Gulf War of 1990–1991* Cairo: Cairo Papers in Social Science, 1998.

Aykan, M. B., 'The Palestinian Question in Turkish Foreign Policy from the 1950s to the 1980s', *International Journal of Middle East Studies*, vol. 25, 1993, pp. 91–110.

——'Turkey's Policy in Northern Iraq, 1991–95', *Middle Eastern Studies*, vol. 32, 1996, pp. 343–66.

——'Turkish Perspectives on Turkish-US Relations Concerning Persian Gulf Security in the Post-Cold War Era', *Middle East Journal*, vol. 50, 1996, pp. 344–58.

——'The Turkey-US-Israel Triangle: Continuity, Change and Implications for Turkey's Post Cold War Middle East Policy', *Journal of South Asian and Middle Eastern Studies*, vol. XXII, 1999, pp. 1–31.

Ayman, S. G., and Atefloğlu, N., 'I Stratigiki stis Metavalomenes Diethnis Synthikes. I Tourkia ke oi Gitones tis' in F. Sönmezoğlu (ed.), *Mythos ke Pragmatikotita: Analysi tis Tourkikis Exoterikis Politikis*, Athens: Infognomon, 2001, tomos A, pp. 568–87.

Bal, I., *Turkey's Relations with the West and the Turkic Republics: The Rise and Fall of the 'Turkish Model'*, Aldershot: Ashgate, 2000.

Barkey, H. J., 'The Push and Pull of Strategic Cooperation: The US Relationship with Turkey in the Middle East', in D. W. Lesch (ed.), *The Middle East and the United States: A Historical and Political Reassessment,* Boulder, CO: Westview, 2007, pp. 446–61.

Barkey, H. J., and Fuller, G. E., *Turkey's Kurdish Question*, Lanham: Rowman and Littlefield Publishers, 1998.

Barutçuoğu, I., 'Evolution of Turkey's Security Role in the Middle East', in G. S. Harris (ed.), *The Middle East in Turkish-American Relations*, Washington, DC: The Heritage Foundation, 1985, pp. 61–7.

Batu, H., 'Turkish Foreign Policy in a Changing World', *Studies on Turkish-Arab Relations: Special Issue on Turkey and the Gulf Crisis*', Istanbul: Foundation for the Study of Turkish-Arab Relations (TAIV), vol. 6, 1991, pp. 85–93.

Beasley, R., 'Collective Interpretations: How Problem Representations Aggregate in Foreign Policy Groups', in D. A. Sylvan and K. F. Voss (eds), *Problem Representation in Foreign Policy Decision Making*, Cambridge: Cambridge University Press, 1998, pp. 80–115.

Bengio, O., *The Turkish-Israeli Relationship: Changing Ties of Middle Eastern Outsiders*, New York: Palgrave Macmillan, 2004.

Bertram, C., 'Introduction', *America's Security in the 1980s*, London: IISS, Adelphi Papers, vol. 22, 1982, pp. 1–4.

Bir, Ç., 'Nato'nun Yeni Stratejisi ve Türkiye', *Savunma ve Havacılık*, vol. 6, 1992, pp. 16–22.

Birand, M. A., *12 Eylül, Saat: 04.00*, Istanbul: Karacan Yayınları, 1984.

Bishku, M. M., 'Turkey and Its Middle Eastern Neighbours since 1945', *Journal of South Asian and Middle Eastern Studies*, vol. 15, 1992.

Blank, S. J., Pelletiere, S. C. and Johnsen, W. T., *Turkey's Strategic Position at the Crossroads of World Affairs*, Carlisle, PA: Strategic Studies Institute, US Army War College, 1993.

Bölükbaşı, S., 'Turkey Copes with Revolutionary Iran', *Journal of South Asian and Middle Eastern Studies*, vol. 13, 1989, pp. 94–109.

——'Turkey Challenges Iraq and Syria: The Euphrates Dispute', *Journal of South Asian and Middle Eastern Studies*, vol. XVI, 1993, pp. 9–32.

Bozarslan, H., *Istoria tis Syhronis Tourkias: apo tin epanastasi ton Neotourkon mehri simera*, Athens: Savvalas, 2008.

Brady, L. B., 'Working with Allies: Clinton Defense Policy and the Management of Multilateralism', in S. J. Cimbala (ed.), *Clinton and Post-Cold War Defense*, Westport, CT: Praeger, 1996, pp. 71–86.

Brown, H., *U.S. Security Policy in Southwest Asia: A Case Study in Complexity*, Washington DC: Johns Hopkins University School of Advanced International Studies, Johns Hopkins Foreign Policy Institute, Occasional Paper, 1981.

Brown, S., *The Causes and Prevention of War*, New York: St Martin's Press, 1994.

Bulloch, J., and Morris, H., *Saddam's War*, London: Faber and Faber, 1991.

Burt, R., 'Turkey and the Reagan Administration', in G. S. Harris (ed.), *The Middle East in Turkish-American Relations*, Washington, DC: The Heritage Foundation, 1985, pp. 17–21.

Campany, R. C., *Turkey and the United States: The Arms Embargo Period*, New York: Praeger, 1986.

Campbell, J. C., 'The Superpowers and Turkey: An American View', in A. L. Karaosmanoğlu and S. Taşhan (eds), *Middle East, Turkey and the Atlantic Alliance*, Ankara: Foreign Policy Institute, 1987, pp. 58–77.

Çandar, C., 'Some Turkish Perspectives on the United States and American Policy toward Turkey', in M. Abramowitz (ed.), *Turkey's Transformation and American Policy*, New York: The Century Foundation Press, 2000, pp. 117–52.
——'The Post-September 11 United States through Turkish Lenses', in M. Abramowitz (ed.), *The United States and Turkey: Allies in Need*, New York: The Century Foundation Press, 2003, pp. 145–72.
Carley, P., *Turkey's Role in the Middle East*, Washington DC: United States Institute of Peace, Conference Report, 2005.
Celasun, O., *The 1994 Currency Crisis in Turkey*, Washington DC: World Bank Policy Research Working Paper no. 1319, April 1998.
Çelik, Y., *Contemporary Turkish Foreign Policy*, Westport, CT: Praeger, 1999.
Çevic, I., 'A Top Class Diplomat, a Gentleman and a Friend', *Turkish Daily News*, 16 May 1997.
Chase, R. S., Hill, E. M., and Kennedy, P., 'Pivotal States and U.S. Strategy', *Foreign Affairs*, Jan/Feb 1996, vol.75, pp.33–51.
Clarke, D. L., O'Connor, D. B. and Ellis, J. D., *Send Guns and Money: Security Assistance and U.S. Foreign Policy*, Westport, CT: Praeger, 1997.
Çongar, Y., 'The State of Turkish-American Dialogue: Do You Understand What I Am Saying?', *Private View*, vol. 3, no. 7, 1999, available online at www.tusiad.org.tr/yayin/private/spring99/html/sec9.html (accessed 20 June 2007).
Cordesman, A. H., *The Military Balance in the Middle East: An Executive Summary*, Berkeley, CA: Institute on Global Conflict and Cooperation, University of California, 1999, Policy Paper 49.
——*After Desert Fox: Our Policy for the Gulf and Iraq*, Washington DC: CSIS, 1999.
Couloumbis, T., *The U.S., Greece and Turkey: The Troubled Triangle*, New York: Praeger, 1983.
Cowell, A., 'Turkey Tries to Stay Aloof on War', *New York Times*, 10 July 1987.
Cronin, P. M. (ed.), *From Globalism to Regionalism: New Perspectives on U.S. Foreign and Defense Policies*, Washington DC: National Defense University Press, 1993.
Cullather, N., *Illusions of Influence; The Political Economy of United States – Philippines Relations, 1942–1960*, Stanford, CA: Stanford University Press, 1994.
Dagi, I. D., 'Democratic Transition in Turkey, 1980–83: The Impact of European Diplomacy', in S. Kedourie (ed.), *Turkey: Identity, Democracy and Politics*, London: Frank Cass, 1996, pp. 123–41.
David, C.-F., *Dissecting Clinton's Foreign Policy Making: A First Cut*, Montreal: Center for United States Studies, Université du Quebéc, 2004.
Demirsar, M., 'U.S. Upgrades Military Links to Turkey with Eye to Soviet Union and Mideast', *The Wall Street Journal*, 12 January 1983.
Dietrich, J. W., 'Interest Groups and Foreign Policy: Clinton and the China MFN Debates', *Presidential Studies Quarterly*, vol. 29, 1999, pp. 280–96.
Drew, E., 'The Neocons in Power', *The New York Review of Books*, 12 June 2003, available online at www.nybooks.com/articles/16378 (accessed 7 October 2008).
Elegi, S., *Taktik Balisti Füzeler ve Türkiye*, Ankara: Milli Savunma Bakanlığı, 1993.
'Discussion on "Turkey between Alliance and Alienation"', *Diş Politika (Foreign Policy)* vol. 8, 1980, pp. 125–47.
Eralp, Y., 'An Insider's View of Turkey's Foreign Policy and Its American Connection', in M. Abramowitz (ed.), *The United States and Turkey: Allies in Need*, New York: The Century Foundation Press, 2003, pp. 109–43.

Erdem, V., 'Turkish Defense Industries and DIDA', *Diş Politika* (Foreign Policy) vol. XIV, 1988, pp. 111–23.

Ertuğrul, A., and Selçuk, F., 'Turkish Economy: 1980–2000', in Kibritçioğlu, A., Rittenberg, L. and Selçuk, F. (eds), *Inflation and Disinflation in Turkey*, Aldershot, Hampshire: Ashgate, 2002, pp. 13–40.

Evriviades, E. L., *US-Turkey Contingency Planning and Soviet Reaction 1978–1983*, Athens: Themata, Policy and Defense, Defense Analyses Institute, 2001.

Evriviades, M. L., *The U.S. and Cyprus: The Politics of Manipulation in the 1985 U.N. Cyprus High Level Meeting*, Athens: Institute of International Relations, Occasional Research Paper, no. 3, 1992.

——'Turkey's Role in United States Strategy during and after the Cold War', *Mediterranean Quarterly*, vol. 9, 1998, pp.30–51.

——'The Turkish-Israeli Axis: Alliances and Alignments in the Middle East', *ORIENT*, vol. 39, 1998, pp. 565–82.

Fialka, J. F., 'Former Defense Official Creates Firm to Lobby in Washington for Turkey', *The Wall Street Journal*, 16 February 1989.

Friedman, T., 'Foreign Affairs: The Turkish Nightmare', *New York Times*, 17 May 1995.

Gabelnick, T., Hartung, W. D., and Washburn, J., with research assistance by Ciarrocca, M., *Arming Repression: U.S. Arms Sales to Turkey During the Clinton Administration*, a joint report of the World Policy Institute and the Federation of American Scientists, October 1999, available online at www.fas.org/asmp/library/reports/turkeyrep.htm (accessed 4 March 2000).

Gold, S., 'The Costs of Privatization. Turkey in the 1980s', *The Multinational Monitor*, vol. 10, October 1989, available online at www.multinationalmonitor.org/hyper/issues/1989/10/gold.html (accessed 15 February 2005).

Goldberg, J. J., *Jewish Power: Inside the American Jewish Establishment*, Reading, MA: Addison-Wesley, 1996.

Gorenberg, G., 'Israel Demeans Itself in an Affront to Armenians', *Los Angeles Times*, 30 October 1989.

Goshko, J. M., 'From the Allies: Patience', *The Washington Post,* 13 September 1980.

Gözen, R., 'Operation Provide Comfort: Origins and Objectives', *Ankara Üniversitesi Siyasal Bilgiler Fakültesi Dergisi*, vol. 50, 1995, available online at http://dergiler.ankara.edu.tr/search.php (accessed 20 October 2007).

Greene, G., *The Quiet American*, London: Vintage Books, 2004.

Gresh, G., 'Turkish-Israeli-Syrian-Relations and Their Impact on the Middle East', *Middle East Journal,* vol. 52, 1998, pp. 188–203.

Gruen, G. E., 'Ambivalence in the Alliance: U.S. Interests in the Middle East and the Evolution of Turkish Foreign Policy', *Orbis*, vol. 24, 1980, pp. 363–78

——'Dynamic Progress in Turkish-Israeli Relations', *Israel Affairs,* vol. 1, 1995, pp. 40–70.

——'Turkey and the Middle East after Oslo I', in Freedman, R. O., (ed.), *The Middle East and the Peace Process: The Impact of the Oslo Accords*, Gainesville: University Press of Florida, 1998, pp. 169–212.

——'Turkey between the Middle East and the West', in Freedman, R. O., (ed.), *The Middle East from the Iran-Contra Affair to the Intifada*, Syracuse, NY: Syracuse University Press, 1999, pp. 390–422.

Halberstam, D., *War in a Time of Peace: Bush, Clinton, and the Generals*, New York: Simon and Schuster, 2001.

Hale, W., 'Turkey, the Middle East and the Gulf Crisis', *International Affairs*, vol. 68, 1992, pp. 679–92.

——*Turkish Politics and the Military*, London: Routledge, 1994.

——*Turkish Foreign Policy, 1774–2000*, London: Frank Cass, 2000.

Halliday, F., *Iran. Dictatorship and Development*, Harmondsworth: Penguin Books, 1979.

Halperin, M., and Clapp, P. A., with Kanter, A., *Bureaucratic Politics and Foreign Policy*, Washington DC: Brookings Institution Press, 2006.

Handel, M. I., *Weak States in the International System*, London: Frank Cass, 1981.

Harris, G. S., *Troubled Alliance: Turkish-American Problems in Historical Perspective, 1945–1971*, Washington DC: American Enterprise Institute for Public Policy Research, 1972.

——'Turkey between Alliance And Alienation', *Diş Politika* (Foreign Policy), vol. 8, 1980, pp. 117–25.

——*Turkey: Coping with Crisis*, Boulder, CO: Westview Press, 1985.

——'Introduction', in G. S. Harris (ed.), *The Middle East in Turkish-American Relations*, Washington, DC: The Heritage Foundation, 1985, pp. vii–x.

——'The Russian Federation and Turkey', in Rubinstein, A. Z., and Smolansky, O. M. (eds), *Regional Power Rivalries in the New Eurasia: Russia, Turkey, and Iran*, Armonk, NY: M. E. Sharpe, 1995, pp. 3–25.

——'Turkish-American Relations since the Truman Doctrine', in Aydin, M., and Erhan, Ç. (eds), *Turkish American Relations: Past, Present and Future*, London: Routledge, 2004, pp. 66–88.

Heilbrunn, J., *They Knew They Were Right: The Rise of the Neocons*, New York: Doubleday, 2008.

Helsinki Watch, *Human Rights in Turkey's 'Transition to Democracy': A Helsinki Watch Report*, New York and Washington DC: US Helsinki Watch Committee, 1983.

——*State of Flux: Human Rights in Turkey, December 1987 Update*, New York: Helsinki Watch, 1987.

Heraclides, A., *The Greek-Turkish Conflict in the Aegean: Imagined Enemies*, Houndmills, Basingstoke: Palgrave Macmillan, 2010.

Hershlag, Z. H., *The Contemporary Turkish Economy*, London: Routledge, 1988.

Hickok, M. R., 'Peace Onyx: A Story of Turkish F-16 Co-production', in Wood, P. C., and Sorenson, D. S. (eds), *International Military Aerospace Collaboration*, Aldershot: Ashgate Press, 1999, pp. 153–81.

——'Hegemon Rising: The Gap between Turkish Strategy and Military Modernization', *Parameters*, vol. XXX, 2000, pp. 105–19.

Hill, C., *The Changing Politics of Foreign Policy*, Houndmills, Basingstoke: Palgrave, 2003.

Hubel, H., 'Turkey and the Crisis in the Middle East', in Karaosmanoğlu, A. L., and Taşhan, S. (eds), *Middle East, Turkey and the Atlantic Alliance*, Ankara: Foreign Policy Institute, 1987, pp. 97–121.

Hudson, V. M., *Foreign Policy Analysis: Classic and Contemporary Theory*, Lanham, MD: Rowman and Littlefield Publishers, Inc., 2007.

Human Rights Watch, *U.S. Cluster Bombs for Turkey?*, vol. 6, no. 19, December 1994, available online at www.hrw.org/reports/1994/Turkey2 (accessed 12 June 2006).

——*Weapons Transfers and Violations of the Laws of War in Turkey*, New York: Human Rights Watch, 1995.

Hunter, S., 'Bridge or Frontier? Turkey's Post-Cold War Geopolitical Posture', *The International Spectator*, vol. XXXIV, 1999, pp. 63–78.

——'The Gulf Cooperation Council. Security in the Era Following the Iran-Contra Affair', in Freedman, R. O., (ed.), *The Middle East from the Iran-Contra Affair to the Intifada*, Syracuse, NY: Syracuse University Press, 1999, pp. 145–66.

Hyland, W. G., 'A Mediocre Record', *Foreign Policy*, vol. 101, 1996, pp. 370–74.

——*Clinton's World: Remaking American Foreign Policy*, Westport, CT: Praeger, 1999.

Ilkin, S., 'Les tentatives de cooperation économique en mer Noire', *Cahiers d' Études sur la Méditerranée Orientale et le Monde Turco-Iranien*, vol. 15, 1993, pp. 51–75.

Ibrahimov, R., 'Israeli Pipeline. Ashelon-Eilat-The Second Breath', *Journal of Turkish Weekly*, 9 April 2007, available online at www.turkishweekly.net (accessed 20 September 2007).

Inbar, E., *The Israeli-Turkish Entente*, London: King's College Mediterranean Studies, 2001.

'Industrial Allies Offer Turkey $1,45 Billion', *The New York Times*, 31 May 1979.

Jabber, P., 'U.S. Interests and Regional Security in the Middle East', *Daedalus*, 1980, vol. 109, pp. 67–80.

Jacoby, T., 'The Reagan Turnaround on Human Rights', *Foreign Affairs*, vol. 64, 1986, pp. 1066–86.

JINSA's Mandate, [n.d.], available online at www.jinsa.org/about/agenda/agenda.html (accessed 20 February1999).

Joffe, J., 'European-American Relations: The Enduring Crisis', *Foreign Affairs*, vol. 59, 1981, pp. 836–51.

Joseph, J., 'Pipeline Diplomacy: The Clinton Administration's Fight for Baku-Ceyhan', WWS Case Study 1/99, Woodrow Wilson School for Public Affairs, Princeton University, [n.d.], available online at http://wws.princeton.edu/research/cases/pipeline.pdf (accessed 2 Februar 2001).

Jung, D., and Piccoli, W., 'The Turkish-Israeli Alignment: Paranoia or Pragmatism?', *Security Dialogue*, vol. 31, 2000, pp. 91–104.

——*Turkey at the Crossroads: Ottoman Legacies and a Greater Middle East*, London: Zed Books, 2001.

Karaosmanoğlu, A. L., 'Turkey's Security Policy in the Middle East', *Dış Politika* (Foreign Policy), vol. X, 1983, pp. 3–17.

——'Turkey's Security and the Middle East', *Foreign Affairs*, vol. 62, 1983, pp. 157–75.

——'Turkey's Discreet Foreign Policy between Western Europe and the Middle East', in Karaosmanoğlu, A. L., and Taşhan, S. (eds), *Middle East, Turkey and the Atlantic Alliance*, Ankara: Foreign Policy Institute, 1987, pp. 78–96.

——'European Security and Turkey in a Changing Strategic Environment', *Year Book 1989*, Athens: Hellenic Foundation for Defense and Foreign Policy, 1990, pp. 177–86.

——'The Evolution of the National Security Culture and the Military in Turkey', *Journal of International Affairs*, vol. 54, 2000, pp. 199–216.

Karpat, K. H., 'Turkish and Arab-Israeli Relations', in Karpat, K. H. *et al.*, *Turkey's Foreign Policy in Transition, 1950–1974*, Leiden: E. J. Brill, 1975, pp. 108–34.

——'Discussion On "Turkey between Alliance and Alienation"', *Dış Politika* (Foreign Policy), vol. 8, 1980.

Kaylan, M., *The Kemalists: Islamic Revival and the Fate of Secular Turkey*, Amherst, NY: Prometheus Books, 2005.

Kemp, G., 'Strategic Problems in the Persian Gulf Region', in Wise, G. S., and Issawi, C. (eds), *Middle East Perspectives: The Next Twenty Years*, Princeton, NJ: Darwin Press, 1981, pp. 71–9.

Kesic, O., 'American-Turkish Relations at a Crossroads', *Mediterranean Quarterly*, vol. 6, 1995, pp. 97–108.

Keskin, F., 'Turkey's Trans-Border Operations in Northern Iraq: Before and after the Invasion of Iraq', *Research Journal of International Studies*, issue 8, 2008, pp. 59–75.

Kirişci, K., 'U.S.-Turkish Relations: New Uncertainties in a Renewed Partnership', in Rubin, B., and Kirişci, K. (eds), *Turkey in World Politics: An Emerging Multiregional Power*, Boulder, CO: Lynne Rienner Publishers, 2001, pp. 129–49.

Kirişci, K., and Winrow, G. M., *The Kurdish Question and Turkey: An Example of a Trans-state Ethnic Conflict*, London: Routledge Curzon, 2004.

Kissinger, H. A., 'Bureaucracy and Policymaking: The Effects of Insiders and Outsiders on the Policy Process', in Kissinger, H. A., and Brodie, B., *Bureaucracy, Politics, and Strategy*, Los Angeles: University of California, Security Studies Project, Security Studies Paper no. 17, 1968, pp. 1–14.

Knorr, K., *Power and Wealth: The Political Economy of International Power*, New York: Basic Books, 1973.

Köni, H., 'Gulf Savaşı Sonrasında Orta Doğunun Durumu', in *Değişen Dünyada Türkiye ve Türk Dünyası Sempozyumu*, Ankara: Hacettepe Üniversitesi Atatürk İlkeleri ve İnkılap Tarihi Enstitüsü, 1993, pp. 41–54.

Kuniholm, B. R. 'Turkey and NATO: Past, Present, Future', *Orbis*, 1983, pp. 421–45.

——'Turkey in the World', in Harris, G. S. (ed.), *The Middle East in Turkish-American Relations*, Washington DC: The Heritage Foundation, 1985, pp. 9–16.

——'East or West? The Geopolitics of Turkey and Its NATO Alliance', in Karaosmanoğlu, A. L., and Taşhan, S. (eds), *Middle East, Turkey and the Atlantic Alliance*, Ankara: Foreign Policy Institute, 1987, pp. 134–57.

——'Turkey and the West since World War II', in Mastny, V., and Nation, R. C. (eds), *Turkey between East and West: New Challenges for a Rising Regional Power*, Boulder, CO: Westview Press, 1996, pp. 45–69.

Kürkçüoğlu, Ö., 'Turkey's Attitude towards the Middle East Conflict', *Foreign Policy*, vol. 5, 1976.

——'The Evolution of Turkish-Arab Relations', in Harris, G. S. (ed.), *The Middle East in Turkish-American Relations*, Washington DC: The Heritage Foundation, 1985, pp. 45–9.

——'Development of Turkish-Arab Relations: A Historical Appraisal', in Karaosmanoğlu, A. L., and Taşhan, S. (eds), *Middle East, Turkey and the Atlantic Alliance*, Ankara: Foreign Policy Institute, 1987, pp. 8–27.

Laciner, S., 'Turgut Özal Period in Turkish Foreign Policy: Özalism', Ankara: USAK Yearbook of International Politics and Law, 2009, vol. 2, pp. 153–205.

Laipson, E. B., *Congressional-Executive Relations and the Turkish Arms Embargo*, Congress and Foreign Policy Series, Washington DC: US Government Printing Office, 1981.

——'Turkey and the U.S. Congress', in Harris, G. S. (ed.), *The Middle East in Turkish-American Relations*, Washington DC: The Heritage Foundation, 1985, pp. 27–33.

——'Thinking about the Mediterranean', *Mediterranean Quarterly*, vol. 1, 1990, pp. 50–66.

——'US Policy towards Greece and Turkey since 1974', in D. Constas (ed.), *The Greek-Turkish Conflict in the 1990s: Domestic and External Influences*, Houndmills, Basingstoke: Macmillan, 1991, pp. 164–82.

Laqueur, W., *The Struggle for the Middle East: The Soviet Union in the Mediterranean 1958–1968*, New York: The Macmillan Company, 1969.

Larrabee, F. S., and Lesser, I. O., *Turkish Foreign Policy in an Age of Uncertainty*, Santa Monica, CA: RAND, 2003.

Lesser, I. O., *Changes in the Character of East-West Relations: Implications for NATO's Southern Region*, Santa Monica, CA: RAND, June 1990.

——*Southern Region Perspectives on Security and International* Affairs, Santa Monica, CA: RAND, 1991.

——*Bridge or Barrier? Turkey and the West after the Cold War*, Santa Monica, CA: RAND, 1992.

——'Turkey and the West after the Gulf War', *International Spectator*, vol. 72, 1992, pp. 33–42.

——'Turkey's Strategic Options', *The International Spectator*, vol. XXXIV, 1999, pp. 79–88.

——'Western Interests in a Changing Turkey', in Khalilzad, Z., Lesser, I. O. and Larrabee, F. S. (eds), *The Future of Turkish-Western Relations,* Santa Monica, CA: RAND, 2000, pp. 53–78.

LeVine, S., *The Oil and the Glory: The Pursuit of Empire and Fortune on the Caspian Sea*, New York: Random House, 2007.

Lockman, S., *Contending Visions of the Middle East: The History and Politics of Orientalism*, Cambridge: Cambridge University Press, 2004.

Ludington, N. S., and Spain, J. W., 'Dateline Turkey: The Case for Patience', *Foreign Policy*, no. 50, 1983, pp. 150–68.

McCormick, J. M., 'Assessing Clinton's Foreign Policy at Midterm', *Current History*, vol. 94, 1995, pp. 370–74.

——*American Foreign Policy and Process*, Boston: Wadsworth, 2010.

McDowall, D., *Palestine and Israel: The Uprising and Beyond*, Berkeley: University of California Press, 1989.

Makovsky, A., 'Israeli-Turkish Relations. "A Turkish Periphery Strategy"?', in Barkey, H. J. (ed), *Reluctant Neighbor: Turkey's Role in the Middle East*, Washington DC: United States Institute of Peace Press, 1996, pp. 147–70.

——'How to Deal with Erbakan', *Middle East Quarterly*, vol. IV, 1997, pp. 3–8.

——'Israeli-Turkish Co-operation: Full Steam Ahead', *Policywatch*, 1998, p. 292.

——'The New Activism in Turkish Foreign Policy', *Insight Turkey*, vol. 1, 1999, pp. 92–113.

——'U.S. Policy toward Turkey: Progress and Problems', in Abramowitz, M. (ed.), *Turkey's Transformation and American Policy,* New York: The Century Foundation Press, 2000, pp. 219–66.

Malanczuk, P., 'The Kurdish Crisis and Allied Intervention in the Aftermath of the Second Gulf War', *European Journal of International Law*, vol. 2, 1991, pp. 114–32.

Mango, A., 'Turkey and the Middle Eastern Market', in Manisalı, E. (ed.), *Turkey's Place in the Middle East*, Istanbul: Middle East Business and Banking Publications, 1989, pp. 36–41.

Mann, J., *Rise of the Vulcans: The History of Bush's War Cabinet*, New York: Viking, 2004.

Mearsheimer, J. J., and Walt, S. M., *The Israel Lobby and U.S. Foreign Policy*, New York: Farrar, Straus and Giroux, 2007.

Miller, A. D., *The Much Too Promised Land: America's Elusive Search for Arab-Israeli Peace*, New York: Bantam Books, 2008.

Mufti, M., 'Daring and Caution in Turkish Foreign Policy', *Middle East Journal*, vol. 52, 1998, pp. 32–50.

——*Daring and Caution in Turkish Strategic Culture: Republic at Sea*, Houndmills, Basingstoke: Palgrave, Macmillan, 2009.

Nachmani, A., 'Bridge across the Middle East: Turkey and Israel in the 1990s', unpublished paper, Jerusalem 1997.

——'The Remarkable Turkish-Israeli Tie', *Middle East Quarterly*, vol. 5, 1998, pp. 19–29.

——*Turkey: Facing a New Millennium; Coping with Intertwined Conflicts*, Manchester: Manchester University Press, 2003.

Newman, B., 'At the Crossroads: Turkey Seems to Be on the Road to Democracy, But Its Route There Appears Very Undemocratic', *The Wall Street Journal,* 15 June 1982.

Olson, R., *Turkey's Relations with Iran, Syria, Israel, and Russia, 1991–2000. The Kurdish and Islamist Questions*, Costa Mesa, CA: Mazda Publishers, 2001.

Önis, Z., and Özmucur, S., *Capital Flows and the External Financing of Turkey's Imports*, Paris: OECD Development Centre, Working Paper no. 36, July 1991.

Öniş, Z., and Webb, S. B., *Political Economy of Policy Reform in Turkey in the 1980s*, Washington DC: The World Bank, Policy Research Working Papers, WPS 1059, 1992.

Özcan, G., 'Apologismos 50 Hronon ton Sheseon Tourkias-Israil', in Sönmezoğlu, F. (ed.), *Mythos ke Pragmatikotita: Analysi tis Tourkikis Exoterikis Politikis*, Athens: Infognomon, 2001, tomos A, pp. 227–51.

——'Politiko Kathestos ke Exoteriki Politiki stin Tourkia (1983–93)', in Sönmezoğlu, F. (ed.), *Mythos ke Pragmatikotita: Analysi tis Tourkikis Exoterikis Politikis*, Athens: Infognomon, 2001, tomos B, pp. 99–133.

——'The Military and the Making of Foreign Policy in Turkey', in Rubin, B., and Kirişci, K. (eds), *Turkey in World Politics: An Emerging Multiregional Power*, Boulder, CO: Lynne Rienner Publishers, 2001, pp. 13–30.

Palmer, D. R., 'Paradigms Lost: A Retrospective Assessment of the NATO-Warsaw Pact Military Competition in the Alliance's Southern Region', *Comparative Strategy*, vol. 9, 1990, pp. 265–86.

Parris, M., 'The U.S. and Turkey', in Maddy-Weitzman, B., and Susser, A. (eds), *Turkish-Israeli Relations in a Trans-Atlantic Context: Wider Europe and the Greater Middle East*, Tel Aviv: Conference Proceedings, The Moshe Dayan Center for Middle Eastern and African Studies, 2005, pp. 27–31.

Peres S., and Naor, A., *The New Middle East*, New York: Henry Holt, 1993.

Perle, R, 'Turkey and US Military Assistance', in Harris, G. S. (ed.), *The Middle East in Turkish-American Relations*, Washington DC: The Heritage Foundation, 1985, pp. 23–6.

——'A Turkish Story', the First Annual Robert Strausz-Hupé Lecture, Foreign Policy Research Institute, FPRI Wire, September 1999, vol. 7, available online at http://fpri.org/fpriwire/0711.19909.perle.turkishstory.html (accessed 20 June 2010).

Perle, R., and McNamara, M., J., 'The U.S. Security Assistance for Turkey and the Challenge of Aid for the Southern Flank', *NATO's Sixteen Nations,* vol. 32, 1987, pp. 94–7.

Peterson, J. E., *Defending Arabia*, London: Croom Helm, 1986.

Phillips, J., *Afghanistan: The Soviet Quagmire*, Washington DC: The Heritage Foundation, 1979, backgrounder 101.

——'Turkey: An Increasingly Key Strategic Asset for the U.S.', Washington DC: The Heritage Foundation, 1987, backgrounder 609.

Putnam, R. D., 'Diplomacy and Domestic Policy: The Logic of Two Level Games', *International Organization*, vol. 42, 1988, pp. 427–60.

Rabi, Y., 'An Unprecedented Meeting: Foreign Ministers of Israel and Turkey to Meet for the First Time', *Jewish Telegraphic Agency*, 22 September 1987, available online at http://archive.jta.org/article/1987/09/22/3007669/an-unprecedented-meeting-foreign-ministers-of-israel-and-turkey-to-meet-for-the-first-time (accessed 6 March 2010).

Rabinovich, I., *The Brink of Peace; The Israeli-Syrian Negotiations*, Princeton, NJ: Princeton University Press, 1998.

Reiter, D., 'Learning, Realism, and Alliances: The Weight of the Shadow of the Past,' *World Politics*, vol. 46, 1994, pp. 490–526.

Robins, P., *Turkey and the Middle East*, London: The Royal Institute of International Affairs, 1991.

——*Suits and Uniforms: Turkish Foreign Policy since the End of the Cold War*, London: Hurst and Co, 2003.

Rodrik, D., 'Premature Liberalization, Incomplete Stabilization: The Ozal Decade in Turkey', in Bruno, M., Fischer, S., Helpman, E. and Liviatan, N. (eds), *Lessons of Economic Stabilization and Its Aftermath*, London: MIT Press, 1991, pp. 323–53.

Rosenau, J. N., 'Pre-Theories and Theories of Foreign Policy', in Farrell, R. B. (ed.), *Approaches in Comparative and International Politics,* Evanston, IL: Northwestern University Press, 1966, pp. 27–92.

Rotter, A. J., *Comrades at Odds: The United States and India, 1947–1964*, Ithaca, NY: Cornell University Press, 2000.

Roy, J., 'The Turkish Economy: Assessment of a Recovery under a Structural Adjustment Program', Washington DC: The Economic Development Institute of the World Bank, EDI Working Papers, 1989.

Rubin, B., 'U.S. Middle East Policy in the Turkish Context', in Harris, G. S. (ed.), *The Middle East in Turkish-American Relations*, Washington DC: The Heritage Foundation, 1985, pp. 75–80.

Rubinstein, A. Z., 'New World Order or Hollow Victory?', *Foreign Affairs*, vol. 70, 1991, pp. 53–65.

Rustow, D. A., 'Turkey's Travails', *Foreign Affairs*, vol. 58, 1979, pp. 87–102.

——*Turkey, America's Forgotten Ally*, New York: Council on Foreign Relations, 1987.

Sariibrahimoglu, L., 'Building an Industry: The Turkish Dimension', *Jane's Defence Weekly*, 9 November 1991.

——'Turkey Seeks Review of US Defence Agreement', *Jane's Defence Weekly*, 30 January 1993.

Sayari, S., 'Turkey: The Changing European Security Environment and the Gulf Crisis', *Middle East Journal*, vol. 46, 1992, pp. 9–22.

——'Regional Security Issues and U.S.-Turkish Relations in the 1980s', paper presented at Boğaziçi University conference,'The History of American-Turkish Relations, 1833–1989', Istanbul, June 2006.

Schmidt, H., 'A Policy of Reliable Partnership', *Foreign Affairs*, vol. 59, 1981, pp. 744–55.

Sezer, D., 'Discussion on "Turkey between Alliance and Alienation"', *Dış Politika* (Foreign Policy), vol. 8, 1980, pp. 125–28

——'Turkish Foreign Policy in the Year 2000', in *Turkey in the Year 2000*, Ankara: Turkish Political Science Association, 1989, pp. 61–117.

——'Turkey and the Western Alliance in the 1980s', in Eralp, A., Tünay, M. and Yeşilada, B. (eds), *The Political and Socioeconomic Transformation of Turkey*, Westport, CT: Praeger, 1993, pp. 215–30.

Sick, G., 'The Evolution of U.S. Strategy toward the Indian Ocean and Persian Gulf Regions', in Rubinstein, A. Z. (ed.), *The Great Game: Rivalry in the Persian Gulf and South Asia,* New York: Praeger, 1983, pp. 49–80.

Sigler, J. H., 'Evaluating Reagan's Middle East Policy: A First Term Balance Sheet', in Marantz, P., and Steinberg, B. S. (eds), *Superpower Involvement in the Middle East: Dynamics of Foreign Policy,* Boulder, CO: Westview Press, 1985, pp. 249–62.

Şenesen, G. G., 'Mia Axiologisi tou Programmatos Eksyhronismou ton Tourkikon Enoplon Dynameon', in Sönmezoğlu, F. (ed.), *Mythos ke Pragmatikotita: Analysi tis Tourkikis Exoterikis Politikis,* Athens: Infognomon, 2001, tomos B, pp. 209–33.

Şimşek, M., 'Defense Industry in Turkey', *Foreign Policy* (Diş Politika), vol. XV, 1989, pp. 36–66.

Sönmezoğlu, F., *ABD'nin Türkiye Politikası (1964–1980)*, Istanbul: Der Yayinevi, 1995.

Spain, J. W., 'The United States, Turkey and the Poppy', *Middle East Journal,* vol. 29, 1975, pp.295–309.

Stern, F., 'Germany in a Semi-Gaullist Europe', *Foreign Affairs,* vol. 58, 1980, pp. 867–86.

Stern, L., *The Wrong Horse: The Politics of Intervention and the Failure of the American Diplomacy,* New York: Times Books, 1977.

Strange, S., *States and Markets: An Introduction to International Political Economy,* London: Pinter Publishers, 1988.

Talbot, S., *Deadly Gambits: The Reagan Administration and the Stalemate in Nuclear Arms Control,* New York: Vintage Books, 1985.

Taşhan, S., 'Turkey's Relations with the U.S.A. and Possible Future Developments', *Diş Politika* (Foreign Policy), vol. 8, 1979, pp. 11–32.

Thomson, P. L., 'United States-Turkey Military Relations: Treaties and Implication', *The International Journal of Kurdish* Studies, vol. 9, 1996, pp. 103–13.

Tirman, J., 'Improving Turkey's "Bad Neighborhood": Pressing Ankara for Rights and Democracy', *World Policy Journal,* vol. 15, 1998, pp. 60–67.

Tovias, A., and Inbar, E., 'Potential Effects of Turkey's Membership in the EC on Israel's Economy', in Bağış, A. I. (ed.), *Actual Situation and Prospects of Turkey's Bilateral Relations with Israel: Potential and Opportunities,* Ankara: TES-AR Yayınları, 1992, pp. 105–42.

Treverton, G. F., 'Managing Alliance Politics', in Karaosmanoğlu, A. L., and Taşhan, S. (eds), *Middle East, Turkey and the Atlantic Alliance,* Ankara: Foreign Policy Institute, 1987, pp. 158–81.

Turan, I., 'Discussion on "Turkey between Alliance and Alienation"', *Diş Politika* (Foreign Policy), vol. 8, 1980, pp. 128–31.

Türkmen, I., *The Middle East Policy of the Republic of Turkey,* Istanbul: Bilgesam, 2010, vol. 4.

The Turkish Yearbook of International Relations, Ankara: Ankara Üniversitesi Basımevi, 2000, vol. XXXI.

Uslu, N., *The Turkish-American Relationship between 1947 and 2003: The History of a Distinctive Alliance,* New York: Nova Science Publishers, Inc., 2003.

Vital, D., *The Inequality of States,* Oxford: Clarendon Press, 1967.

Walsh, E., 'Turkey Tests "Controlled Democracy"', *The Washington Post*, 6 November 1983.

Walt, S., *The Origins of Alliances*, Ithaca, NY: Cornell University Press, 1987.

Wamsted, D. J., 'Supplemental Funding Requested for Desert Storm and Aid to Israel', *Washington Report on Middle East Affairs*, 26 March 1991, available online at www.wrmea.com/backissues/0391/9103037.htm (accessed 10 February 2007).

'Washington Talk: Greece and Turkey, The Local War', *The New York Times*, 26 March 1987.

Wedel, J. R., *Shadow Elite: How the Wold's New Power Brokers Undermine Democracy, Government, and the Free Market*, New York: Basic Books, 2009.

Weiker, W., *The Modernization of Turkey. From Ataturk to the Present Day*, New York: Holmes and Meier Publishers, 1981.

Weisman, A., *Prince of Darkness: Richard Perle. The Kingdom, the Power and the End of Empire in America*, New York: Union Square Press, 2007.

Welch, D. A., *Painful Choices: A Theory of Foreign Policy Change* Princeton, NJ: Princeton University Press, 2005.

Whetten, L. L., 'Turkey and NATO's Second Front', *Strategic Review*, 1981, pp. 57–64.

White, T. H., 'Weinberger on the Ramparts', *New York Times Magazine*, 6 February 1983.

Wilson, G., 'US – Turkey Sets Air Forces Nearer USSR', *The Washington Post*, 7 November 1982.

Wohlstetter, A., 'Lift the Turkish Embargo', *Wall Street Journal*, 14 June 1978.

Vordermark, J., 'Security Assistance Mission in the Republic of Turkey', *Defense Institute of Security Assistance Management Journal*, 22 December 2003, available online at www.thefreelibrary.com/Security+assistance+mission+in+the+Republic+of+Turkey.-a0116525416 (accessed 10 March 2007).

Yavuz, M. H., 'O Diismos stis Tourkoaravikes Sxesis ke to Palestiniako Zitima', in Sönmezoğlu, F. (ed.), *Mythos ke Pragmatikotita: Analysi tis Tourkikis Exoterikis Politikis*, Athens: Infognomon, 2001, tomos B, pp. 183–207.

Yavuz, M. H., and Khan, M. R., 'Turkish Foreign Policy toward the Arab-Israeli Conflict: Duality and the Development (1950–91)', *Arab Studies Quarterly*, vol. 14, 1992, pp. 69–94.

Yilanci, V., and Özcan, B., 'External Debt Sustainability of Turkey: A Nonlinear Approach', *International Research Journal of Finance and Economics*, issue 20, October 2008, pp. 91–8.

Zarate, R., and Sokolski, H. (eds), *Nuclear Heuristics: Selected Writings of Albert and Roberta Wohlstetter*, Carlisle, PA: Stategic Studies Institute, 2009.

Zürcher, E. J., *Turkey: A Modern History*, London: I.B. Tauris, 1993.

Newspapers/periodic publications

Anadolu Agency: News in English (daily news review)

BBC Summary of World Broadcasts

Foreign Broadcast Information Service, Daily Report, Western Europe [FBIS-WEU]

The Guardian

Hurriyet Daily News

The Independent

Info Türk

International Herald Tribune

Jewish Telegraphic Agency
The Jerusalem Post
MEED
Middle East International
Milliyet
The New York Times
Turkey Briefing
Turkish Daily News
Turkish Press Review, Directorate General of Press and Information, Ankara.
U.S. News and World Report
The Wall Street Journal
The Washington Post

Index of names

General index

Made in the USA
Las Vegas, NV
06 November 2024

10868451R00129